COMPUTER SCIENCE, TECHNOLOGY AND APPLICATIONS

CLOUD COMPUTING AND GOVERNMENT: BACKGROUND, BENEFITS, RISKS

COMPUTER SCIENCE, TECHNOLOGY AND APPLICATIONS

Additional books in this series can be found on Nova's website under the Series tab.

Additional E-books in this series can be found on Nova's website under the E-books tab.

DEFENSE, SECURITY AND STRATEGIES

Additional books in this series can be found on Nova's website under the Series tab.

Additional E-books in this series can be found on Nova's website under the E-books tab.

COMPUTER SCIENCE, TECHNOLOGY AND APPLICATIONS

CLOUD COMPUTING AND GOVERNMENT: BACKGROUND, BENEFITS, RISKS

GEORGE I. NIKOLOV
EDITOR

Nova Science Publishers, Inc.

New York

LIBRARY OF CONGRESS Cataloging-in-Publication Data
Cloud computing and government : background, benefits, risks / editor,
George I. Nikolov.
p. cm.
Includes index.
ISBN 978-1-61761-784-3 (hardcover)
1. Administrative agencies--Information technology--United States. 2.
Cloud computing. 3. Executive departments--Information technology--United
States. 4. Electronic government information--United States--Management. 5.
Information technology--United States. I. Nikolov, George I.
JK468.A8C56 2010
352.3'80285436--dc22
2010036415

Published by Nova Science Publishers, Inc. † New York

CONTENTS

PREFACE

Cloud computing, an emerging form of computing where users have access to scalable, on-demand capabilities that are provided through Internet-based technologies, has the potential to provide information technology services more quickly and at a lower cost, but also to introduce information security risks. Cloud computing can both increase and decrease the security of information systems in federal agencies. Potential information security benefits include those related to the use of virtualization, such as faster deployment of patches, and from economies of scale, such as potentially reduced costs for disaster recovery. Risks include dependence on the security practices and assurances of a vendor, dependency on the vendor, and concerns related to sharing of computing resources. This book provides an overview of the background, benefits, and risks of cloud computing and government usage.

Chapter 1- Cloud computing, an emerging form of computing where users have access to scalable, on-demand capabilities that are provided through Internet-based technologies, has the potential to provide information technology services more quickly and at a lower cost, but also to introduce information security risks. Accordingly, GAO was asked to (1) identify the models of cloud computing, (2) identify the information security implications of using cloud computing services in the federal government, and (3) assess federal guidance and efforts to address information security when using cloud computing. To do so, GAO reviewed relevant publications, white papers, and other documentation from federal agencies and industry groups; conducted interviews with representatives from these organizations; and surveyed 24 major federal agencies.

Chapter 2- The Obama Administration is changing the way business is done in Washington and bringing a new sense of responsibility to how we manage taxpayer dollars. We are working to bring the spirit of American innovation and the power of technology to improve performance and lower the cost of government operations.

The United States Government is the world's largest consumer of information technology, spending over $76 billion annually on more than 10,000 different systems. Fragmentation of systems, poor project execution, and the drag of legacy technology in the Federal Government have presented barriers to achieving the productivity and performance gains found when technology is deployed effectively in the private sectors.

Chapter 3- The purpose of today's hearing is to examine the benefits and risks of cloud computing for the federal government. At the most basic level, cloud computing is web-based computing whereby computing resources are shared and accessible over the Internet on demand. In this way, cloud computing is like most utility services.

Before the electric grid was developed, business owners who wanted to use machinery also needed to produce enough energy to run that machinery. That meant investing heavily to build and maintain a power source. The electric grid revolutionized the country by centralizing the resource and allowing businesses to simply purchase electricity.

Cloud computing promises the same for computing power. Instead of building and maintaining an entire IT system in house, businesses can purchase computing power and tap into that resource over the Internet.

Chapter 4- At its most basic level the term "cloud computing" is a metaphor for internet-based computing. Some have described it as a new name for an old concept: the delivery of computing services from a remote location, similar to the way electricity and other utilities are provided to most customers. A preponderance of technology experts believe that by 2020 most people will access software applications online and share and retrieve information through the use of remote server networks. This is a dramatic departure from today's environment where we depend on software housed on individual computers.

Chapter 5- Information technology (IT) has transformed how the private sector operates and has revolutionized the efficiency, convenience, and effectiveness with which it serves its customers.In our everyday lives, we can track the status of a shipment, buy goods and services, make travel, hotel and restaurant reservations, and collaborate with friends and colleagues – all online, anytime and anywhere.

Yet, when it comes to dealing with our government, we have to stand in line, hold on the phone, or mail in a paper form. The Federal Government has largely missed out on the transformation in the use of IT due to poor management of its technology investments.Government IT projects all too often cost millions of dollars more than they should, take years longer than necessary to deploy, and deliver technologies that are obsolete by the time they are completed.

Chapter 6- Cloud computing enables convenient, rapid, and on-demand computer network access—most often via the Internet--to a shared pool of configurable computing resources (in the form of servers, networks, storage, applications, and services). Quite simply, it is the way computing services are delivered that is revolutionary. Cloud computing allows users to provision computing capabilities rapidly and as needed; that is, to scale out and scale back as required, and to pay only for services used. Users can provision software and infrastructure cloud services on demand with minimal, if any, human intervention. Because cloud computing is based on resource pooling and broad network access there is a natural economy of scale that can result in lower costs to agencies. In addition, cloud computing offers a varied menu of service models from a private cloud operated solely for one organization to a public cloud that is available to a large industry group and the general public and owned by an organization that is selling cloud computing services.

Chapter 7- As one of the major research components within NIST, the ITL accelerates the development and deployment of information and communication systems that are reliable, usable, interoperable, and secure; advances measurement science through innovations in mathematics, statistics, and computer science; and conducts research to develop the measurements and standards infrastructure for emerging information technologies and applications.

NIST works with federal agencies, industry, and academia to research, develop and deploy information security standards and technology to protect information systems against threats to their confidentiality, integrity and availability. NIST researches technologies such as identity management and verification, metrics for complex systems, automation of discovery and maintenance of system security configurations and status, and techniques for specification and automation of access authorization in support of many different kinds of access policies.

Chapter 8- Cloud computing, an emerging form of computing where users have access to scalable, on-demand capabilities that are provided through Internet-based technologies, reportedly has the potential to provide information technology services more quickly and at a lower cost, but also to introduce information security risks. Accordingly, GAO was asked to testify on the benefits and risks of moving federal information technology into the cloud. This testimony summarizes the contents of a separate report that is being released today which describes (1) the models of cloud computing, (2) the information security implications of using cloud computing services in the federal government, and (3) federal guidance and efforts to address information security when using cloud computing. In preparing that report, GAO collected and analyzed information from industry groups, private-sector organizations, and 24 major federal agencies.

Chapter 9- My name is Scott Charney, and I am the Corporate Vice President for Trustworthy Computing at Microsoft Corporation. I also serve as one of four Co-Chairs of the Center for Strategic and International Studies (CSIS) Commission on Cybersecurity for the 44th Presidency. Prior to joining Microsoft, I was Chief of the Computer Crime and Intellectual Property Section in the Criminal Division of the United States (U.S.) Department of Justice. I was involved in nearly every major hacker prosecution in the U.S. from 1991 to 1999; worked on legislative initiatives, such as the National Information Infrastructure Protection Act that was enacted in 1996; and chaired the G8 Subgroup on High Tech Crime from its inception in 1996 until I left government service in 1999.

Chapter 10- Chairman Towns and Chairwoman Watson, Ranking Member Issa and Ranking Member Bilbray, Members of the Committee, thank you for holding this hearing on cloud computing and for inviting me to share my views with you. Cloud computing is a revolutionary and disruptive new technology that is having a profound impact on how we use, manage and build computing applications. As the Senior Vice President for Global Public Policy at Salesforce.com, I am deeply involved in government discussions about cloud computing, and I applaud the efforts of this Committee and the Administration to enable federal agencies to take advantage it.

Chapter 11- Cloud computing is a relatively new term for some, but the cloud is being used today by significant numbers of consumers, businesses, and – increasingly – the public sector. In fact, more than two million businesses use our cloud service, Google Apps. In the cloud, everyday processes and information that are typically run and stored on local computers – email, documents, calendars – can be accessed securely anytime, anywhere, and with any device through an Internet connection. The cloud enables government agencies to replace in-house information technology – which is costly and complex to own, maintain, and secure – with externally provided computing power that offers better and secure performance at dramatically reduced costs.

Chapter 12- My name is Nick Combs and I am the Chief Technology Officer for EMC Corporation's Federal Division. EMC is a global leader in cloud computing infrastructure and services. We enable the full realization of the inherent power of information by creating complete information environments that are reliable, efficient, and secure. With EMC, users and organizations can bring the power of information to life...information that illuminates what is possible and that moves the world forward. Prior to joining EMC, I served for more than 25 years in the Federal Government as a senior leader in the Army, Senior IT leader in the Defense Intelligence Agency and as an IT Director and CIO with the Director of National Intelligence. During my career in government and the IT industry, I personally experienced many of the IT the challenges facing federal agencies today, particularly as agencies transition to cloud services. In both the public and private sectors, I have worked with different types of cloud computing models, each of which had its own risk management, interoperability, and data portability requirements.

Chapter 13- I have been conducting research on large-scale computing and storage infrastructures (e.g., cloud computing) and their operation/administration for over a decade. Among the cloud computing projects I lead are CMU's Data Center Observatory (DCO) and the CMU portion of OpenCirrus. The DCO was conceived as a consolidated data center and private cloud for research computing/storage needs, but heavily instrumented and forward-looking to enable research into efficiency, and it is being realized with active collaboration from several of the PDL sponsor companies. OpenCirrus (https://opencirrus.org/) is an open cloud computing testbed currently consisting of ten sites worldwide, each of which provides public cloud computing resources via open interfaces and open source software.

Chapter 14- Cloud computing is an emerging trend which has progressed to the point of serious adoption in both public and private sector organizations, yet it remains a relatively immature paradigm, one which dictates a revision to the traditional characterization of risk in information technology environments. As a means of an introduction to those changes, this paper offers an overview of the information assurance aspects of cloud computing with a focus on potential security advantages and pitfalls. While many of the security concerns associated with cloud computing are shared with traditional computing models, this paper will focus on those issues unique to cloud computing or that are exacerbated by it. The intended audience is anyone who is considering the adoption of cloud computing and who needs to understand the security risks and potential opportunities cloud computing provides as part of a risk management process.

Chapter 15- Advancing technology has the potential of dramatically changing the security posture of the federal enterprise and, if engineered correctly, the entire IT fabric of the globe. Potential security enhancements in the communications infrastructure, the software codebase, and cloud computing all hold great potential for dramatic positive change. This paper provides an overview of the cloud computing components relevant to security and proposes items for both awareness and action by the Federal IT team.

What is cloud computing? The term is used two different ways in the IT community. To most users, cloud computing is any capability delivered over the network. If it is not local computing it is from the cloud. To these users, almost all enterprise IT is cloud computing. Technologists and enterprise architects use the term in a different way. To them, cloud computing implies new ways of providing capability on demand by use of virtualized resources. It involves pools of storage, network, processing and other computational resources that can be efficiently allocated on demand. It also implies far more agility in support of operational missions. Technologists view cloud computing as a means to most efficiently deliver computer power via an application program interface (API).

What follows is a snapshot of the current glideslope of technology in this area, an update on relevant activities in the private sector which can further federal enablement of cloud computing security, and a new look at key principles for federal implementation of cloud computing.

Chapter 16- Note 1: Cloud computing is still an evolving paradigm. Its definitions, use cases, underlying technologies, issues, risks, and benefits will be refined in a spirited debate by the public and private sectors. These definitions, attributes, and characteristics will evolve and change over time.

Note 2: The cloud computing industry represents a large ecosystem of many models, vendors, and market niches. This definition attempts to encompass all of the various cloud approaches.

In: Cloud Computing and Government: Background, Benefits...   ISBN: 978-1-61761-784-3
Editor: George I. Nikolov   © 2011 Nova Science Publishers, Inc.

Chapter 1

INFORMATION SECURITY: FEDERAL GUIDANCE NEEDED TO ADDRESS CONTROL ISSUES WITH IMPLEMENTING CLOUD COMPUTING

United States Government Accountability Office

WHY GAO DID THIS STUDY

Cloud computing, an emerging form of computing where users have access to scalable, on-demand capabilities that are provided through Internet-based technologies, has the potential to provide information technology services more quickly and at a lower cost, but also to introduce information security risks. Accordingly, GAO was asked to (1) identify the models of cloud computing, (2) identify the information security implications of using cloud computing services in the federal government, and (3) assess federal guidance and efforts to address information security when using cloud computing. To do so, GAO reviewed relevant publications, white papers, and other documentation from federal agencies and industry groups; conducted interviews with representatives from these organizations; and surveyed 24 major federal agencies.

WHAT GAO RECOMMENDS

GAO is recommending that the Office of Management and Budget, General Services Administration, and the Department of Commerce take several steps to address cloud computing security, including completion of a strategy, consideration of security in a planned procurement of cloud computing services, and issuance of guidance related to cloud computing security. In comments on a draft of this chapter, these agencies generally concurred with GAO's recommendations and described efforts under way to implement them.

WHAT GAO FOUND

Cloud computing has several service and deployment models. The service models include the provision of infrastructure, computing platforms, and software as a service. The deployment models relate to how the cloud service is provided. They include a private cloud, operated solely for an organization; a community cloud, shared by several organizations; and a public cloud, available to any paying customer.

Cloud computing can both increase and decrease the security of information systems in federal agencies. Potential information security benefits include those related to the use of virtualization, such as faster deployment of patches, and from economies of scale, such as potentially reduced costs for disaster recovery. Risks include dependence on the security practices and assurances of a vendor, dependency on the vendor, and concerns related to sharing of computing resources. However, these risks may vary based on the cloud deployment model. Private clouds may have a lower threat exposure than public clouds, but evaluating this risk requires an examination of the specific security controls in place for the cloud's implementation.

Federal agencies have begun efforts to address information security issues for cloud computing, but key guidance is lacking and efforts remain incomplete. Although individual agencies have identified security measures needed when using cloud computing, they have not always developed corresponding guidance. For example, only nine agencies reported having approved and documented policies and procedures for writing comprehensive agreements with vendors when using cloud computing. Agencies have also identified challenges in implementing existing federal information security guidance and the need to streamline and automate the process of implementing this guidance. These concerns include having a process to assess vendor compliance with government information security requirements and the division of information security responsibilities between the customer and vendor. Furthermore, while several governmentwide cloud computing security initiatives are under way by organizations such as the Office of Management and Budget (OMB) and the General Services Administration (GSA), little has been completed as a result of these efforts. For example, OMB has not yet finished a cloud computing strategy. GSA has begun a procurement for cloud computing services, but has faced challenges in completing the procurement due in part to information security concerns. In addition, while the Department of Commerce's National Institute of Standards and Technology has begun efforts to address cloud computing information security, it has not yet issued cloud-specific security guidance. Until specific guidance and processes are developed to guide agencies in planning for and establishing information security for cloud computing, they may not have effective information security controls in place for cloud computing programs.

ABBREVIATIONS

CARS	Car Allowance Rebate System
CIO	chief information officer
DOD	Department of Defense
DOT	Department of Transportation

FIPS   Federal Information Processing Standards
FISMA   Federal Information Security Management Act
GSA   General Services Administration
IT   information technology
NASA   National Aeronautics and Space Administration
NIST   National Institute of Standards and Technology
RACE   Rapid Access Computing Environment
SAS   Statement on Auditing Standards
SP   Special Publication

May 27, 2010

Congressional Requesters

Cloud computing, an emerging form of delivering computing services, has been highlighted by the current administration as having the potential to provide information technology (IT) services both more quickly and at a lower cost. Although exact definitions vary, cloud computing can, at a high level, be described as a form of computing where users have access to scalable, on-demand IT capabilities that are provided through Internet-based technologies.

Cloud computing has been reported to have several potential benefits over current systems, including faster deployment of computing resources, a decreased need to buy hardware or to build data centers, and more robust collaboration capabilities. However, along with these benefits are the potential risks that any new form of computing services can bring, including information security breaches, infrastructure failure, and loss of data. Several media reports have described security breaches of cloud infrastructure. Furthermore, other reports have identified security as the major concern hindering federal agencies from adopting cloud computing.

Given these concerns, you asked us to (1) identify the models of cloud computing, (2) identify the information security implications of using cloud computing services in the federal government, and (3) assess federal guidance and efforts to address information security when using cloud computing.

To identify the models of cloud computing, we reviewed publications, guidance, and other documentation from the National Institute of Standards and Technology (NIST), industry groups, and private-sector organizations and then conducted interviews with representatives from these organizations to identify commonly expressed characteristics of cloud computing. To identify information security implications of using cloud computing services in the federal government, we obtained and reviewed publications and guidance from the preceding sources and analyzed them to identify positive and negative information security implications of using cloud computing. We also obtained perceptions of security implications from federal agencies by developing, pretesting, and distributing a survey to 24 major federal agencies.[1] To assess federal guidance and efforts to address information security when using cloud computing, we obtained and analyzed federal information security guidance relevant to cloud computing, identified federal agencies that have implemented cloud computing services, and examined relevant agency security practices related to cloud computing for consistency with existing federal guidance. Appendix I contains additional details on the objectives, scope, and methodology of our review.

We conducted this performance audit from September 2009 through May 2010 in accordance with generally accepted government auditing standards. Those standards require that we plan and perform the audit to obtain sufficient, appropriate evidence to provide a reasonable basis for our findings and conclusions based on our audit objectives. We believe that the evidence obtained provides a reasonable basis for our findings and conclusions based on our audit objectives.

BACKGROUND

Cloud computing is an emerging form of computing that relies on Internet-based services and resources to provide computing services to customers, while freeing them from the burden and costs of maintaining the underlying infrastructure. Examples of cloud computing include Web-based e-mail applications and common business applications that are accessed online through a browser, instead of through a local computer. The President's budget has identified the adoption of cloud computing in the federal government as a way to more efficiently use the billions of dollars spent annually on IT.[2] As part of the 2011 budget, the administration plans to deploy cloud computing in a series of pilot projects across the government. According to the President's budget, these pilots could potentially lead to significant savings in federal IT spending. However, along with the potential benefits of using cloud computing come the potential risks and challenges of adopting a new model for delivering IT services.

Federal Systems and Infrastructure Are at Risk from Cyber Threats

We have previously reported that cyber threats to federal information systems and cyber-based critical infrastructures are evolving and growing.[3] Without proper safeguards, computer systems are vulnerable to individuals and groups with malicious intentions who can intrude and use their access to obtain and manipulate sensitive information, commit fraud, disrupt operations, or launch attacks against other computer systems and networks. The threat is substantial and increasing for many reasons, including the ease with which intruders can obtain and use hacking tools and technologies.

Our previous reports and those by agency inspectors general describe serious and widespread information security control deficiencies that continue to place federal assets at risk of inadvertent or deliberate misuse, mission-critical information at risk of unauthorized modification or destruction, sensitive information at risk of inappropriate disclosure, and critical operations at risk of disruption. Accordingly, we have designated information security as a governmentwide high-risk area since 1997,[4] a designation that remains in force today.[5]

Further, the growing interconnectivity among information systems, the Internet, and other infrastructure presents increasing opportunities for attacks. For example, in 2009, several media reports described incidents that affected cloud service providers such as Amazon and Google. According to these reports, in December 2009, Amazon's Elastic Compute Cloud experienced two attacks on its cloud infrastructure. Google reported that in December 2009, an attack was made on e-mail accounts that it provided, which resulted in the inadvertent release of sensitive information. Adoption of cloud computing will require federal agencies to implement new protocols and technologies and interconnect diverse networks and systems while mitigating and responding to threats.

Policies, Procedures, and Required Controls Have Been Established to Protect Federal Information and Information Systems

Federal laws and guidance specify requirements for protecting federal systems and data. This includes systems used or operated by a contractor or other organization on behalf of a federal agency, which would include cloud computing. Recognizing the importance of securing federal systems and data, Congress enacted the Federal Information Security Management Act of 2002 (FISMA) to strengthen the security of federal information and information systems within federal agencies. FISMA requires each agency to develop, document, and implement an agencywide information security program to provide security for the information and information systems that support operations and assets of the agency, including those provided or managed by another agency, contractor, or other source. Specifically, FISMA requires that information security programs include, among other things, the following:

- risk-based policies and procedures that cost-effectively reduce information security risks to an acceptable level and ensure that information security is addressed throughout the life cycle of each information system;
- periodic testing and evaluation of the effectiveness of information security policies, procedures, and practices that include testing of management, operational, and technical controls for every system identified in the agency's required inventory of major information systems;
- a process for planning, implementing, evaluating, and documenting remedial actions to address any deficiencies in the information security policies, procedures, and practices of the agency;
- procedures for detecting, reporting, and responding to security incidents; and
- plans and procedures to ensure continuity of operations for information systems that support the operations and assets of the agency.

FISMA assigns certain responsibilities to the Office of Management and Budget (OMB) and other responsibilities to NIST. FISMA states that the Director of OMB shall oversee agency information security policies and practices, including

- developing and overseeing the implementation of policies, principles, standards, and guidelines on information security;
- requiring agencies to identify and provide information security protections commensurate with the risk and magnitude of harm resulting from the unauthorized access, use, disclosure, disruption, or destruction of information collected or

maintained by or on behalf of an agency, or information or information systems used or operated by an agency, or by a contractor or other organization on behalf of an agency;

- overseeing agency compliance with FISMA to enforce accountability; and
- reviewing, at least annually, and approving or disapproving agency information security programs.

Each year, OMB provides instructions to federal agencies regarding FISMA reporting. In this guidance, for example, OMB has stated that agencies are permitted to utilize private sector data services, provided that appropriate security controls are implemented and, more generally, that agencies ensure that their information security programs apply to all organizations that possess or use federal information, including contractors.

Under FISMA, NIST is tasked with developing, for systems other than national security systems, standards and guidelines that must include, at a minimum, (1) standards to be used by all agencies to categorize all of their information and information systems based on the objectives of providing appropriate levels of information security, according to a range of risk levels; (2) guidelines recommending the types of information and information systems to be included in each category; and (3) minimum information security requirements for information and information systems in each category.

Specifically, NIST has developed a risk management framework of standards and guidelines for agencies to follow in developing information security programs. Key publications are

- NIST Special Publication (SP) 800-37, Revision 1, *Guide for Applying the Risk Management Framework to Federal Information Systems: A Security Life Cycle Approach.*[6]
- Federal Information Processing Standard (FIPS) 199, *Standards for Security Categorization of Federal Information and Information Systems.*[7]
- FIPS 200, *Minimum Security Requirements for Federal Information and Information Systems.*[8]
- NIST SP 800-53, *Recommended Security Controls for Federal Information Systems and Organizations.*[9]

NIST SP 800-37 provides agencies with guidance for applying a risk management framework to federal information systems to include security categorization, security control selection and implementation, security control assessment, information system authorization, and security control monitoring. This framework includes the preparation of a security assessment report and authorization package.[10]

FIPS 199 provides agencies with criteria to identify and categorize all of their information and information systems based on the objectives of providing appropriate levels of information security according to a range of risk levels.

FIPS 200 requires a baseline of minimum information security controls for protecting the confidentiality, integrity, and availability of federal information systems and the information processed, stored, and transmitted by those systems. FIPS 200 directs agencies to implement these baseline control recommendations as follows:

- *Access control*: limit information system access to authorized users and to the types of transactions and functions that authorized users are permitted to exercise.
- *Certification, accreditation, and security assessments*: periodically assess security controls, develop and implement plans of action designed to correct deficiencies and reduce or eliminate vulnerabilities, authorize operation of systems and any associated system connections, and monitor system security controls on an ongoing basis.
- *Risk assessment*: periodically assess the risk to operations, assets, and individuals, resulting from the operation of systems and the associated processing, storage, or transmission of information.

In applying the provisions of FIPS 200, agencies first categorize their information and systems as required by FIPS 199, and then typically select an appropriate set of security controls from NIST SP 800-53 to satisfy their minimum security requirements. This helps to ensure that appropriate security requirements and security controls are applied to all federal information and information systems including cloud computing.

Selected Organizations Have Established Information Security Guidance for Cloud Computing

As stated previously in this chapter, federal laws, such as FISMA, and guidance such as that issued by NIST, specify requirements for protecting federal systems and data. Other organizations have developed security models and guidance that specifically apply to cloud computing services. These groups include the Cloud Security Alliance and the European Network and Information Security Agency.

The Cloud Security Alliance is a nonprofit organization formed to promote the use of leading practices for providing security assurance when using cloud computing. In December 2009, the alliance issued Security Guidance for Critical Areas of Focus in Cloud Computing, v2.1.[11] The guidance provides recommendations in 13 cloud computing domains:

- *Architectural framework*: provides a conceptual framework focusing on cloud computing.
- *Governance and enterprise risk management*: ability of an organization to govern and measure enterprise risks.
- *Legal and electronic discovery*: potential legal issues including protection requirements for information and computer systems.
- *Compliance and audit*: proving compliance when using cloud computing during an audit.
- *Information life cycle management*: managing data that is placed in the cloud and determining responsibility for data confidentiality, integrity, and availability.
- *Portability and interoperability*: the ability to move data and services from one provider to another or bring it back in-house.
- *Traditional security, business continuity, and disaster recovery*: identifying where cloud computing may assist in lowering security risks, while potentially increasing it in other areas.

- *Data center operations*: common data center characteristics that could be detrimental to ongoing services, and those that are fundamental to long-term stability.
- *Incident response, notification, and remediation*: addresses complexities that cloud computing brings to an incident handling program and forensics for both the provider and customer.
- *Application security*: securing application software that is either running on or being developed in the cloud.
- *Encryption and key management*: identifying proper encryption usage and scalable key management.
- *Identity and access management*: focuses on issues encountered when extending an organization's identity into the cloud.
- *Virtualization*: risks associated with items such as multitenancy, or the sharing of computing resources by different organizations.

For each domain, the guidance documents areas of concern for cloud computing.

The European Network and Information Security Agency is an organization established by the European Union that specializes in information security. In November 2009, the agency issued Cloud Computing: Benefits, Risks, and Recommendations for Information Security,[12] which provides a set of information requirements and includes questions that a customer can ask a cloud computing service provider in order to evaluate the service provider's information security practices. The requirements address

- *Personnel security*: policies and procedures when hiring IT administrators or others with system access.
- *Supply chain assurance*: defining and detailing services outsourced or subcontracted, inquiring about the measures taken to ensure third-party service levels are met and maintained, and confirmation that security policy and controls are applied to third party providers.
- *Operational security*: ensuring a provider employs appropriate controls to mitigate unauthorized disclosure of information in addition to defined agreements.
- *Identity and access management*: controls that apply to both the cloud providers and the customer, including access control, authorization, frameworks, identity provisioning, management of personal data, key management, encryption, authentication, and credential compromise or theft.
- *Asset management*: ensuring cloud providers maintain an inventory of the assets under their control.
- *Data and services portability*: clarifying the risks related to becoming dependent on one vendor.
- *Business continuity management*: maintaining a documented method to determine the impact of a disruption and the relevant response and restoration process.
- *Physical security*: ensuring the vendor provides adequate physical security for the customers' data.
- *Environmental controls*: policies and procedures to ensure environmental issues such as fires, floods, and power failures do not cause an interruption of service.
- *Legal requirements*: compliance with regulatory frameworks.

In addition, the agency's Information Assurance Framework[13] states the need for a clear definition and understanding of security-relevant roles and responsibilities between the customer and the provider.

Cloud Computing Is a Form of Shared Computing with Several Service and Deployment Models

According to NIST, cloud computing is a means "for enabling convenient, on-demand network access to a shared pool of configurable computing resources that can be rapidly provisioned and released with minimal management effort or service provider interaction."[14] This definition has been generally adopted throughout the federal government. Cloud computing is a form of delivering IT services that takes advantage of several broad evolutionary trends in IT, including the use of virtualization;[15] the decreased cost and increased speed of networked communications, such as the Internet; and overall increases in computing power. As such, any definition of cloud computing will be somewhat broad and subject to interpretation. While several other organizations have developed definitions of cloud computing, many of the elements of these definitions are encompassed in the NIST definition.

Cloud computing is further defined by its service and deployment models. There are three service models: infrastructure as a service, platform as a service, and software as a service (see figure1).

- *Infrastructure as a service* provides various infrastructure components such as hardware, storage, and other fundamental computing resources.
- *Platform as a service* provides a service that runs over an underlying infrastructure. A platform vendor offers a ready-to-use platform, such as an operating system like Microsoft Windows or Linux, which runs on vendor-provided infrastructure. Customers can build applications on a platform using application development frameworks, middleware capabilities, and functions such as databases.
- *Software as a service* runs on an underlying platform and infrastructure managed by the vendor and provides a self-contained operating environment used to deliver a complete application such as Web-based e-mail and related management capabilities.

In addition to the service models that describe what can be provided, NIST and other entities describe four deployment models that relate to how the cloud service is provided. These four cloud models are private, community, public, and hybrid (see figure 2). In a private cloud, the service is set up specifically for one organization, although there may be multiple customers within that organization, and the cloud may exist on or off the premises. In a community cloud, the service is set up for related organizations that have similar requirements. A public cloud is available to any paying customer and is owned and operated by the service provider. A hybrid cloud is a composite of the deployment models.

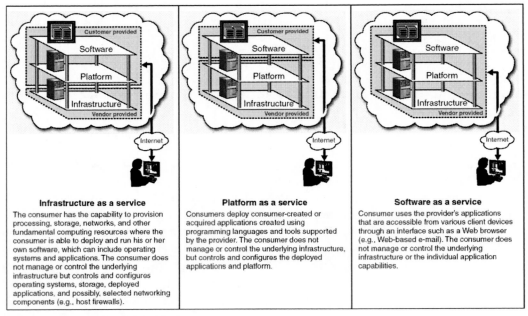

Source: GAO analysis of NIST data.

Figure 1. Cloud Computing Service Models

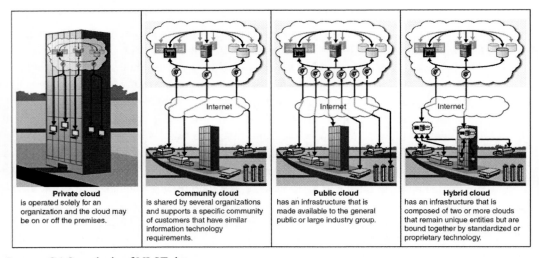

Source: GAO analysis of NI ST data.

Figure 2. Cloud Computing Deployment Models

According to NIST, cloud computing includes each of the characteristics listed in table 1 and in figure 3.

While NIST states that all five of its essential characteristics should be present for an application to be considered cloud computing, other federal officials and experts stated that an application that has some but not all of these characteristics could still be considered cloud computing.

Table 1. NIST Essential Characteristics of Cloud Computing

Essential characteristic	Description
On-demand self service	Consumer can unilaterally provision computing capabilities as needed automatically, without interaction with the service's provider.
Broad network access	Capabilities are available over the network and accessed through standard mechanisms such as desktop computers, laptops, mobile phones, and personal digital assistants.
Resource pooling	Provider's computing resources are pooled to serve multiple consumers using a multitenant model, with different physical and virtual resources dynamically assigned and reassigned according to consumer demand.
Rapid elasticity	Capabilities can be rapidly and elastically provisioned, in some cases automatically, to quickly scale out (increase) and rapidly released to quickly scale back in (decrease).
Measured service	Cloud systems automatically control and optimize resource use by leveraging a metering (measured use) capability at some level of abstraction appropriate to the type of service.

Source: GAO analysis of NIST data.

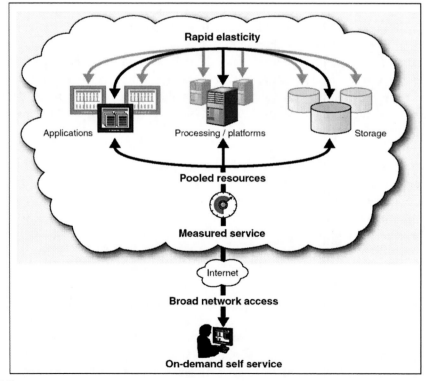

Source: GAO.

Figure 3. NIST Essential Characteristics

CLOUD COMPUTING HAS BOTH POSITIVE AND NEGATIVE INFORMATION SECURITY IMPLICATIONS

Cloud computing can both increase and decrease the security of information systems. Potential information security benefits include those related to the use of virtualization, such as faster deployment of patches, and from economies of scale, such as potentially reduced costs for disaster recovery. Risks include those related to dependence on the security assurances of a vendor; dependence on the vendor; and concerns related to multitenancy, or sharing computing resources among different organizations. However, these risks may vary based on the cloud deployment model.

Cloud Computing Can Provide Potential Information Security Benefits

The use of cloud computing has the potential to provide several benefits related to information security. These benefits are related to the attributes of cloud computing—specifically, its use of virtualization and automation, broad network access, potential economies of scale, and use of self-service technologies.

The use of virtualization and automation in cloud computing can expedite the implementation of secure configurations for virtual machine images. Department of Defense (DOD) officials responsible for one cloud computing program stated that virtualization allows a cloud computing provider to rapidly replicate secure configurations for cloud-based virtual servers, rather than manually applying secure configurations to physical servers, which could be required in a traditional environment that has not employed virtualization techniques. Private sector representatives also stated that virtualization can allow faster deployment of secure server configurations, security upgrades, and patches for security vulnerabilities than a traditional computing infrastructure can.

Other advantages relate to cloud computing's broad network access and use of Internet-based technologies. For example, several agencies stated that cloud computing provided a reduced need to carry data in removable media because of the ability to access the data through the Internet, regardless of location. NIST officials stated that shifting public data to a public cloud using the Internet that is separate from the agency's internal network is a means of network segmentation that may reduce exposure of sensitive data on the agency's internal network.

Additional advantages relate to the potential economies of scale and distributed nature of cloud computing. For example, in response to our survey, 22 of the 24 agencies identified low-cost disaster recovery and data storage as a potential benefit. Specifically, cloud computing may provide a cheaper way to store backup copies of information. Agencies also stated that a cloud provider may have more resources to devote to security than the agency may have available. The large-scale and mitigation techniques that cloud providers offer may also reduce vulnerability to denial of service attacks. Department of Transportation (DOT) officials responsible for a cloud computing program noted that the program's Web site, which used a cloud computing service provider, was better able to withstand a denial of service attack because of the use of the cloud provider. The National Aeronautics and Space Administration (NASA) officials responsible for another cloud computing program stated that it may require less effort for cloud computing customers to ensure effective information security if information security controls were already implemented by the provider. Customers could also be freed from the responsibility of maintaining a physical infrastructure, as well as resolving management, operational, and technical issues related to the underlying cloud platform, although the customers would still be responsible for ensuring these issues are addressed and that data are adequately protected.

The self-service aspect of cloud computing may also provide benefits. For example, 20 out of the 24 agencies identified the ability to apply security controls on demand as a potential benefit. A private sector representative stated that cloud computing provided the ability for more flexible and granular control of security. For example, features such as encryption and monitoring could be individually applied as needed. Table 2 lists potential benefits of cloud computing grouped by cloud computing attribute.

Cloud Computing Can Create Information Security Risks

In addition to benefits, the use of cloud computing can create numerous information security risks for federal agencies. Twenty-two of the 24 agencies reported that they are either concerned or very concerned about the potential information security risks associated with cloud computing. These concerns include risks related to being dependent on a vendor's security assurances and the vendor, and risks related to the use of multitenancy.

Several cloud computing information security risks relate to the ability to rely on a vendor's security assurances and practices. Specifically, several agencies stated concerns about

- the possibility of ineffective or noncompliant service provider security controls—which could lead to vulnerabilities affecting the confidentiality, integrity, and availability of agency information;
- the potential loss of governance and physical control over agency data and information—that is, in using cloud computing services, the agency cedes control to the provider for the performance of certain security controls and practices;

Table 2. Potential Benefits of Cloud Computing

Attribute	Potential benefit
Virtualization and automation	Rapid replication of securely configured servers, security upgrades, and patches
Broad network access	Reduced need to carry data in removable media Ability to shift data needed by public away from internal agency network
Economies of scale and distributed infrastructure	Low-cost disaster recovery and storage Resistance to denial of service attack
On-demand self-service	Apply security controls on demand Individually apply features such as encryption and monitoring

Source: GAO analysis of agency and private sector data.

- the insecure or ineffective deletion of agency data by cloud providers once services have been provided and are complete; and
- potentially inadequate background security investigations for service provider employees—which could lead to an increased risk of wrongful activities by malicious insiders.

Of particular concern is dependency on a vendor. All 24 agencies specifically noted concern about the possibility of loss of data if a cloud computing provider terminated its services. For example, the provider and the customer may not have agreed on terms to transfer or duplicate the data. The European Network and Information Security Agency also identified dependency on a vendor as a high risk, noting the lack of tools, procedures, or standard data formats to ensure data, application, and service portability. The agency stated that this can make it difficult for the customer to migrate from one provider to another or to migrate data and services back to an in-house IT environment. One member of GAO's Executive Council on Information Management and Technology[16] stated that if an agency chooses to implement cloud computing, at some point in the future the vendor may want to raise the cost for use of the cloud. The agency may then have no alternative to paying the cost because it lacks the technical ability to bring the service back in-house.

Multitenancy and use of shared resources can also increase risk. Twenty-three out of the 24 agencies identified multitenancy as a potential information security risk because one customer could intentionally or unintentionally gain access to another customer's data, causing a release of sensitive information.

Additional concerns relate to exchanging authentication information on users and responding to security incidents. For example, NASA officials responsible for a cloud computing program stated that identity management and user authentication are a concern because customers and a provider may need to establish a means to securely exchange and rely on authentication and authorization information for system users. In addition, responding to security incidents may be more difficult in a shared environment because there could be confusion over who performs the specific tasks—the customer or the provider. The Nuclear Regulatory Commission emphasized the importance of a clear delineation of responsibilities as they relate to incident response management, whereby the cloud computing service provider has the responsibility to report the security incident to the agency and the agency is responsible for reporting the incident to the appropriate government entity.

Another concern is the increased volume of data transmitted across agency and public networks. This could lead to an increased risk of the data being intercepted in transit and then disclosed.

NIST also stated that cloud computing security is dependent on the security of a user's Internet browser, and that vulnerabilities in the browser can create vulnerabilities for the cloud computing service.

Although there are numerous potential information security risks related to cloud computing, these risks vary based on the particular deployment model. For example, NIST states that private clouds may have a lower threat exposure than community clouds, which may have a lower threat exposure than public clouds. Officials from another agency stated that they are considering implementing a private cloud behind their agency's firewall because of the moderate-to-high impact classification of sensitive data they were considering placing into this system.[17] Several agency officials and industry representatives stated that initial use of public clouds may be focused on low-impact information. However, several industry representatives also stated that making general statements based on cloud deployment models may be misleading and that an agency would need to examine the specific security controls of the vendor they were evaluating. Table 3 lists potential risks of cloud computing.

FEDERALAGENCIES HAVE BEGUN EFFORTS TO ADDRESS INFORMATION SECURITY ISSUES FOR CLOUD COMPUTING, BUT SPECIFIC GUIDANCE IS LACKING AND EFFORTS REMAININCOMPLETE

Federal agencies have started to address information security when using cloud computing; however, they have not always developed corresponding guidance. Furthermore, agencies that have implemented cloud computing efforts have faced challenges in implementing existing federal information security guidance and identified the need to streamline and automate the process of implementing this guidance. While several governmentwide cloud computing security activities are under way by organizations such as OMB and the General Services Administration (GSA), significant work remains to be completed. In addition, NIST has begun certain efforts related to cloud computing information security, but its existing guidance is not specific to cloud computing issues, and it has only begun plans to issue cloud-specific security guidance.

Table 3. Potential Risks of Cloud Computing

Risk	Explanation
Reliance on vendor's security assurances and practices	An agency is dependent on a provider's ability to ensure effective security. A provider may have security weaknesses such as ineffective or noncompliant security controls. For example, a provider may not maintain adequate physical control over agency data and information or may have inadequate background investigations for provider employees.
Dependence on a vendor	If the agency and provider do not agree on a means to transfer or duplicate data, data may be lost if a provider ends its service. An agency that uses a cloud computing provider may also lose the technical ability to bring the information system back in-house.
Insecure or ineffective identity management	Agencies and a cloud provider may need to securely exchange and rely on sensitive authentication and authorization information for system users.
Unclear responsibilities for incident response	There may be confusion over roles and responsibilitiesbetween agency and provider.

Source: GAO analysis of agency and private sector data.

Agencies Have Taken Steps to Address Information Security Issues for Cloud Computing, but Have Not Always Developed Corresponding Policies or Procedures and Face Challenges in Implementing Existing Guidance and Processes

About half of the 24 agencies we asked reported using some form of cloud computing for obtaining either infrastructure, platform, or software services. These agencies identified measures they are taking or plan to take when using cloud computing. Specifically, 23 of the 24 agencies reported that they currently write or plan to write and enforce comprehensive service-level agreements to include information security control requirements and currently use or plan to use appropriate encryption when using cloud computing. Further, 22 of the 24 agencies responded that they currently limit or plan to limit the type of information placed in a cloud, while 21 of the 24 agencies currently limit or are planning to limit the type of cloud deployment model used. Appendix II includes descriptions of three case studies of cloud computing implementations in the federal government, including steps taken to address information security.

However, these actions have not always been accompanied by the development of related policies or procedures. Of the 23 agencies that reported writing and enforcing or planning to write and enforce comprehensive service-level agreements when using cloud computing, 9 agencies have approved and documented policies and procedures for doing so. Fifteen agencies have documented policies and procedures for the use of encryption. Just four agencies responded that they have documented policies and procedures limiting the type of information placed in a cloud and two agencies responded that they have documented policies and procedures limiting the type of cloud deployment model used. The lack of approved and documented policies and procedures to ensure effective information security when using cloud computing could place sensitive information in a cloud environment at risk.

Agencies Have Concerns about Ensuring Vendor Implementation of Information Security Requirements

Most agencies identified challenges and concerns in implementing existing information security laws and guidance. For example, 20 of the 24 agencies identified concerns about service provider compliance with and implementation of government information security requirements. Agencies also expressed concerns about limitations on their ability to conduct independent audits and assessments of security controls of cloud computing service providers.

Several industry representatives agreed that compliance and oversight issues are a concern. However, the representatives also stated that requiring each individual agency that uses a service provider to conduct its own assessment of controls and audits and complete a separate assessment and authorization process would be burdensome and remove the cost advantages offered by cloud computing. In response, representatives raised the idea of having a single government entity or other independent entity conduct security oversight and audits for cloud computing service providers. The process could be similar to the Statement on Auditing Standards (SAS) 70 audit process often used as part of financial audits.[18] A SAS 70 report is issued by an independent auditor for a service provider that processes financial data on behalf of others; it discusses the effectiveness of the service provider's internal controls over the processing of transactions that may be relevant to the financial reporting of customers. Management of the customer organization and its auditor may use this chapter to assess the internal control policies and procedures at the service provider as part of the overall evaluation of the internal control at the customer organization. Some cloud computing service providers have obtained a SAS 70 audit for use and review by its customers. In discussing the use of SAS 70 reports to meet information security requirements, OMB Memorandum M-09-29[19] states that it is the agency's responsibility to ensure that

- the scope of the SAS 70 audit is sufficient and fully addresses the specific contractor system requiring FISMA review, and
- the audit encompasses all controls and requirements of law, OMB policy, and NIST guidance.

There are attestation standards, similar to those in SAS 70, that could be used to provide an assessment of controls at a service provider that relates to the effective implementation of security and compliance with specified requirements of laws and guidance. However, the scope of an audit based on a standard such as SAS 70 is defined by the service provider and could exclude key controls essential to effectively protecting agency information. Therefore, if an attestation report on security effectiveness and compliance with laws and guidance is used, it is critical that the scope of the controls addressed by the attestation report is sufficient to meet agency requirements.

Agencies also stated that having a cloud service provider that had been precertified as being in compliance with government information security requirements through some type of governmentwide approval process would make it easier for them to consider using cloud computing. For example, DOT officials implementing the Car Allowance Rebate System program stated that having a cloud service provider that was precertified to process federal financial transactions may have made implementation of the payment processing system for the program easier. Until such precertified providers are in place, the adoption of cloud computing may be limited.

Processes, Documentation, and Division of Roles and Responsibilities for Cloud ComputingCreate Challenges

In their efforts to ensure information security in cloud computing, agencies have had to re-examine and, at times, change related processes, documentation, and roles and responsibilities. For example, DOD officials implementing a cloud computing program identified the need to improve related DOD business processes, including those related to security. The existing DOD process required for risk assessment and assessment and authorization for information systems created challenges because of its focus on stand-alone systems and multiple levels of organizational review. In response, the program office worked with a contractor to re-engineer the process and reduce the time needed to complete information security requirements for new systems. NASA officials also noted the increased complexity of information security-related document maintenance in a shared owner environment and took steps to address this issue.

Other agency concerns related to the division of information security responsibilities between customer and vendor. For example, both DOD and NASA officials responsible for cloud computing implementations at their agencies stated that a clear division of security roles and responsibilities in cloud computing was important. For example, NASA officials divided responsibility for the security controls in NIST SP 800-53 Revision 3 for low-impact systems into customer and provider controls and found that the customer had primary responsibility for 47 of the 112 total controls. Similarly, DOD officials also divided responsibilities for the corresponding DOD information assurance controls between customers and service providers. Both sets of agency officials commented on the challenges in analyzing and maintaining such a division of responsibilities but noted that clear assignment of responsibilities was important for effective information security.

Several Governmentwide Cloud Computing Information Security Initiatives Have Been Started, but Key Guidance and Efforts Have Not Been Completed

To address cloud computing security issues, the executive branch has begun several initiatives. However, these initiatives have not yet been completed. For example, OMB stated that it began a federal cloud computing initiative in February 2009; however, it does not yet have an overarching strategy or an implementation plan. According to OMB officials, the initiative includes an online cloud computing storefront managed by GSA and will likely contain three pilot cloud computing projects, each with a lead agency: (1) a voucher payment portal led by the Department of the Treasury; (2) a tool for citizen interaction to support open government led by GSA; and (3) a citizen services dashboard led by GSA. However, as of March 2010, a date had not been set for the release of the strategy or for any of the pilots. In addition, OMB has not yet defined how information security issues, such as a shared assessment and authorization process, will be addressed in this strategy.

Federal agencies have stated that additional guidance on cloud computing security would be helpful. Addressing information security issues as part of this strategy would provide additional direction to agencies looking to use cloud computing services. Until this strategy has been completed, agencies will lack clear direction in how to ensure information security while implementing cloud computing services.

GSA Has Established Program Office and Cloud ComputingStorefront, but Key Procurement Has Been Delayed in Part Due to Information Security Concerns

GSA has established a Cloud Computing Program Management Office that manages several cloud computing activities within GSA and provides administrative support for cloud computing efforts by the federal Chief Information Officers (CIO) Council. Specifically, the program office manages a storefront, www.apps.gov, established by GSA to provide a central location for federal agencies to purchase several software as a service cloud computing applications, including

- business applications, such as data analysis, human resources, and financial management software, and tools for tracking and monitoring various types of activities;

- office productivity applications, which include standard word processing and spreadsheet applications, and also applications used for brainstorming, collaboration, document management, and project management; and
- social media applications that are focused on making it easier to create and distribute content and that enable people to communicate easily and share information.

GSA plans to expand the storefront by also providing infrastructure as a service cloud computing offerings such as storage, virtual machines, and Web hosting. To this end, GSA began a procurement process by issuing a request for quotations in July 2009. The request asked for quotations to provide the government with required documentation on vendors' offerings of cloud storage services, virtual machines, or cloud Web hosting. These services would be available through the www.apps.gov storefront. The procurement closed in September 2009, with nine vendors submitting quotations.

However, addressing information security issues has been a significant challenge in the procurement. GSA officials stated that as they were analyzing the submitted quotations, one issue they were attempting to resolve was establishing a process for federal agencies to work with GSA to complete the information security assessment and authorization process when using these services. In early March 2010, GSA canceled the request and announced plans to begin a new request process, in part due to concerns and challenges in addressing information security. Specifically, the new request will ask for services that meet the level of security for both low- and moderate-impact systems as defined in FIPS 199 and NIST SP 800-53. The canceled request required only low-level security. GSA stated that providing cloud computing services that meet both low- and moderate-impact information security controls would allow a broader range of services and customers. GSA officials also stated that they need to work with vendors after a new procurement has been completed to develop a shared assessment and authorization process, but have not yet developed specific plans to do so.

Adding moderate-impact controls to the request may increase demand for the infrastructure services when the procurement is completed; however, establishing both an assessment and authorization process for customers of these services and a clear division of security responsibilities will help ensure that these services, when purchased and effectively implemented, protect sensitive federal information.

Federal CIO Council Has Established Cloud ComputingExecutiveSteeringCommittee but Has Not Finalized Key Process or Guidance

The CIO Council established the Cloud Computing Executive Steering Committee to promote the use of cloud computing in the federalgovernment. The GSA Cloud Computing Program Management Office provides technical and administrative support for the committee. The committee consists of an overall advisory council and these four subgroups:

- The communications subgroup provides information on the status of cloud computing in the federal government and is planning an information portal for the www.apps.gov storefront.
- The operational excellence subgroup examines cloud computing implementations at federal agencies, assists agencies in evaluating potential applications for cloud computing, and identifies possible improvements to the storefront.

- The standards subgroup is helping develop standards related to interoperability and portability of cloud computing services.
- The security subgroup is addressing several issues related to information security and cloud computing.

The security subgroup has begun developing recommendations for a streamlined assessment and authorization process through the Federal Risk and Authorization Management Program. This process would address authorizing operation of a system, including the development and implementation of risk assessments and security controls. For example, according to GSA, the program is to provide joint authorizations and continuous monitoring services for all federal agencies with an initial focus on cloud computing. The process would rely on several key steps of the process being performed by a governmentwide organization, while the final authorization to operate a system would still be made by a designated official at the agency purchasing the service. According to a summary provided by GSA, the goals for this process include providing better security and privacy, clearer communication of security requirements for government and industry, improved efficiency and broad acceptance for agencies, and compliance with existing federal information security guidance and legislation. Officials involved in the process have noted the need to clearly delineate security control responsibilities between providers and customers. The group is currently working with its members to define interagency security requirements for cloud systems and services and related information security controls from both the moderate and low baselines specified in NIST SP 800-53 Revision 3.

According to GSA, a draft of the new assessment and authorization process has been approved by the Cloud Computing Executive Steering Committee. However, a deadline for completing development and implementation of this process had not been established. A particular concern of the committee is the requirement for agency CIOs to certify the adequacy of information security controls for systems that they do not own or operate. GSA officials involved in this effort stated that it may be up to OMB to clearly establish that agencies will be able to rely on the shared process.

In addition to the Executive Steering Committee and its subgroups, another component of the CIO Council is working on information security issues related to cloud computing. The group, which is part of the CIO Council's Information Security and Identity Management Committee, is currently developing a white paper on guidelines for the secure use of cloud computing for federal departments and agencies, according to a cochair of this group. The paper is intended to provide agencies with guidelines, use cases, and scenarios to help program managers make risk-based decisions when selecting cloud deployment and service models.

Federal agencies responding to our information request, officials of the cloud computing case studies described in appendix II, and private sector representatives have all identified concerns with how to properly and efficiently complete activities related to the assessment and authorization process, including control selection and testing, when using cloud computing. Until a clear, comprehensive, and efficient process has been established, adoption of cloud computing in the federal government may be limited, and cloud computing programs that are implemented may not have appropriate information security controls in place.

NIST Is CoordinatingActivitieswith CIO Council but has not Established Cloud-Specific Guidance

NIST is responsible for establishing information security guidance for federal agencies to support FISMA. Cloud computing is an emerging model for IT, and NIST has not yet established guidance specific to cloud computing. However, according to its officials, the institute has begun several other activities related to cloud computing. For example, it has developed a definition of cloud computing and is participating in the activities of the CIO Council subgroups.

The NIST official leading the institute's cloud computing activities stated that existing NIST requirements apply to cloud computing and can be tailored to the information security issues specific to cloud computing. However, as previously discussed in this chapter, both federal and private sector officials have made clear that existing guidance is not sufficient. At the conclusion of our review, NIST officials stated that the institute is planning to issue guidance on cloud computing and virtualization but had not yet finalized the topics that it would cover and had not determined a date for issuing this guidance.

Our analysis also indicates areas where existing NIST guidance does not clearly address information security issues specifically related to cloud computing. While NIST SP 800-53 covers general security areas important to cloud computing to some extent, the guidance lacks specificity in key security areas. For example, NIST guidance does not directly address key cloud computing security issues such as portability and interoperability, data center operations, and virtualization. Both public and private sector officials identified interoperability issues and concerns about virtualization as challenges agencies face when making decisions on whether to implement cloud computing. At the end of our review, NIST officials stated that SP 800-53 was not intended to be specific to a particular type of computing, such as cloud computing, but agreed that areas such as portability and interoperability were important in implementing cloud computing and they were considering including them in future NIST publications.

Furthermore, federal agencies stated that establishing a clear delineation of security control responsibilities between providers and customers is a challenge, but existing NIST guidance does not fully address these issues or establish a process for doing so. Existing NIST guidance addresses the establishment of interconnection security agreements between different organizations; however, the guidance is not specific to issues related to cloud computing. For example, NIST guidance does not address the division of information security responsibilities when several organizations are involved in cloud computing or possible variations in these roles and responsibilities due to the use of different cloud deployment and service models. Until federal guidance addresses information security issues specific to cloud computing and provides information on how to divide responsibilities between providers and customers, agencies may not be able to effectively ensure the security of their systems when using cloud computing.

CONCLUSIONS

About half of the 24 agencies are using various models of cloud computing, and many others are interested in using it; however, implementation of this emerging technology presents both information security benefits and risks. Agencies have taken steps to address cloud computing security but have not always developed corresponding guidance. The use of attestation standards and precertification of cloud service providers may provide a way for agencies to ensure information security when using cloud computing service providers. However, OMB has not yet developed a strategy that addresses the information security issues related to cloud computing, and guidance from individual agencies and NIST to ensure information security is insufficient. While the federal CIO Council is developing a shared assessment and authorization process, which could help foster adoption of cloud computing, this process remains incomplete, and GSA has yet to complete its procurement of cloud computing infrastructure as a service offerings for its storefront, in part due to security concerns. Until federal guidance and processes that specifically address information security for cloud computing are developed, agencies may be hesitant to implement cloud computing, and those programs that have been implemented may not have effective information security controls in place.

RECOMMENDATIONS FOR EXECUTIVE ACTION

To assist federal agencies in identifying uses for cloud computing and information security measures to use in implementing cloud computing, we recommend that the Director of OMB take the following three actions:

- Establish milestones for completing a strategy for implementing the federal cloud computing initiative.
- Ensure the strategy addresses the information security challenges associated with cloud computing, such as needed agency-specific guidance, the appropriate use of attestation standards for control assessments of cloud computing service providers, division of information security responsibilities between customer and provider, the shared assessment and authorization process, and the possibility for precertification of cloud computing service providers.
- Direct the CIO Council Cloud Computing Executive Steering Committee to develop a plan, including milestones, for completing a governmentwide security assessment and authorization process for cloud services.

To assist federal agencies in selecting and acquiring precertified cloud computing products and services, we recommend that the Administrator of GSA, as part of the procurement for infrastructure as a service cloud computing technologies, ensure that full consideration is given to the information security challenges of cloud computing, including a need for a shared assessment and authorization process.

To assist federal agencies in implementing appropriate information security controls when using cloud computing, we recommend that the Secretary of Commerce direct the Administrator of NIST to issue cloud computing information security guidance to federal agencies to more fully address key cloud computing domain areas that are lacking in SP 800-53, such as virtualization, data center operations, and portability and interoperability, and include a process for defining roles and responsibilities of cloud computing service providers and customers.

List of Congressional Requesters

The Honorable Joseph I. Lieberman
Chairman
The Honorable Susan M. Collins
Ranking Member
Committee on Homeland Security and Governmental Affairs
United States Senate

, The Honorable Tom R. Carper
Chairman
Subcommittee on Federal Financial Management, Government
Information, Federal Services, and International Security
Committee on Homeland Security and Governmental Affairs

United States Senate
The Honorable Diane E. Watson
Chairwoman
Subcommittee on Government Management, Organization,
and Procurement
Committee on Oversight and Government Reform
House of Representatives

APPENDIX I: OBJECTIVES, SCOPE, AND METHODOLOGY

The objectives of our review were to (1) identify the models of cloud computing; (2) identify the information security implications of using cloud computing services in the federal government; and (3) assess federal guidance and efforts to address information security when using cloud computing.

To identify cloud computing models, we reviewed publications, white papers, and other documentation from public and private sector organizations. We then obtained relevant information through interviews with officials from the National Institute of Standards and Technology (NIST) and private sector organizations that offer cloud computing services. We compared cloud computing descriptions and definitions of cloud computing from these sources to identify similarities and differences.

To identify the information security implications of using cloud computing services in the federal government, we reviewed documentation from the public and private sectors. Our documentation review focused on identifying the positive and negative information security implications (risks and benefits) of cloud computing. We supplemented this review by interviewing representatives of public and private sector organizations to prioritize these implications and identify information security challenges associated with federal agenciesworking with cloud computing service providers. We interviewed representatives of several of the 24 major federal agencies[20] and private sector organizations that provide cloud computing services. In addition, we issued a survey and data request to the 24 federal agencies. We pretested the survey at three agencies to ensure that the questions were relevant and easy to comprehend. For each agency surveyed, we identified the appropriate point of contact, notified each one of our work, and distributed the survey along with a data request to each via e-mail in November 2009. All 24 agencies responded to our survey and data request from December 2009 to February 2010; results are reported as of this date. We contacted agency officials when necessary for additional information or clarification of agency responses. We did not verify the accuracy of the agencies' responses; however, we reviewed supporting documentation that agencies provided to corroborate information provided in their responses. We then analyzed the results of the survey and data request responses to identify

- the potential information security implications agencies might consider positive or negative for cloud computing;
- the techniques agencies are using to ensure that effective information security measures are being implemented when using cloud computing;
- the extent to which the agency has procured or plans to procure cloud computing products or services using www.apps.gov; and
- the concerns agencies faced when working with cloud computing providers.

Conducting any survey may introduce errors. For example, differences in how a particular question is interpreted, the sources of information that are available to respondents, or how the data are entered or were analyzed can introduce variability into the survey results. We took steps in the development of the survey instrument, the data collection, and the data analysis to minimize errors.

To assess federal guidance and efforts to address information security when using cloud computing, we gathered and analyzed information at federal entities with specific governmentwide responsibilities, including the Office of Management and Budget (OMB), General Services Administration (GSA), NIST, and the federal Chief Information Officers Council. We further reviewed federal information security guidance to determine the extent to which the guidance addressed concerns specifically related to cloud computing and relevant information security areas. For example, we compared NIST Special Publication 800-53 Revision 3 to key cloud computing security areas specified by other IT security organizations such as the Cloud Security Alliance and European Network and Information Security Agency. We also conducted case studies on three federal cloud computing programs, the Department of Defense's (DOD) Rapid Access Computing Environment (RACE) program, the National Aeronautics and Space Administration's (NASA) Nebula program, and the Department of Transportation's (DOT) Car Allowance Rebate System (CARS) program. We selected these agency case studies based on cloud computing experts' and agency officials' referrals, and any references in the documentation we reviewed. We also relied on the survey of the 24 major federal agencies to identify the techniques federal agencies stated they used to ensure that effective information security measures are in place when they use cloud computing.

We conducted this performance audit from September 2009 through May 2010 in accordance with generally accepted government auditing standards. Those standards require that we plan and perform the audit to obtain sufficient, appropriate evidence to provide a reasonable basis for our findings and conclusions based on our audit objectives. We believe that the evidence obtained provides a reasonable basis for our findings and conclusions based on our audit objectives.

APPENDIX II: CLOUD COMPUTING CASE STUDIES

The following is a description of three federal cloud computing programs: the DOD's RACE program; NASA's Nebula program; and Department of Transportation's CARS program, including lessons learned related to information security.

DOD's RACE Program Provides Platforms for DOD Systems Development Efforts

The RACE program was started by DOD's Defense Information Systems Agency in October 2008 to provide platform as a service to support DOD systems development efforts. The goal of the program is to provide the service through a streamlined process including system provisioning, development, testing, assessment and authorization, and deployment of applications to DOD customers within a private cloud. RACE customers purchase one or many virtual machines[21] through a self-service portal. The RACE program is managed by both government and contractor personnel within existing DOD data centers and operates only on DOD's internal network.

According to program officials, users can acquire server capacity rapidly for short- or long-term use without the need for approval for a capital acquisition expense. Initial provisioning in RACE takes a few days, while traditional purchasing can take a month or longer. RACE currently has about 120 virtual machines in use. Program officials state that they hope to expand RACE to the classified environment in the future. Currently, DOD uses three information system impact levels,[22] which are equivalent to low, moderate, and high, as defined by NIST. RACE is currently certified to operate at the moderate-impact level, although the current use is for data at the lowest impact level.

Information Security Controls and LessonsLearned

DOD officials emphasized the need for a clear division of responsibilities among its customers and cloud service providers when implementing cloud computing. For RACE, potential customers must agree to meet minimum information security requirements before becoming customers of the RACE program, including resolving any open vulnerabilities or documenting them in a plan of action and milestones. The program also has documentation that divides information security control responsibilities between controls managed by the RACE program and controls managed by the customer. Using a matrix containing the appropriate DOD information assurance controls, RACE officials determined that out of 106 controls, 62 were the responsibility of the customer, 31 of the service provider, and 13 were not applicable. Of the 106 controls, 37 were classified as inheritable controls, meaning the customer application inherits several predefined information assurance controls from RACE.

During the initial stages of RACE implementation, program officials recognized the need to improve related DOD business processes, including those related to security. The existing DOD process required for risk assessment and assessment and authorization for information systems created challenges because of its focus on stand-alone systems and multiple levels of organizational review. In response, the program office worked with a contractor to re-engineer the process to complete information security requirements for new systems. Program officials estimate that the total time required to complete the assessment and authorization process will be reduced from 80 days to 40 days for RACE customers, but the process is too new to be verified. A subsequent release is planned to further reduce this time to 7 days. The officials stated that overall implementation of the RACE program and other cloud efforts would have been faster if guidance and processes related to assessment and authorization for cloud computing had already been in place.

NASA's Nebula Pilot Uses Open-Source Technologies to Enhance Collaboration

Nebula is a cloud computing pilot under development at NASA's Ames Research Center in Mountain View, California. It is an infrastructure as a service implementation for scientific data and Web-based applications. Platform as a service capability is planned for the future. According to NASA, Nebula is to provide high-capacity computing, storage, and network connectivity using a virtualized, scalable approach to achieve cost and energy savings. Currently, NASA's Nebula is considered a private cloud and is operated at Ames Research Center on NASA equipment using both government and contractor personnel. Nebula is housed in a standard shipping container that is mounted in place, but could be transported if needed (see figure 4). Program officials chose this design as a means to easily replicate the Nebula equipment as the program expands. The officials state that a future goal is for Nebula to become a hybrid cloud as a way to eventually foster collaboration in analysis of NASA-sponsored research with the academic community and the public. As a result, Nebula relies on open-source cloud computing technologies so that data can be easily transferred to other cloud service providers if required. The officials stated that when NASA data is first generated, its sensitivity must be evaluated to see if it is appropriate for public release. Once the decision has been made to share the data, the use of Nebula makes sharing information easier.

The officials also stated that Nebula will provide other benefits. For example, according to NASA, researchers who use Nebula will not have to purchase their own servers, hardware, and computing infrastructure, which can be time-consuming. Nebula is currently authorized to handle only low-impact data as defined in FIPS 199; however, officials noted that they may migrate to a moderate-impact system in the future. Currently, Nebula's customers include the World Wide Telescope from Ames Research Center and the Climate Grid led by NASA's Goddard Space Flight Center.

Information Security Controls and LessonsLearned

NASA officials said that a major challenge in their implementation of Nebula was determining how to apply federal information security policies and guidance because current federal guidance does not clearly address specific controls for a cloud computing environment like Nebula. Examples included how to track, schedule, and report compliance with the Federal Information Security Management Act of 2002 when customers are responsible for some controls and the provider is responsible for others, and how to address security and service-level agreements. Nebula officials noted challenges in determining responsibilities and identifying the necessary documentation for interconnection security agreements[23] between customers and third-party systems used by the customers.

Additionally, officials noted the need to clearly define the information security controls for which the cloud provider is responsible and those for which the customer is responsible. For example, effective incident response in a cloud environment requires delineation of customer and provider responsibilities, which is information that is not currently addressed in federal guidance. NASA Nebula officials noted that the exact number of controls for which the customer is responsible varies depending on the cloud computing service model. In Nebula's current infrastructure as a service offering, the customer is responsible for 47 of the 112 total controls in NIST SP 800-53 Revision 3 for low-impact systems. They noted further that many of the responsibilities under the customer controls are actually shared between the customer and Nebula, as the service provider, because the provider will still have responsibility for the parts of the infrastructure under the provider's control.

DOT's CARS Program Made Partial Use of Cloud Computing, but Was Limited by Security Concerns

The CARS program used a public cloud for part of its system. CARS was administered by DOT under the authority of the Consumer Assistance to Recycle and Save Act of 2009. The program allowed owners of certain less fuel-efficient vehicles to receive a credit for trading in a vehicle and purchasing or leasing a new, more fuel-efficient vehicle. Dealers were reimbursed for this credit by the government. According to program officials, the program faced a number of challenges, including having only about 1 month to develop and deploy the system and an unexpectedly high demand for the program; users of the program tripled in number within 12 days of the start of the program.

The program, which operated from July 24 to August 24, 2009, had two major information technology components: a publicly accessible Web site with content for consumers, dealers, and salvage facilities, and a payment processing system used by dealers to submit applications to the program. The Web site was considered a low-impact system under FIPS 199, but the payment processing system, which contained personal information, was considered a moderate-impact system.

The public Web site used a cloud computing service provider that hosted the Web site and provided additional surge capabilities to cope with spikes in demand for Web content. Effective communication through the Web site was vital to implementation of the CARS program. According to department officials, because of the use of a cloud service provider, the CARS Web site was not affected by the July 4, 2009, cyber attacks.[24] Also, using the cloud service provider for Web content allowed the CARS program information to be accessible while protecting DOT's primary Web site from being overwhelmed and potentially disabled by the high demand for information about the program. The department's agreement with the cloud service provider allowed it to quickly and easily increase capacity as needed.

In contrast, the payment-processing system used a more traditional database and financial management system containing commercial off-the-shelf software and, according to DOT officials, was not able to cope with increases in demand for the program. Although the payment processing system was originally designed to process up to 250,000 transactions over 4 months, the system actually processed approximately 690,000 transactions in about 1 month. Partly as a result of the overwhelming interest in the program, the department encountered several technical issues and capacity-related deficiencies with the payment system. Specifically, the system had numerous outages and periods of slow operation, causing frustration among dealers and disrupting the department's ability to review submissions. Since the payment processing system did not use cloud computing, expanding the system's capacity was more challenging.

Information Security Controls and LessonsLearned

Officials said they briefly considered use of a cloud computing model for the payment processing system, but were reluctant to do so because of programmatic constraints to using applications already in use by the department. They also were concerned about processing personal information in a cloud environment without the environment having been precertified to handle the information. The officials acknowledged that many characteristics of the CARS program would have made the payment processing system a good candidate for cloud computing. These included the program's limited time available for deployment, short duration, and need to cope with sudden peaks in demand. However, the need to interface with existing department computing infrastructure, including using expertise from the existing vendor and the lack of an already developed and deployed cloud that had been certified to handle personal information made them hesitant to use a cloud computing solution and led them to instead use a more traditional application. As it was, the short time available to deploy the system made completion of information security processes, such as authorization and accreditation, a challenge.

Source: NASA.

Figure 4. NASA Nebula Container

A program official added that successful implementation of cloud computing in the federal government will be dependent on several information security-related factors, including the ability to ensure continuous monitoring of security controls and the ability to independently verify the security of cloud computing providers.

APPENDIX III: COMMENTS FROM THE OFFICE OF MANAGEMENT AND BUDGET

EXECUTIVE OFFICE OF THE PRESIDENT
OFFICE OF MANAGEMENT AND BUDGET
WASHINGTON, D.C. 20503

Gregory Wilshusen
Director
The Government Accountability Office
441 G Street, Northwest
Washington, D.C. 20548

Dear Mr. Wilshusen:

Thank you for the opportunity to comment on your draft report, "INFORMATION SECURITY: Federal Guidance Needed to Address Control Issues with Implementing Cloud Computing" (GAO-10-153).

As an initial matter, OMB appreciates GAO's focus on this important issue, and we agree with GAO on the need for an overarching Federal cloud computing strategy with milestones. However, cloud computing is in its early stages. OMB has been deliberate in making sure a unified cloud strategy does not thwart innovation by prematurely hardwiring and institutionalizing cloud technologies, standards and security requirements. Accordingly, OMB, Federal agencies and private industry are partnering together to observe, test and deploy best practices as the cloud sector matures. OMB feels it would be appropriate to develop, over the next six months, a Federal cloud strategy that covers a planning horizon of five to 10 years and is based on lessons learned in the near term. Additionally, the strategy and related milestones may need to evolve over time, as cloud computing technologies establish market strongholds.

As noted above, we agree that the strategy must address the security challenges associated with implementing cloud computing. For this reason the National Institute of Standards and Technology (NIST), at the direction of the Federal CIO, is convening a cloud summit on May 20th, 2010. The Summit, which will feature a broad array of speakers from government, industry and academia, will broaden the dialogue on key cloud issues, including data interoperability, portability and security standards. Outputs from the Summit will be used to guide the development of appropriate security controls and inform a future Federal cloud computing strategic plan.

OMB is committed to the Federal government developing and implementing secure cloud environments, and we are actively working to make this a reality. To that end, the Federal CIO has established the Cloud Computer Security Workgroup (led by NIST) to study, propose and implement a solution for government-wide security assessment and authorization. This Workgroup has already established a process for government-wide assessments and authorizations.

Moreover, agency-specific guidance must address standards and the appropriate division of roles and responsibilities. The Federal CIO has also activated a standards workgroup, and OMB is working with NIST to propose and implement standards for implementing cloud computing environments in support of government programs and activities. Agencies recognize the need for agency-specific guidance in this area, and they are collaborating with OMB to align our cloud computing initiatives with agency business needs.

Thank you again for the opportunity to comment on the draft report and to discuss our work on the development and implementation of a secure cloud computing environment.

Sincerely,

Vivek Kundra
Federal Chief Information Officer

APPENDIX IV: COMMENTSFROM THE GENERAL SERVICES ADMINISTRATION

GSA Administrator

May 7, 2010

The Honorable Gene L. Dodaro
Acting Comptroller General of the United States
U.S. Government Accountability Office
Washington, DC 20548

Dear Mr. Dodaro:

The U.S. General Services Administration (GSA) appreciates the opportunity to review and comment on the draft report entitled "Federal Guidance needed to Address Control Issues with Implementing Cloud Computing" (GAO-10-513).

We agree in part to the findings and recommendations. Substantive comments to the findings and recommendations are provided below:

1. **The report recommends that "the CIO Council Cloud Computing Executive Steering Committee develop a plan, including milestones, for completing a government wide security assessment and authorization process for cloud services.**

The Security Working Group has developed the Federal Risk and Authorization Management Program (FedRAMP) that addresses this recommendation. The Security Working Group, as part of GSA's Cloud Computing Program with members from over 15 agencies, is led by the National Institute of Standards and Technology (NIST). FedRAMP is a government-wide program to provide joint authorizations and continuous security monitoring services for all Federal agencies with an initial focus on cloud computing. It is a major element in the strategy to facilitate the use of cloud computing by the Federal Government. FedRAMP is a central office that performs certification and authentications, recommends authority to operate, and supports continuous monitoring of systems in compliance with Federal laws and regulations. Agencies can leverage the Certification and Authorization (C&A) and Authority to Operate (ATO) without having to repeat the process for each system. We expect that FedRAMP will be operational in May 2010.

As detailed in the GAO Report, agencies have expressed the following concerns: (a) depending on vendors ability to provide and maintain adequate security controls; (b) implementing and maintaining adequate security controls and monitoring; and (c) meeting the requirements of Federal information security requirements and guidance. Each agency is responsible to independently select appropriate security controls, implement and assess security, develop appropriate plans of action, and conduct ongoing security monitoring.

U.S. General Services Administration
1800 F Street, NW
Washington, DC 20405-0002
Telephone: (202) 501-0800
Fax: (202) 219-1243
www.gsa.gov

2

As background, FedRAMP is a unified government-wide risk management for enterprise level IT systems. It enables agencies to leverage authorizations with:

- Unified interagency C&A process;
- Consistent application of Federal security requirements;
- Consolidated risk management; and
- Increased effectiveness and management cost savings.

FedRAMP has three components:

- Security Requirement Authorities to create governmentwide baseline security requirements that are interagency developed and approved;
- FedRAMP Office to coordinate authorization packages, manage authorized system list, and provide continuous monitoring oversight; and
- Joint Authorization Board to perform authorizations and on-going risk determinations that can be leveraged government-wide. Members of the Board are GSA, DoD, DHS and the sponsoring agency for the system to be authorized.

Figure 1 presents a concept of operations and high level workflow for FedRAMP.

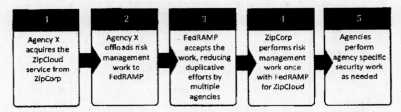

1	2	3	4	5
Agency X acquires the ZipCloud service from ZipCorp	Agency X offloads risk management work to FedRAMP	FedRAMP accepts the work, reducing duplicative efforts by multiple agencies	ZipCorp performs risk management work once with FedRAMP for ZipCloud	Agencies perform agency specific security work as needed

Figure 1. FedRAMP Workflow

FedRAMP will create a unified risk management process that:

- **increases security** through focus assessments;
- **eliminates duplication of effort** and associated cost savings;
- **enables rapid acquisition** by leveraging pre-authorized solutions;
- provides agency vetted **transparent security** requirements and authorization packages;
- facilitates **multi-agency use** of shared systems; and
- ensures **integration with governmentwide security** efforts.

3

FedRAMP allows agencies to leverage authorizations which reduces agency effort for authorizations and monitoring. With FedRAMP agencies will only have to review security details, leverage the existing authorization, and secure agency usage of system. This will greatly reduce cost, enable rapid acquisition, and reduce effort (diagrams that illustrate FedRAMP processes are enclosed).

Currently, it is anticipated that FedRAMP will be operational in May 2010.

2. **The GAO report recommends that "the Administrator of GSA complete the procurement for pre-certified infrastructure as a service cloud computing technologies at the low and moderate impact levels and ensure that it includes full considerations of the information security challenges of cloud computing, including a need for a shared assessment and authorization process."**

GSA will reissue the Request for Quote for Infrastructure as a Service (IaaS) in May 2010. The RFQ will result in a multi-award blanket purchase agreement (BPA) for IaaS providers. Awardees of this BPA will be included in FedRAMP. FedRAMP is a government-wide program to provide joint authorizations and continuous security monitoring services for all Federal agencies with an initial focus on cloud computing. Upon successful completion of the FedRAMP process and approval by the Joint Approval Board, the IaaS services will be granted an Authority to Operate (ATO) at the moderate impact level as defined by the Federal Information Security Management Act. An ATO at the moderate level includes approval of operation at low impact level.

Before reissuing the RFQ, GSA is working to improve the statement of work and to clarify the bidding instructions. As a result, the RFQ will better reflect customer requirements and vendors will be able to more accurately bid their services against requirements.

If you have any additional questions or concerns, please do not hesitate to contact me. Staff inquiries may be directed to Ms. Katie Lewin, Director, Cloud Computing Program, Office of Citizen Services and Communications. She can be reached at (202) 219-0394.

Sincerely,

Martha Johnson
Administrator

Enclosure

cc: Gregory C. Wilshusen

APPENDIX V: COMMENTSFROM THE DEPARTMENT OF COMMERCE

UNITED STATES DEPARTMENT OF COMMERCE
The Secretary of Commerce
Washington, D.C. 20230

May 4, 2010

Mr. Gregory C. Wilshusen
Director, Information Security Issues
United States Government Accountability Office
Washington, DC 20548

Dear Mr. Wilshusen:

Thank you for the opportunity to comment on the draft report from the Government Accountability Office (GAO) entitled "Information Security: Federal Guidance Needed to Address Control Issues with Implementing Cloud Computing" (GAO-10-513).

We concur with the report's conclusions that Federal agencies should take several steps to address cloud computing security, including completing the strategy, considering security in a planned procurement of cloud computing services, and issuing guidance related to cloud computing security. The Department of Commerce offers the following comments regarding the GAO's conclusions:

1. Page 14. The draft states that "Infrastructure as a service is the foundation of all cloud services." This is not accurate because one can build cloud services without relying on an "infrastructure as a service" system. We suggest deleting the sentence.

2. Page 24. The NIST point about browser vulnerability (from page 23) should be part of table 3.

3. Page 24. Delete "and it does not currently have finalized plans or milestones to issue cloud-specific security guidance" and replace it with "NIST has two documents in preparation: a guide on virtualization and a guide on cloud computing. NIST expects the virtualization document to be released for public comment in June 2010 and the cloud computing document to be released for public comment in September 2010."

4. Page 32. Replace "stated that existing NIST guidance applies" with "stated that existing NIST requirements apply."

Note: NIST publication 800-53 is a catalogue of controls that represent security requirements for information systems. It is designed to be flexible and adaptable to a variety of computing models and technologies, including cloud computing. We agree that guidance specific to cloud computing is needed.

Mr. Gregory C. Wilshusen
Page 2

5. Page 33. NIST believes portability and interoperability are not "security issues," as the text implies in the second paragraph on the page. We suggest replacing the sentence "For example, NIST guidance does not clearly address key cloud computing security issues such as portability and interoperability, data center operations, and virtualization" with "Current NIST guidance does not directly address key cloud computing issues such as portability and interoperability, data center operations, and virtualization."

We welcome further communications with GAO regarding its conclusions and look forward to receiving the final report. Please contact Rachel Kinney at (301) 975-8707 if you have any questions regarding this response.

Sincerely,

Gary Locke

End Notes

[1] The 24 major federal agencies are the Agency for International Development; the Departments of Agriculture, Commerce, Defense, Education, Energy, Health and Human Services , Homeland Security, Housing and Urban Development, the Interior, Justice, Labor, State, Transportation, the Treasury, and Veterans Affairs; the Environmental Protection Agency; the General Services Administration; the National Aeronautics and Space Administration; the National Science Foundation; the Nuclear Regulatory Commission; the Office of Personnel Management; the Small Business Administration; and the Social Security Administration.

[2] For fiscal year 2011, the administration has proposed about $79 billion for IT projects.

[3] GAO, *Continued Efforts Are Needed to Protect Information Systems From Evolving Threats*, GAO-10-230T (Washington D.C.: Nov. 17, 2009) and *Cyber Threats and Vulnerabilities Place Federal Systems at Risk*, GAO-09-661T (Washington, D.C.: May 5, 2009).

[4] GAO, *High-Risk Series: Information Management and Technology*, GAO/HR-97-9 (Washington, D.C.: February 1997).

[5] GAO, *High-Risk Series: An Update,* GAO-09-271 (Washington, D.C.: January 2009).

[6] NIST, *Guide for Applying the Risk Management Framework to Federal Information Systems: A Security Life Cycle Approach*, SP 800-37 Revision 1 (Gaithersburg, Md., February 2010).

[7] NIST, *Standards for Security Categorization of Federal Information and Information Systems*, FIPS Publication 199 (Gaithersburg, Md., February 2004).

[8] NIST, *Minimum Security Requirements for Federal Information and Information Systems*, FIPS Publication 200 (Gaithersburg, Md., March 2006).

[9] NIST, *Recommended Security Controls for Federal Information Systems and Organizations*, SP 800-53 Revision 3 (Gaithersburg, Md., August 2009).

[10] NIST, *Guide for Applying the Risk Management Framework to Federal Information Systems*, SP 800-37 Revision 1 was formerly NIST, *Guide for the Certification and Accreditation of Federal Information Systems*, SP 800-37. The assessment and authorization process replaces the process known as certification and accreditation described in the previous version of SP 800-37.

[11] Cloud Security Alliance, *Security Guidance for Critical Areas of Focus in Cloud Computing*, version 2.1 (December 2009).

[12] The European Network and Information Security Agency, *Cloud Computing: Benefits, Risks and Recommendations for Information Security* (November 2009).

[13] The European Network and Information Security Agency, *Cloud Computing: Information Assurance Framework* (November 2009).

[14] NIST began developing its definition of cloud computing in November 2008, and its most recent version, version 15, was released in October 2009. See NIST, *The NIST Definition of Cloud Computing*, version 15 (Gaithersburg, Md., Oct. 7, 2009).

[15] Virtualization is a technology that allows multiple, software-based virtual machines, with different operating systems, to run in isolation, side-by-side, on the same physical machine. Virtual machines can be stored as files, making it possible to save a virtual machine and move it from one physical server to another. Virtualization is often used as part of cloud computing.

[16] The Executive Council on Information Management and Technology members include experts from the public and private sectors and representatives of related professional organizations who are widely recognized in IT and information management areas. Council members provide expert perspectives to senior GAO executives on performance goals contained in GAO's strategic plan that guide GAO's work in the areas of information security, information management, and IT management.

[17] FIPS Special Publication 199 defines three levels of potential impact on organizational operations, assets, or individuals should there be a breach of security. Low applies when the loss of confidentiality, integrity, or availability could be expected to have a limited adverse effect; moderate applies when the loss could be expected to have a serious adverse effect on operations, assets, or individuals; and high applies when the loss could be expected to have a severe or catastrophic adverse effect.

[18] SAS 70 will soon be superseded by two new standards: a new audit standard for audits of entities that use service providers and a new attestation standard for reporting on controls at a service provider.

[19] OMB, *FY 2009 Reporting Instructions for the Federal Information Security Management Act and Agency Privacy Management*, Memorandum M-09-29 (Washington, D.C., Aug. 20, 2009).

[20] The 24 agencies are the Agency for International Development; the Departments of Agriculture, Commerce, Defense, Education, Energy, Health and Human Services , Homeland Security, Housing and Urban Development, the Interior, Justice, Labor, State, Transportation, the Treasury, and Veterans Affairs; the Environmental Protection Agency; the General Services Administration; the National Aeronautics and Space Administration; the National Science Foundation ; the Nuclear Regulatory Commission; the Office of Personnel Management; the Small Business Administration; and the Social Security Administration.

[21] A virtual machine is a software image of a computer that executes programs in the same manner as a physical computer or server. Multiple virtual machine images can run on one physical computer.

[22] DOD categorizes system impact levels using Mission Assurance Category I, II, and III: category I systems are considered high impact and handle information that is vital to mission success, category II systems are considered medium impact and handle information that is important for mission success, and category III systems are considered low impact and handle information that does not materially affect mission success.

[23] An interconnection security agreement documents security roles and responsibilities and technical requirements related to the connection of two information systems.

[24] In July 2009, press accounts reported that a widespread and coordinated attack over the course of several days had targeted Web sites operated by major government agencies, causing disruptions to the public availability of government information.

In: Cloud Computing and Government: Background, Benefits...   ISBN: 978-1-61761-784-3
Editor: George I. Nikolov   © 2011 Nova Science Publishers, Inc.

Chapter 2

STATE OF PUBLIC SECTOR CLOUD COMPUTING

Vivek Kundra

EXECUTIVE SUMMARY

The Obama Administration is changing the way business is done in Washington and bringing a new sense of responsibility to how we manage taxpayer dollars. We are working to bring the spirit of American innovation and the power of technology to improve performance and lower the cost of government operations.

The United States Government is the world's largest consumer of information technology, spending over $76 billion annually on more than 10,000 different systems. Fragmentation of systems, poor project execution, and the drag of legacy technology in the Federal Government have presented barriers to achieving the productivity and performance gains found when technology is deployed effectively in the private sectors.

In September 2009, we announced the Federal Government's Cloud Computing Initiative. Cloud computing has the potential to greatly reduce waste, increase data center efficiency and utilization rates, and lower operating costs. This chapter presents an overview of cloud computing across the public sector. It provides the Federal Government's definition of cloud computing, and includes details on deployment models, service models, and common characteristics of cloud computing.

As we move to the cloud, we must be vigilant in our efforts to ensure that the standards are in place for a cloud computing environment that provides for security of government information, protects the privacy of our citizens, and safeguards our national security interests. This chapter provides details regarding the National Institute of Standards and Technology's efforts to facilitate and lead the development of standards for security, interoperability, and portability.

Furthermore, this chapter details Federal budget guidance issued to agencies to foster the adoption of cloud computing technologies, where relevant, and provides an overview of the Federal Government's approach to data center consolidation.

This chapter concludes with 30 illustrative case studies at the Federal, state and local government levels. These case studies reflect the growing movement across the public sector to leverage cloud computing technologies.

FEDERALGOVERNMENTAPPROACH

Cloud computing is still in its early stages and we have a long journey ahead. This chapter provides information on our approach to leverage cloud computing to help close the Government's technology gap. Specifically, this chapter presents:

- Definition of Cloud Computing
- Data Center Consolidation
- Standards Development
- Federal Budget Planning

Definition of Cloud Computing

As defined by the National Institute of Standards and Technology (NIST)[1], cloud computing is a model for enabling convenient, on-demand network access to a shared pool of configurable computing resources (e.g., networks, servers, storage, applications, and services) that can be rapidly provisioned and released with minimal management effort or service provider interaction. This cloud model promotes availability and is composed of essential characteristics, deployment models, and various service models.

Characteristics of the Cloud

- *On-demand self-service.* A consumer can unilaterally provision computing capabilities, such as server time and network storage, as needed automatically without requiring human interaction with each service's provider.
- *Broad network access.* Capabilities are available over the network and accessed through standard mechanisms that promote use by heterogeneous thin or thick client platforms (e.g., mobile phones, laptops, and PDAs).
- *Resource pooling.* The provider's computing resources are pooled to serve multiple consumers using a multi-tenant model, with different physical and virtual resources dynamically assigned and reassigned according to consumer demand. There is a sense of location independence in that the customer generally has no control or knowledge over the exact location of the provided resources but may be able to specify location at a higher level of abstraction (e.g., country, state, or datacenter). Examples of resources include storage, processing, memory, network bandwidth, and virtual machines.
- *Rapid elasticity.* Capabilities can be rapidly and elastically provisioned, in some cases automatically, to quickly scale up and rapidly released to quickly scale down.

To the consumer, the capabilities available for provisioning often appear to be unlimited and can be purchased in any quantity at any time.

- *Measured Service.* Cloud systems automatically control and optimize resource use by leveraging a metering capability at some level of abstraction appropriate to the type of service (e.g., storage, processing, bandwidth, and active user accounts). Resource usage can be monitored, controlled, and reported providing transparency for both the provider and consumer of the utilized service.

Benefits of Cloud Computing

There was a time when every household, town, farm or village had its own water well. Today, shared public utilities give us access to clean water by simply turning on the tap; cloud computing works in a similar fashion. Just like the water from the tap in your kitchen, cloud computing services can be turned on or off quickly as needed. Like at the water company, there is a team of dedicated professionals making sure the service provided is safe and available on a 24/7 basis. Best of all, when the tap isn't on, not only are you saving water, but you aren't paying for resources you don't currently need.

- *Economical.* Cloud computing is a pay-as-you-go approach to IT, in which a low initial investment is required to get going. Additional investment is incurred as system use increases and costs can decrease if usage decreases. In this way, cash flows better match total system cost.
- *Flexible.* IT departments that anticipate fluctuations in user load do not have to scramble to secure additional hardware and software. With cloud computing, they can add and subtract capacity as its network load dictates, and pay only for what they use.
- *Rapid Implementation.* Without the need to go through the procurement and certification processes, and with a near-limitless selection of services, tools, and features, cloud computing helps projects get off the ground in record time.
- *Consistent Service.* Network outages can send an IT department scrambling for answers. Cloud computing can offer a higher level of service and reliability, and an immediate response to emergency situations.
- *Increased Effectiveness.* Cloud computing frees the user from the finer details of IT system configuration and maintenance, enabling them to spend more time on mission-critical tasks and less time on IT operations and maintenance.
- *Energy Efficient.* Because resources are pooled, each user community does not need to have its own dedicated IT infrastructure. Several groups can share computing resources, leading to higher utilization rates, fewer servers, and less energy consumption.

DeploymentModels

- *Private cloud.* The cloud infrastructure is operated solely for one organization. It may be managed by the organization or a third party and may exist on premises or off premises.

- *Community cloud.* The cloud infrastructure is shared by several organizations and supports a specific community that has shared concerns (e.g., mission, security requirements, policy, and compliance considerations). It may be managed by the organizations or a third party and may exist on premises or off premises.
- *Public cloud.* The cloud infrastructure is made available to the general public or a large industry group and is owned by an organization selling cloud services.
- *Hybrid cloud.* The cloud infrastructure is a composition of two or more clouds (private, community, or public) that remain unique entities but are bound together by standardized or proprietary technology that enables data and application portability (e.g., cloud bursting for load-balancing between clouds).

Service Models

- *Cloud Software as a Service (SaaS).* Provides the consumer the ability to use the provider's applications running on a cloud infrastructure. The applications are accessible from various client devices through a thin client interface such as a web browser (e.g., web-based e-mail). The consumer does not manage or control the underlying cloud infrastructure including network, servers, operating systems, storage, or even individual application capabilities, with the possible exception of limited user-specific application configuration settings.
- *Cloud Platform as a Service (PaaS).* Provides the consumer the ability to deploy onto the cloud infrastructure consumer-created or acquired applications created using programming languages and tools supported by the provider. The consumer does not manage or control the underlying cloud infrastructure including network, servers, operating systems, or storage, but has control over the deployed applications and possibly application hosting environment configurations.

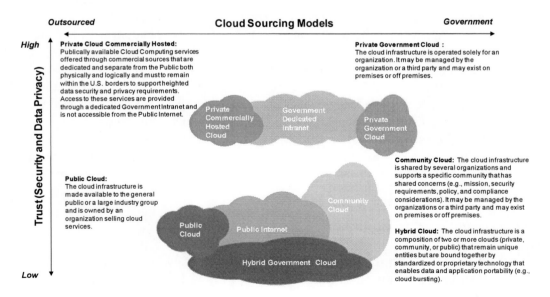

Figure 1. Cloud Sourcing Models[2]

- *Cloud Infrastructure as a Service (IaaS).* Provides the consumer the ability to provision processing, storage, networks, and other fundamental computing resources where the consumer is able to deploy and run arbitrary software, which can include operating systems and applications. The consumer does not manage or control the underlying cloud infrastructure but has control over operating systems, storage, deployed applications, and possibly limited control of select networking components (e.g., host firewalls).

Data Center Consolidation

The transition to cloud computing is also supported by Federal data center consolidation efforts. The consolidation of Federal data centers will reduce energy consumption, space usage, and environmental impacts, while increasing the utilization and efficiency of IT assets. Data center consolidation will also play an important role in meeting the goals of the Energy Security and Independence Act of 2007[3] and various executive orders directing increased energy efficiencies. The effort will promote shared Government-wide, cost effective, green, and sustainable Federal data centers in support of agency missions.

In February 2010, the Federal CIO issued data center consolidation guidance[4] to agencies regarding creation of agency data center consolidation plans. The guidance directed agencies to consider agency data center performance and utilization metrics, energy efficiency use data, physical facility, operational cost and asset information, best practices, open standards, and security. Agencies will develop their data center consolidation plans and incorporate them into their Fiscal Year 2012 budgets by August 30, 2010.

Standards Development

As we move to the cloud, we must be vigilant in our efforts to ensure the standards are in place for a cloud computing environment. As part of the Federal Cloud Computing Initiative, the National Institute of Standards and Technology (NIST)[5] is leading and facilitating the development of cloud computing standards which respond to high priority security, interoperability, and portability requirements.

Current cloud computing standards development activities, conducted by the NIST Information Technology Laboratory (ITL), include:

- **Special Publications:** In 2009, NIST made the widely adopted and referenced NIST Definition of Cloud Computing publicly available. NIST is in the process of developing a series of Special Publications (SP) related to cloud computing. These Special Publications are informed by the activities which are described below.
- **Standards Acceleration to Jumpstart Adoption of Cloud Computing (SAJACC):** The SAJAAC goal is to facilitate the development of cloud computing standards. SAJACC will include a publicly accessible NIST hosted portal which facilitates the exchange of verifiable information regarding the extent to which pre-standard candidate interface specifications satisfy key cloud computing requirements. The

expectation is that SAJACC will help to accelerate the development of cloud computing standards and, as a bi-product of its information dissemination function, increase the level of confidence to enable cloud computing adoption.

- **Federal Risk and Authorization Management Program (FedRAMP):** NIST's role is to support the definition of a consistent technical process that will be used by FedRAMP to assess the security posture of specific cloud service implementations. NIST serves as a technical advisor for the FedRAMP process that will be implemented by the Federal CIO Council.

Description of NIST Cloud Computing Standards Development Activities

NIST serves as the government lead, working with other government agencies, industry, academia, Standards Development Organizations (SDO), and others to leverage appropriate existing standards and to develop cloud computing standards where gaps exist. While cloud computing services are currently being used, security, interoperability, and portability are cited as major barriers to further adoption. The expectation is that standards will shorten the adoption cycle, enabling cost savings and an increased ability to quickly create and deploy enterprise applications. The focus is on standards which support interoperability, portability, and security to enable important usage scenarios.

NIST scientific expertise and its diverse group of NIST IT scientists yield a collective knowledge, research, and technical guidance capability which is aligned with the bureau's mission to support industry and advise government, acting impartially and providing credible technical insights.

Special Publications on Cloud Computing and SelectedTopics
NIST plans to issue an initial SP on cloud computing. The purpose is to provide insight into the benefits and considerations, and the secure and effective uses of cloud computing. More specifically, the document will provide guidance on key considerations of cloud computing: interoperability, portability, and security. To present these issues, the document will use the broadly recognized and adopted NIST Definition of Cloud Computing as a basis, given informal models of the major cloud computing service categories (Software as a Service, Platform as a Service, and Infrastructure as a Service). The publication will outline typical terms of use for cloud systems, will synopsize future research areas in cloud computing, and will provide informal recommendations.

NIST is also in the process of developing an SP on securing virtualization solutions for servers and desktops which are widely used in cloud computing technologies. The publication will provide an overview of full virtualization technologies, discuss the security concerns associated with full virtualization for servers, and provide recommendations for addressing them. The publication will also give an overview of actions that organizations should perform throughout the lifecycle of a server virtualization solution.

Standards Acceleration to Jumpstart Adoption of Cloud Computing (SAJACC)
There is often a gap between the time when formal standards for a new technology are needed and when they become available. The development of standards is inherently

dependent on the time consuming process of consensus building through broad participation. There is also a need to ensure due diligence in producing a standard of quality and completeness such that it will be effective and broadly adopted.

The SAJAAC strategy and approach is to accelerate the development of standards and to increase the level of confidence in cloud computing adoption during the interim period before cloud computing standards are formalized. SAJACC will provide information about interim specifications and the extent that they support key cloud computing requirements through a NIST hosted SAJACC portal.

More specifically, SAJACC will provide a public Internet-accessible repository of cloud computing usage scenarios (i.e., use cases), documented cloud system interfaces, pointers to cloud system reference implementations, and test results showing the extent to which different interfaces can support individual use cases.

The project is in the process of formulating an initial set of draft use cases and vetting these with cloud computing stakeholders in academia, government, and industry. The use cases are being developed to demonstrate portability, interoperability, and achievable security for users of cloud systems. After the use cases have been refined, they will be published on the portal. The project will then identify candidate legacy cloud system interfaces, along with their reference implementations, for validation against the use cases. After an initial set of legacy interfaces have been identified, NIST will conduct validation tests and publish the results. The process of identifying new interfaces (with corresponding reference implementations) and new use cases will be ongoing.

SAJACC leverages, coordinates, and is heavily dependent on input from all stakeholders with an interest in cloud computing standards.

FederalRisk and Authorization Management Program (FedRAMP)

NIST, in the technical advisory role to the interagency Federal Cloud Computing Advisory Council (CCAC) Security Working Group will define an initial technical approach and process for FedRAMP consistent with NIST security guidance in the context of the Federal Information System Management Act (FISMA). To clarify the role of NIST with respect to FedRAMP, while NIST is supporting the definition of the FedRAMP process from a technical perspective, NIST is not the implementing organization. The governance and operational implementation of FedRAMP will be completed under the auspices of the Federal CIO Council.

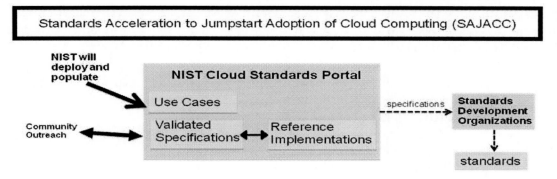

Figure 2. Standards Acceleration Overview[6]

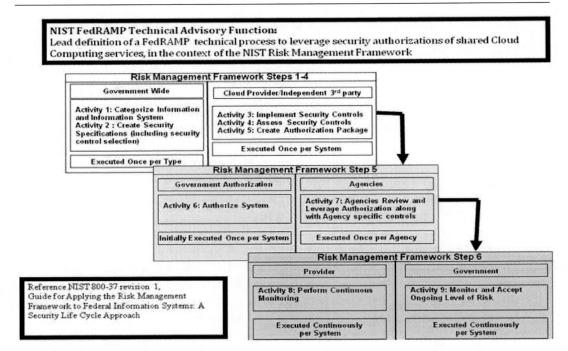

Figure 3. FedRAMP Overview[7]

As part of its Technical Advisory effort NIST will:

- Provide technical support and leadership to the working groups supporting the Federal CIO Council
- Create guidance to facilitate leveraged Government authorization of cloud systems and on the application of FISMA and 800-53 to cloud computing

Federal Budget Planning

The President's FY 2011 Budget highlights cloud computing as a major part of the strategy to achieve efficient and effective IT. Federal agencies are to deploy cloud computing solutions to improve the delivery of IT services, where the cloud computing solution has demonstrable benefits versus the status quo. OMB, as part of the FY 2011 Budget Process, requested all agencies to evaluate cloud computing alternatives as part of their budget submissions for all major IT investments, where relevant. Specifically:

- By September 2011 – all newly planned or performing major IT investments acquisitions must complete an alternatives analysis that includes a cloud computing based alternative as part of their budget submissions.
- By September 2012 – all IT investments making enhancements to an existing investment must complete an alternatives analysis that includes a cloud computing based alternative as part of their budget submissions.

- By September 2013 – all IT investments in steady-state must complete an alternatives analysis that includes a cloud computing based alternative as part of their budget submissions.

ILLUSTRATIVE CASE STUDIES

Cloud computing provides tremendous opportunities for the public sector to improve the delivery of services to the American people, reduce the cost of government operations and make more effective use of taxpayer dollars, and lower energy consumption. While the public sector is just at the beginning of the journey to cloud computing, we are already seeing innovative examples at all levels of government.

For example, on April 26, 2010, Recovery.gov became the first Government-wide system to migrate to a cloud-based environment. With the cost savings gained from using a cloud computing infrastructure, the Recovery Board plans to redirect more than $1 million in computer equipment and software to its accountability mission to help identify fraud, waste, and abuse. The City of Los Angeles is anticipating savingsof $5.5 million over five years as a result of moving e-mail and productivity tools to the cloud for over 34,000 City employees, and the State of Wisconsin's Department of Natural Resources is increasing collaboration through a hosted online meeting space that supports conference calls, interactive meetings, and information sharing.

These are a handful of illustrative examples that are part of a larger movement to leverage cloud computing across the public sector.

FEDERAL CLOUD COMPUTING CASE STUDIES

The following case studies provide recent examples of how Federal agencies are using cloud computing technologies.

- Department of Defense (United States Army) - Army Experience Center
- Department of Defense (Defense Information Systems Agency) - Rapid Access Computing Environment
- Department of Defense (Defense Information Systems Agency) - Forge.mil
- Department of Defense (United States Air Force) - Personnel Services Delivery Transformation
- Department of Energy (Lawrence Berkeley National Labs) - Cloud Computing Migration
- Department of Health and Human Services - Supporting Electronic Health Records
- Department of the Interior - Agency-wide E-mail
- General Services Administration (Office of Citizen Services) - USA.gov
- General Services Administration - Agency-wide E-mail
- National Aeronautics and Space Administration (Ames Research Center) - World-Wide Telescope
- National Aeronautics and Space Administration (Jet Propulsion Laboratory) - Be A Martian
- National Aeronautics and Space Administration - Enterprise Data Center Strategy
- Social Security Administration - Online Answers Knowledgebase
- Federal Labor Relations Authority - Case Management System
- Recovery Accountability and Transparency Board - Recovery.gov Cloud Computing Migration
- Securities and Exchange Commission - Investor Advocacy System

Department of Defense

Project: Army Experience Center
(United States Army)

The Army Experience Center (AEC), located in Philadelphia, PA, is an Army pilot program designed to explore new technologies and techniques that the Army can leverage to improve the efficiency and effectiveness of its marketing and recruiting operations. The AEC uses touch screen career exploration kiosks, state-of-the-art presentation facilities, community events, virtual reality simulators, and social networking to help potential recruits learn about the Army and make informed decisions about enlisting. The Army required a customer relationship management system that would track personal and electronic engagements with prospects and would help recruiting staff manage the recruiting process.

Improving communications and relationship management with potential recruits through a cloud-based CRM solution

Army's legacy proprietary data system, the Army Recruiting Information Support System (ARISS), was over 10 years old. Despite regular upgrades over the years, it was infeasible to modify ARISS to meet the AEC's requirements; including integration with Social Networking and other Web 2.0 applications, real time data access from multiple platforms including handheld devices, ability to track AEC visitor and engagement data, and integration of marketing and recruiting data. Initial bids from traditional IT vendors to provide required functionality ranged from $500,000 to over $1 million.

Instead, the Army chose a customized version of the cloud-based Customer Relationship Management tool Salesforce.com as its pilot solution to manage recruiting efforts at the Army Experience Center. The Army is piloting this cloud-based solution at an annual cost of $54,000. With the new system, the Army is able to track recruits as they participate in multiple simulations at the Army Experience Center. The solution integrates directly with e-mail and Facebook, allowing recruiters to connect with participants more dynamically after they leave the Army Experience Center. By using Salesforce.com's mobile solution, Army recruiters can access recruit information from anywhere.

The Army is currently in the second year of a two year pilot of the customized Salesforce.com application. Using the cloud-based solution, the Army was able to have fewer recruiters handle the same workload as the five traditional recruiting centers the Army Experience Center replaced. The cloud application has resulted in faster application upgrades, dramatically reduced hardware and IT staff costs, and significantly increased staff productivity.[8,9]

Project: Rapid Access Computing Environment
(Defense Information Systems Agency)

The Defense Information Systems Agency (DISA) provides Information Technology support to the Department of Defense (DoD). DISA began leveraging cloud computing in 2008 by creating its own secure private cloud, the Rapid Access Computing Environment (RACE).

RACE, which uses virtual server technology to provide on-demand server space for development teams, aims to be more secure and stable than a traditional public cloud.

Using cloud computing technology to provide on-demand virtual server space for development teams

RACE consists of many virtual servers inside a single physical server. By using virtualization technologies, DISA has divided the costs of provisioning and operating a single physical server among the users of the various virtual servers. This system passes cost savings on to individual teams. Within this virtual environment, users can use a self-service portal to provision computing resources in 50 GB increments with the guarantee that the environment will be secure to DoD standards. At DoD, a dedicated server environment used to take three to six weeks to provision due to lengthy procurement processes. However, RACE is able to provision functional server space to users in 24 hours. The cost for a user to obtain an environment on RACE is reasonable and can be set up with an approved Government credit card.

According to DISA, personnel can expect the same level of service and availability when using RACE over a traditional environment. Additionally, for security purposes RACE has built-in application separation controls so that all applications, databases and Web servers are separate from each other. DISA also has a strict data cleansing process for when an application needs to be removed completely from the RACE platform. Since the inception of this cloud-based solution, hundreds of military applications including command and control systems, convoy control systems, and satellite programs have been developed and tested on RACE.[10]

Project: Forge.mil
(Defense Information Systems Agency)

Typical implementation of new software and systems at DoD requires large amounts of time and money due to licensing, acquisition, and support demands. Non-cloud based software development does not typically allow for the utilization of economies of scale, ubiquitous delivery, or cross collaboration on projects. Recognizing that such benefits can be found in the cloud, DISA established the software development environment Forge.mil. Through Forge.mil, DISA provides the entire Department of Defense with the tools and services necessary for rapid development, testing, and deployment of new software and systems.

Software development environment for rapid access to the tools and services needed to quickly develop, test and deploy software and systems

Forge.mil teamed with cloud provider CollabNet to provide for a software development platform to allow users to reuse and collaborate on software code. Currently, Forge.mil has over 5,000 users, with over 300 open source projects, over 500 file release posts, and over 30,000 downloads. Forge.mil's collaborative environment and open development platform allow DISA to avoid large start-up costs and enable additional return on investment (ROI) through software reuse.

With rapid project start-ups at minimal cost, Forge.mil estimates new projects developed in its environment save DISA between $200,000 and $500,000 per project. Also, DISA estimates about $15 million in cost avoidance by utilizing an open source philosophy that allows for software reuse and collaborative development. This open source philosophy of Forge.mil not only saves money on licensing and support, but provides improved software by giving version control, traceability, and having multiple stakeholders from various projects work on the same software code.

Forge.mil hosts an array of projects for different areas of DoD including the Army, Navy, Air Force, Marine Corps and the Joint Chiefs, all within a secure environment that appropriately protects DoD software assets. Forge.mil allows DISA and its customers to reduce their costs and shorten the time required to develop new software and systems by using a cloud environment that promotes collaboration, reuse of developed software, rapid delivery, and shortened time-to-market for projects.[11]

Project: Personnel Services Delivery Transformation (PSDT)
(United States Air Force)

Faced with a mandate to reshape the personnel community, the Air Force Personnel Center needed to reduce the time spent searching for documentation and allow personnel to support war-fighting missions. The Air Force Personnel Center created a program to transform the way Human Resource tools and services were delivered. The primary goal was to create a better customer experience by providing self-service solutions and tracking customer service needs.

The Air Force implemented the Software as a Service (SaaS) solution by RightNow to support its knowledge management, case tracking, contact center tracking and customer survey mission needs. Using tools available in the RightNow solution the Air Force focused on solving fundamental problems, with the way information was organized.

RightNow empowered the Air Force to complete its manpower reduction initiative and save over $4 million annually. Searches on the knowledge base have increased to nearly 2 million per week and customer engagement has increased 70 percent. By using a cloud-based solution, the site has been able to scale to meet fluctuating demand without compromising the customer experience. Customers can now find answers from over 15,000 documents within two minutes, an improvement on the 20 minute wait they faced before the implementation of this solution.[12]

Improving operations of human resources management through a cloud-based CRM solution that includes knowledge management, case tracking, contact center tracking and customer survey tools

Department of Energy

Project: Cloud Computing Migration
(Lawrence Berkeley National Labs)

The Department of Energy is exploring cost and energy efficiencies that can result from leveraging cloud computing. This initiative explores how to use cloud computing to address needs across the enterprise, in specific business services, and in scientific study. Although started in 2009, these efforts at Lawrence Berkeley National Labs (LBL) are already showing promise.

LBL has already deployed over 2,300 mailboxes on Google Federal Premier Apps, and will end up with 5,000 e-mail accounts deployed by August 2010. This solution uses a LBL Identity Management System to provide authentication. Additionally, Google Docs and Google Sites have already been deployed and are being used by small and medium-sized scientific research teams to foster collaboration and community documentation.

Exploring cost and energy efficiencies of cloud computing solutions

Presently, LBL is evaluating the use of Amazon's EC2 to handle excess capacity for mid-range computers during peak usage periods. LBL is also investigating the use of a federated identity to provide access for the scientific community to a wide range of cloud computing offerings. LBL estimates they will save $1.5 million over the next five years in hardware, software and labor costs from the deployments they have already made.[13,14]

Department of Health and Human Services

Project: Supporting Electronic Health Records

The Department of Health and Human Services (HHS) is leveraging cloud computing to support the implementation of Electronic Health Records (EHR) systems. HHS is planning for 70 Regional Extension Centers which will assist over 100,000 Primary Care Practitioners. To coordinate healthcare providers' implementation of new EHR systems, HHS is deploying a cloud-based customer relationship and project management solution provided by Salesforce.com. The solution will support HHS's Regional Extension Centers in the selection, implementation, and meaningful use of EHRs. Various implementation approaches can be analyzed to quickly identify best practices for EHR implementation as they emerge.

After reviewing internal and cloud-based solutions, the Office of the National Coordinator (ONC) decided that Salesforce.com offered the best CRM solution for a quick, inexpensive, and rapidly scalable implementation. The review process concluded that it would have taken over a year to implement an internally-based system. Leveraging the cloud solution, ONC was able to stand up the first phase of the Salesforce solution in less than three months after the award.

One of the advantages ONC anticipates from deploying a cloud-based CRM system is the ability to update the system as Regional Extension Centers start using it. More implementation phases are already planned to ensure that users' needs are met. ONC expects to be able to quickly update future phases of the system in substantially less time, while doing it collaboratively with end users.[15]

Leveraging cloud-based CRM tools to support HHS in allocating grant funding for implementation of electronic health record

Department of the Interior

Announced Project: Agency-wide E-mail

The Department of the Interior is pursuing a Software as a Service (SaaS) cloud computing model for e-mail. DOI has 80,000 e-mail users who are widely dispersed across the United States. They are currently supported by a very complex messaging infrastructure comprised of more than a dozen different e-mail systems. The Department had already determined that a single e-mail infrastructure would reduce the complexity of the overall system and improve the level of service provided to their users when it decided to explore cloud-based solutions.

When considering how best to deliver a single e-mail system, the Department analyzed the opportunities for cost savings presented by cloud computing. The numbers were compelling: by implementing e-mail using an external commercial SaaS model, the Department expects to provide improved service to its 80,000 users for one-third the amount of money that it spends today. The Department is moving forward with this project with a completion date in Fiscal Year 2011.[16]

Migrating 80,000 mailboxes (from 13 specific systems) to one unified cloud provider

General Services Administration

Project: USA.gov
(Office of Citizen Services)

As the Federal Government's primary information portal, USA.gov, presents the American people with a vast body of information and resources including topics like benefits and grants, taxes, jobs, education, health, voting, technology, and business and nonprofit guides.

As the Federal Government encourages citizens to become more involved and active with local, state, and federal politics, key sites like USA.gov see vastly increasing and decreasing website traffic as key issues are debated in the national public forum, natural disasters come and go, and voting season approaches. These spikes in traffic made a cloud computing-based solution very attractive, as a cloud infrastructure is much better able to deal with on-demand scalability than most traditional IT infrastructures. This increased flexibility positions USA.gov to better serve emerging needs.

By moving to Terremark's Enterprise Cloud service, the General Services Administration (GSA) reduced site upgrade time from nine months (including procurement) to a maximum of one day. Monthly downtime moved from roughly two hours with the traditional hosting setup to near zero with the cloud solution (99.9 percent availability). With its legacy setup, GSA paid $2.35 million annually for USA.gov, including total hardware refresh and software relicensing costs of $2 million, in addition to personnel costs of $350,000. By moving to a cloud service, GSA now pays an annual total of $650,000 for USA.gov and all associated costs, a costs savings of $1.7 million, or 72 percent.[17]

Migrating over 15,000 mailboxes to a cloud solution with features commonly available in commercially solutions

Announced Project: Agency-wide E-mail

GSA's current environment lacks the level of integrated features commercially available. GSA requires a greater use of features such as integrated messaging and collaborative tools to support its mission. E-mail archiving is currently implemented inconsistently, is difficult to use, and does not meet information retrieval (e-discovery) requirements. The storage associated with e-mail archiving continues to grow and is costly to manage. Recent regulations for handling e-mail litigation hold and discovery demand that GSA implement a more effective and expedient process. Additionally, GSA is seeking a solution that will reduce it's in-house system maintenance burden and provide GSA users with more timely implementations of new versions and features.

GSA's e-mail effort will migrate over 15,000 mailboxes to a cloud-based solution, eliminating the redundant and disparate infrastructure presently housed at 17 different locations around the world.

Although still in the information gathering phase, initial estimates indicate that over the first two years, GSA will realize a 30 percent cost savings.[18]

National Aeronautics and Space Administration

Project: World-Wide Telescope
(Ames Research Center)

Nebula, NASA's cloud-computing platform, is helping NASA to engage the public through the viewing and exploration of the Moon and Mars in unprecedented resolution. Nebula allows NASA to process, store and upload thousands of high-resolution images and over 100 terabytes of data. In a traditional IT environment, it would have taken several months to procure new infrastructure and another one to two months of full-time work by two full-time employees to configure the new equipment to handle this data. By utilizing Nebula, NASA saved four to five months of time and roughly 800 hours of labor, allowing the agency to focus on expanding the content accessible to the public instead of building IT infrastructure.

Reducing costs and improving service by moving USA.gov to a cloud-based hosting environment

The nature of NASA's activities requires strict security policies, creating a challenge in providing a collaborative environment to share data with outside partners or the public. Nebula's architecture is designed from the ground up for interoperability with commercial cloud service providers, offering NASA researchers the ability to port data sets and code to run on commercial clouds. Nebula provides a secure way for NASA to make its data accessible to partners, avoiding the need to grant access to internal networks. Each researcher needs a varying amount of storage space and compute power to process his or her data sets. In the old operational model, these resources took months to procure and configure and required constant monitoring and frequent upgrades. Using Nebula's cloud computing infrastructure, researchers will be able to provision these services in just a matter of minutes.

NASA space exploration missions can take over 10 years to develop and the resources needed to process the data coming back are usually scheduled and procured well before launch. Missions, however, have a varying degree of success: some are delayed at a late stage, some are cancelled altogether, and some last much longer than originally anticipated.

Nebula's cloud services allow NASA to be much more flexible and responsive to actual mission needs, scaling resources up or down as the actual requirements of the mission develop. In addition to supporting NASA's missions, the Nebula cloud-computing platform has demonstrated additional versatility and has become the home of the Federal Government's flagship transparency website USAspending.gov. USAspending.gov 2.0 was completely reengineered to leverage the cloud-computing platform at Nebula, and growing the amount of storage as Federal spending data grows will now be a quick and easy process.[19,20]

Using NASA's Nebula cloud platform to store, process and provide access to high-resolution images of the Moon and Mars

Project: Be A Martian
(Jet Propulsion Laboratory)

NASA's Jet Propulsion Laboratory (JPL) brings science to the American people by inspiring interest in the planet Mars. The laboratory sought to increase the impact of its education and outreach program by using technology. It wanted not just to give Mars data to the public, but rather to excite the public about Mars.

To meet this challenge, JPL developed an interactive website, BeAMartian.jpl.nasa.gov, using the Microsoft Azure cloud computing platform. An application programming interface (API) connects website visitors with 250,000 pictures of Mars, available without having to store any additional data on JPL computers. On the cloud, individuals can virtually explore the planet by browsing pictures, watching videos, and creating tags. They can post questions, read responses, and send messages to Mars. The more content a visitor contributes to the site, the more reputation points they earn in their account. For participants, this is a fun way to learn more about Mars.

"JPL chooses to keep it real through early exploration of multiple clouds." said Tom Soderstrom, Chief Technology Officer of NASA's JPL. "In other words, JPL wants to be an intelligent user of clouds and the only way we can do that is by being proactive and trying them out, end-to-end with real mission data. We've been exploring the clouds by partnering with JPL missions and industry partners for about two years now and have several very good use cases and stories."

With this cloud computing solution, NASA has successfully engaged a crowd of users. Users have created over 2,000 pieces of social media and inspired 200 stories on TV, radio, and in print. There have been 2.5 million API queries from NASA crowd-sourcing applications and 500,000 API queries from developers. The Town Hall area of the website has received over 40,000 votes and 5,000 individuals and teams have registered for a NASA sponsored competition. This crowd has also helped NASA identify craters and other features of the Martian surface. JPL has benefited from this outreach by having engaged users and by exploring and learning about new cloud-based technologies.[21]

Engaging the public in citizen science with social media and crowd-sourcing on a scalable cloud platform

Announced Project: Enterprise Data Center Strategy

NASA recently announced that it is re-evaluating its enterprise data center strategy and has halted a request for proposals that would have yielded an indefinite delivery/indefinite quantity contract with a maximum value up to $1.5 billion for outsourced data center services over multiple years.

Concurrently, a number of organizations within NASA are evaluating the use of Nebula, NASA's scientific cloud solution for possible application in satisfying their mission data center needs:

The Flight Vehicle Research & Technology Division at Ames Research Center is exploring using Nebula for their Message Passing Interface (MPI) implementation. This group performs flight vehicle air flow computation. Data from each piece of the aircraft surface runs on a different compute node and each node communicates edge conditions to its neighboring nodes using MPI. Currently, it takes a very expensive suite of equipment to do that work: NASA's 60000-core Pleiades computer. Although Nebula does not compete on performance with Pleiades, the setup time and money saved by self-provisioning compute power makes Nebula an attractive alternative.

A second mission organization with enormous memory and storage requirements is interested in Nebula because the Infrastructure as a Service (IaaS) beta version, scheduled for release June 2010, will allow them to specify the amount of memory and storage needed for their virtual machines. One of the group's storage-heavy applications requires 12 GB of memory, which can be accommodated on the Nebula IaaS cloud solution.

A third organization is evaluating Nebula to create virtual workstations for software developers to write and test-compile their code. Nebula would give them more fine-grained control over the development environment and allow developers to share the many modules and libraries currently running on their local desktops.

And yet another organization is evaluating Nebula as a service platform for interaction with non-NASA partners. Nebula would enable anonymous but controlled FTP for large file transfers and run an in-house, web-based java application that analyzes and visualizes data produced by NASA's Airspace Concept Evaluation System.[22]

Cancelled proposal requests that would have yielded up to $1.5 billion in enterprise data center contracts and now exploring cloud alternatives

Social Security Administration
Project: Online Answers Knowledgebase (SOASK)

The Social Security Administration (SSA) handles millions of questions and inquiries from citizens every year. For example, inquirers want to know what they can do online, or how to get a social security number, file for benefits, locate a field office, get a retirement estimate, or request a proof of income letter. In order to provide the public with a convenient means to answer to their questions, anytime and anywhere Internet access is available, the agency provides an online database of Frequently Asked Questions.

Helping the public easily and efficiently find answers to questions through cloud-based knowledge management and CRM tools

The SSA is leveraging a cloud-based solution from RightNow Technologies to provide this service. Visitors to socialsecurity.gov can search for answers by category, keyword or phrase, which helps them quickly find the information they are looking for. Over a thousand questions and answers are included in the knowledge base. SSA keeps the information contained in the knowledgebase up-to-date and relevant, eliminating the need to call or visit SSA for basic information.

In 2009, the number of answers provided through SSA's Frequently Asked Questions grew to over 34 million. Given current agency staffing levels, it would not have been possible for office staff and 800-number agents to answer even 10 percent of these additional inquiries. By contrast, the Internet solution is highly scalable, allowing SSA to meet increasing demand for online information without impacting service in the office and on the phone.[23]

Federal Labor Relations Authority

Project: Case Management System

The Federal Labor Relations Authority (FLRA) recognized that its decade-old case management system was not supporting its mission to the fullest extent possible. FLRA's users regularly experienced delays in searching and the system couldn't keep up with expected growth. Additionally, the internal system had expensive software licensing costs.

Strategically, FLRA wanted to implement a shared electronic case management tracking system that would allow citizens to file cases and obtain documents electronically and then check the status of their cases. By using the cloud, FLRA intended to improve infrastructure and make existing IT and operations support more responsive to business needs while meeting regulatory compliance.

Providing efficient and cost-effective access to case information by migrating the legacy, in-house case management system to a cloud-based platform

The FLRA selected Intuit's Quickbase system as its platform to implement this new system. From requirements-gathering to completed development, the project took less than 10 months to implement. The cloud-based solution has provided FLRA with more rapid development at 25 percent of the original time to deploy. Users now use a modern browser-based user interface, and information collaboration capabilities have improved work efficiency. FLRA estimates that the total cost of ownership of its case management system has been reduced by nearly $600,000 over five years.[24]

Recovery Accountability and Transparency Board

Project: Recovery.gov Cloud Computing Migration

Launched in February of 2009 after the passage of the American Recovery and Reinvestment Act (Recovery Act), Recovery.gov is designed to "foster greater accountability in the use of funds made available by this Act."[25] The Recovery Accountability and Transparency Board created this public-facing site to allow citizens to track how stimulus funds are spent. The site includes a number of tools including graphs, charts, and maps which are continuously updated and refined to properly reflect stimulus spending. As such, a Government-wide system relies on an agile and substantial infrastructure to ensure that information is accessible, secure, and easy to update with current information.

Leveraging a commercial cloud computing provider to ensure accessibility, security and scalability

On April 26, 2010, Recovery.gov became the first Government-wide system to migrate to a cloud-based environment. The Amazon EC2 infrastructure will provide added security, as the vendor's security will supplement existing measures previously put in place by the Board. The elastic nature of this commercial cloud system means that Recovery.gov is a fully scalable site, ready to handle spikes in usage as needed. In-house personnel currently dedicated to management of the site's associated data center and correspon ding hardware will be able to redirect their resources to oversight and fraud detection.

Moving Recovery.gov to the cloud means a projected cost savings of $334,800 in FY 2010 and $420,000 in FY 2011. This represents 4 percent of the Board's $18 million total budget provided by Congress. Additionally, the Board plans to reallocate more than $1 million worth of hardware and software to its accountability mission to help identify fraud, waste, and abuse. Relocating Recovery.gov to the cloud ensures nearly 100 percent uptime and the ability to continuously backup site information. By implementing cloud technologies, the Board better meets its obligations laid out under Section 1526 of the Recovery Act, and is able to refocus efforts on its mission of transparency and accountability.[26]

Securities and Exchange Commission

Project: Investor Advocacy System

The Office of Investor Education and Advocacy (OIEA) serves individual investors who complain to the SEC about investment fraud or the mishandling of their investments by securities professionals. The staff responds to a broad range of investor contacts through phones, email, web-forms, and US mail with volumes close to 90,000 contacts annually. Case files were previously tracked in a 10 year old in-house system. Like many older systems there were several limitations including the inability attach documents, handle paper files, and provide accurate reports. The older system was also intermittent in regards to up-time and system speed.

To address these issues, the SEC implemented a cloud-based CRM tool called Salesforce.com. The implementation of Software as a Service (SaaS) solution that took less than 14 months from inception to deployment. Since the implementation of OIEA, the SEC has realized improvements in system reliability, efficiency and accuracy. Paper files are scanned into the system and worked electronically. All investor contact channels (email, web-form, US mail, fax, and phone) are brought into a single queue to be assigned and worked electronically. All documentation can now be attached to case files, which allows staff member to build complete chronology of events.

Using this new paperless environment, the time required to complete files has significantly been reduced. In many cases it was decreased up to 75 percent. Lifecycle tracking is now also available, allowing management the ability see at what stage and the chain of events for every case file. The system now also tracks information that is useful for assisting investors as well as reporting on data that is valuable to other SEC divisions.

Improving service for over 90,000 consumer contacts annually by migrating 10-year old legacy investor advocacy system to cloud-based CRM solution

Having this new solution better equips SEC in assisting investors efficiently and accurately, which is even more important as we are still dealing with the financial crisis.[27]

STATE AND LOCAL CLOUD COMPUTING CASE STUDIES

The following case studies provide recent examples of how state and local governments are using cloud computing technologies.

- State of New Jersey (New Jersey Transit Authority) - Customer Relationship Management
- State of New Mexico (Attorney General's Office) - E-mail & Office Productivity
- Commonwealth of Virginia (Virginia Information Technologies Agency) - Application Development Platform
- State of Wisconsin (Department of Natural Resources) - Collaboration
- State of Utah (Department of Technology Services) - Cloud Computing Services
- City of Canton, Georgia- E-mail
- City of Carlsbad, California - Communication & Collaboration Services
- City of Los Angeles, California - E-mail & Office Productivity
- City of Miami, Florida - 311 Service
- City of Orlando, Florida - E-mail
- Klamath County, Oregon - Office Productivity
- Prince George's County, Maryland - School District E-mail
- State of Colorado (Office of Information Technology) - Launching an Enterprise Cloud
- State of Michigan (Department of Technology Management and Budget) – MiCloud

State of New Jersey

Project: Customer Relationship Management
(New Jersey Transit Authority)

NJ Transit is the nation's largest statewide public transportation system providing bus, rail, and light rail services of over 900,000 daily trips on 247 bus routes, 26 bus stations, 11 commuter rail lines, and three light rail lines. NJ Transit links major points in New Jersey, New York, and Philadelphia, serving 164 rail stations, 60 light rail stations and 19,800 bus stops. NJ Transit relies upon its ability to field and respond to customer feedback, and requires a robust customer service system. The agency transformed its customer feedback process from one where issues went unresolved, with no tracking and, in some cases, with multiple executives seeing and responding to the same inquiry to a streamlined, faster, more accurate, and more efficient response system. The legacy infrastructure for tracking customer information and inquiries had limited functionality and not all customer inquiries were properly documented for future use. In addition, customer service representatives were responsible for a wide variety of inquiries, limiting the depth of knowledge they could apply to any given inquiry.

When NJ Transit began the search for a new customer system, the organization found that a hosted CRM system from Salesforce.com service fit its needs. To take full advantage of the software's capabilities, NJT realigned its customer service department to make each member of the staff the expert for a specific customer service area, which decreased communications overhead and improved productivity. The cloud-based system provides workflow rules that route incoming customer questions to the subject area experts. It also enabled customers and internal users the ability to ask questions and submit issues on the existing site via an online "Contact Us" web form, which flows into the solution's central customer information warehouse. The system's applications are linked to a data warehouse, employee information, an e-mail management system, and a data quality system.

Improving responsiveness to citizen inquiries through cloud-based CRM tools

Under the new system, the same number of staff handled 42,323 inquiries in 2006, compared with 8,354 in 2004. During its use, and without an increase in staff, the average response time to inquiries dropped by more than 35 percent and productivity increased by 31 percent. The web form cut down on the time spent handling free-form e-mail; approximately 50 percent of all customer feedback is captured via the online form. Salesforce has allowed NJ Transit to make significant improvements in their customer service capabilities while simultaneously reducing cost, infrastructure, and response time.[28,29]

State of New Mexico

Project: E-mail & Office Productivity Tools
(Attorney General's Office)

The New Mexico Attorney General's Office (NMAGO) has nearly 200 full-time employees, including 120 attorneys. Most work in the office revolves around creating, storing, and accessing documents in a secure IT environment. The office had historically relied upon the case management functionality of its e-mail system to track official documents ranging from legal briefs to news releases. However, this system did not offer a secure back-up function, leaving vital and sensitive documents exposed to possible loss in case of a server failure. One possible solution, migrating to a system of in-house servers, was cost-prohibitive in the short and long term, with the upfront investment calculated at $300,000. For this reason, the office explored alternative IT upgrades.

When investigating alternative email systems, NMAGO selected Google Apps Premier Edition to meet its needs. This solution provides the necessary backup capabilities, and the mail search function also eases the difficulty of locating specific files. Without the need for in-house hardware, employees now have an unlimited ability to access, save, and archive their emails and documents. This transition has also been beneficial from an environmental perspective, as it has reduced the need for paper versions of files. NMAGO is now able to avoid costs such as the $50,000 spent a few years ago for replication software to store data to a disaster recovery site. The office has reduced costs and energy use through reduced hardware acquisitions and reduced workloads for IT staff. Additionally, the office has reduced time and money spent on licensing.

Providing 120 attorneys and 200 full-time employees cloud-based e-mail

NMAGO's successful migration to the cloud is an example of what the office's CIO calls a "fundamental shift in the way information is transported to users." The CIO and his team believe that the sharing platform offered by cloud-based solutions is easily replicable and can be used to meet various government needs. They "believe cloud computing offers a new way for government to be more responsive and helpful to the public, and save more money than ever before."[30,31]

Commonwealth of Virginia

Project: Enterprise Application Development Platforms
(Virginia Information Technologies Agency)

The Virginia Information Technologies Agency (VITA) is the Commonwealth's consolidated information technology organization with responsibility for governance of IT investments and the security, technology procurement, and operations of IT infrastructure. The Agency Outreach group of the Enterprise Applications Division (EAD) at VITA provides software development and integration support and services to small agencies, the secretariat, and projects that require cross-agency collaboration.

In the spring of 2009 this group received a request from the Secretary of the Commonwealth to build and host an online solution for Notary and eNotary applications. At the same time it also received a request from Virginia's Workforce One Stop councils to create and host a low cost solution for a common intake form for the centers. Given the limited resources available, under the constraints of traditional technologies, these custom development projects would have been cost prohibitive.

Improving the application development process through use of virtual environments

To meet this challenge, EAD leveraged cloud computing to quickly provision a virtualized software development platform. Using Amazon EC2 services, the group was able to add and remove development or testing environments with ease. Even after full release to a production environment, EAD uses cloud computing to scale the production environment up as needed and for disaster recovery backups through RackSpace virtual storage services.

Virginia used cloud computing to develop new applications that would have otherwise been cost prohibitive. Instead of going through a process that typically lasts months, EAD was able to stand up a virtualized development platform from the cloud in less than two hours. VITA is still evaluating cloud computing at the agency level, reflecting on this group's recent success delivering service with the speed and flexibility its customers need.[32]

State of Wisconsin

Project: Collaboration
(Department of Natural Resources)

The Wisconsin Department of Natural Resources (DNR) has 200 locations scattered across the State, including some in remote areas. In the past, the department typically conducted business through conference calls and face-to-face meetings with staff from various locations. Outside of e-mail, there were no ad-hoc collaboration tools available to department staff to review documents which required multiple revisions by different staff members. The department's available video-conferencing system ran using outdated technology and cost the DNR $1,330 per month.

The DNR evaluated server-based collaboration software, but due to a recent migration of all of the department's servers to the State's new data center, there were no resources available to purchase an on-premises solution. The DNR began using Microsoft Live Meeting as a web conferencing solution and immediately realized cost savings and improved efficiencies. Staff members are now able to interact and can use dynamic solutions including a 360 degree panoramic video camera to conduct meetings together. The cost of running a web conference is only a fraction of the cost required to use a traditional conference call bridge and the DNR has the flexibility to purchase additional user licenses as needed for other departments.

The DNR has used this cloud-based solution to completely replace on-site meetings, training, and telephone and conference calls among internal staff and with outside agencies. This solution allows remote users to participate in meetings even if they are not at one of the DNR's office locations. The staff is now more efficient because they spend significantly less time on the road travelling to meetings. Since this migration in 2009, the DNR estimates that staff members have participated in nearly 3,500 meetings, saving the department more than $320,000. In the coming years, the DNR expects the return on investment to grow from 270 percent for the first year to over 400 percent in future years.[33]

Increasing collaboration through a hosted online meeting space that supports conference calls, interactive meetings, and information sharing

State of Utah

Project: Cloud Computing Services
(Department of Technology Services)

The State of Utah began an effort to standardize and unify its IT services in 2005 when it merged its technology assets into a single department, moving all IT staff under the state Chief Information Officer. To develop a suitable cloud strategy, the State needed to fulfill specific security requirements unique to the State. If these security challenges were met, Utah could take advantage of an array of cloud benefits including elastic expansion of services, rapidly provisioned computing capabilities, and shared services across multiple users and platforms based on customer demand.

After a wave of data center consolidation, in 2009 Utah decided that a hybrid cloud approach would work best for the State's needs. A hybrid approach combines access to public cloud services that add to or replace existing state infrastructure with private cloud services meeting specialized access and security requirements. This cloud environment includes services hosted both by third-party providers and in-state data centers.

The move to cloud-based solutions has benefited local public sector actors across the state. Although many of the public cloud provisioned services are free, the State of Utah also supports a growing number of paid services where individual county and city governments pay only for their usage. These currently include Force.com for Customer Relationship Management, Google Earth Professional for shared Geographic Information System (GIS) planning, and Wikispaces where there are an increasing number of self-provisioned wikis.

Launching cloud environment to provide enterprise services across the state and local governments at competitive prices

Contracts for these services are centrally managed through the Department of Technology Services (DTS) and make it easy for agencies to use.

Having provided its agencies and local governments with centralized access to the public cloud, the State of Utah is now focused on completing its private cloud. The State's applications previously resided on about 1,800 physical servers in over 35 locations. By

December 2010, the State plans to move these applications to a virtual platform of 400 servers. This initiative is currently over 70 percent complete and is expected to save $4 million in annual costs for a state IT budget of only $150 million. Going forward, DTS plans to extend virtualization to desktops across the state.

By implementing a vast strategy for migrating services to the cloud, the State has created an enterprise where public or private services can be reused and provisioned on demand to meet agency needs as cost-effectively as possible. This effort has had an immediate impact on State agencies and is expected to result in significant future savings.[34,35]

City of Canton, Georgia

Project: E-mail

The City of Canton, GA, approximately 40 miles north of Atlanta, has a population of 21,000 and was recently recognized as the fastest growing city in Georgia and America's 5th fastest growing city. The City's 185 employees were looking to reduce the cost and effort of maintaining an IT infrastructure and increase the reliability of business e-mail and productivity solutions. The legacy e-mail system was difficult to maintain and keep up-to-date.

Migrating 185 city employees to cloud-based e-mail

The City decided to migrate to Google Apps to provide staff members with a more reliable and feature-rich system. Staff members immediately benefited from gaining access to e-mail at home and on mobile devices, and from the increased collaboration available with tools such as group calendar, instant messaging, and shared documents and spreadsheets.

With this cloud-based solution, the City's IT staff no longer has to handle spam filters, a task that took 20 hours a week to manage prior to migration. IT staff members are also able to use powerful e-mail discovery tools in the new cloud-based solution so that e-mails potentially related to legal investigations are securely archived but easily accessible to approved personnel. The City estimates an annual savings of $10,000 by migrating to cloud computing.[36]

City of Carlsbad, California

Project: Communication & Collaboration Services

The City of Carlsbad, California has 1,100 employees across 22 departments who work in 30 different facilities across the city. Until recently, the City's employees used a 15 year-old, non-standard IT system. The City's IT department knew it had to simultaneously standardize its IT infrastructure and cut costs without sacrificing its high level of service. When the City began the process of standardizing its IT infrastructure, officials decided to review options for migrating from an on-premise e-mail and collaboration system to one hosted in the cloud.

The City ended up selecting a cloud-based version of the Microsoft productivity suite, hosted in Microsoft's data centers outside of Carlsbad. It was able to eliminate the costs of maintaining equipment, paying only monthly user fees for this new environment. While the City considered using an on-premises version of the productivity suite instead due to data security concerns, it realized that from a disaster recovery standpoint, their data was more secure being hosted outside of the City's data center.

Serving the city's needs for desktop and mobile e-mail, online collaboration tools, and web conferencing through hosted communication and collaboration services

The City has already realized a 25 percent savings over the past year using the new off-site solution, as there is no longer a need to maintain servers, manage upgrades, implement hardware replacements, or hire a systems administrator. The City realized other immediate benefits after the migration, including better access to e-mail from mobile devices and new, integrated instant messaging and web collaboration for meetings and video conferences.[37]

City of Los Angeles, California

Project: E-mail & Office Productivity

The City of Los Angeles has 34,000 employees across 40+ departments. In 2009, the city faced a $400 million deficit. This budgetary crisis and the resulting IT staff layoffs exacerbated existing frustrations with the city's in-house IT systems. The city's Information Technology Agency sought to find a new e-mail and IT provider which would streamline productivity and create more efficiencies in day-to-day operations. The city received 15 proposals for possible replacements to its in-house system.

Providing over 34,000 employees cloud-based e-mail and productivity tools

In October 2009, the City of Los Angeles announced plans to transition to Google Apps with the help of systems integrator, with a five year services contract. The city plans on having all employees on cloud-based e-mail by June 30, 2010 and has begun initial use of other products within the Google Apps Premier Edition suite and to the cloud as city employees have become more familiar with using the Cloud for workplace productivity.

The City's Chief Technology Officer estimated a direct savings of $5.5 million over five years as a result of the implementation, with the potential ROI for increased productivity possibly reaching $20 to $30 million as city employees become fully trained on cloud-based applications. The city is now able to offer each city employee 25 times more storage space, and can provide much more capability and add new users without ever needing to worry about hardware availability on city servers. City employees will also benefit from cloud-based integrated instant messaging, video conferencing, simultaneous review and editing of documents by multiple people, and the ability to access their e-mail and work data from any computer or mobile device.

While at first some city council members and staff were skeptical about moving city data outside of direct city control, the vendors have ensured that from a security and disaster recovery standpoint, data being stored in the cloud environment exceeds both the City's contractual requirements and current environment. The city's new system and its data will be safe from earthquakes and other potential natural disasters that could and have affected the city. In addition, the City of Los Angeles retains full ownership of all data on the servers and the vendors must request access to see City data, stored in the clear. These were critical hurdles the system had to clear before being recommended by staff and accepted unanimously by the City Council. With these protections and the productivity benefits, moving to cloud computing was a natural step for Los Angeles and in keeping with our focus on innovation as well as fiscal responsibility.[38,39,40]

City of Miami, Florida

Project: 311 Service

The City of Miami, with a population of nearly 5.5 million, has 3,600 employees who work in 83 locations. When the City's centralized IT department needed to cut its budget by nearly 18 percent and was forced to drop nearly 20 percent of its already small staff, continuing to deliver quality and innovative services became a challenge. At the same time, the city sought to supplement its 311 phone line, used by citizens to report non-emergency situations, with an interactive online platform for tracking service requests and mapping them geographically.

The 311 website proposal posed several challenges to the city and its IT staff. The city needed to be sure it had adequate processing power to support its new, processing power-intensive mapping application. The city also needed to take into account disaster recovery measures, since the Miami area is frequently hit with hurricanes. Overall, the city was unsure it could provide the necessary resources to manage the 311 website in-house, so moving to the cloud was the logical next choice.

The City decided to leverage a scalable, cloud-based Windows Azure platform that provides developers with on-demand hosting in Microsoft data centers. From a technical standpoint, the City was able to seamlessly integrate existing technologies in use by development teams on other projects with the cloud-based platform. Also, the pay-as-you-go platform allowed the City to test out the application and only pay for actual usage, which was also beneficial when the application become more popular. Moreover, IT staff members were able to streamline development of the application and move from testing to production simply and quickly. The deployment of the 311 website application on the cloud-based platform was successful and the City is planning additional service offerings to citizens based on the overall value and efficiency of cloud computing. [41,42]

Improving the ability for citizens to report and track requests for city services through its "311" cloud-hosted web application

City of Orlando, Florida

Project: E-mail

To address recent budget and human resource challenges, the City of Orlando moved its e-mail and productivity solution to the cloud. Preparing for the Fiscal Year 2010, the City faced a 12 percent budget cut and the retirement of two mail administrators and an information security officer. As the license renewal deadline approached, the City's CIO confronted these business challenges by leading Orlando into the cloud.

After evaluating several providers, Orlando chose to contract with Google to provide an e-mail solution for all 3,000 City workers. City leadership supported the transition based on several decision factors including projected cost savings of $262,500 per year, centralized document storage and collaboration, increased mail storage from 100MB to 25GB per user, and enhanced support for mobile devices.

Although the City's contract includes Google Docs, the City also retained the Microsoft Office productivity suite in order to avoid the cost to retrain employees.

After piloting with a small number of users, the full roll-out of the solution occurred on January 7, 2010. The City has realized a 65 percent reduction in e-mail costs and provided additional features to increase the productivity of workers. Google is now responsible for the City's e-mail server maintenance and IT support. Security functions and features such as virus checking and spam control are also performed by Google through their Postini services.[43,44]

Providing 3,000 city employees cloud-based e-mail services

Klamath County, Oregon

Project: Office Productivity

Klamath County, Oregon is one of Oregon's geographically largest counties spanning 6,000 square miles. The county has about 70,000 residents and a staff of 600 employees spread across the expansive county. County employees typically leverage video conferencing on a regular basis. When the county's director of IT realized that the need to upgrade IT capacity was imminent, coupled with the fact that the county faced a budget crunch, he began evaluating cloud-based solutions.

Providing county of 6,000 square miles with cloud-based collaboration tools

After considering the options, the county decided to migrate to a hosted solution, and selected Microsoft Online Business Productivity Suite. This would not only free up valuable human resources from managing the server environment, but also cut costs. The county also noted the potential for dependability of the system to improve since performance was not tied to county IT staff's ability to keep the servers optimized.

With this migration, the county was able to keep costs low and ensure that IT personnel and other resources were used appropriately amidst the flat county revenues. The personnel required to manage the e-mail solution decreased by 1.5 full time equivalents, an 86 percent reduction. The county also managed to implement new features including integrated messaging, collaborative tools to increase productivity for the entire county, and the ability to archive emails for a longer period of time.[45]

Prince George's County, Maryland

Project: School District E-mail

The Prince George's County, MD school district is the 18th largest school district in the country, with over 200 schools, 129,000 students and nearly 28,000 faculty/staff. For the 2008-2009 school year, the school district was facing budget cuts of $185 million and projected that a needed upgrade to their on-premises e-mail system would cost $1 million. The existing system required the support of multiple dedicated members of the district's IT staff, and due to the lack of an e-mail archiving system, IT personnel spent an excessive amount of time tracking down electronic records for legal purposes.

Migrating staff e-mails to a cloud-based solution that is offered to public schools free-of-charge

The district decided to migrate staff e-mail accounts to the Google Apps platform, which is offered to public schools at no cost. The school district' faculty and staff are now leveraging Google's cloud computing platform for messaging and collaboration. More than 13,000 of the staff members also use Google Message Discovery, powered by Postini, for archiving and discovery. Due to the cost effectiveness of the cloud computing solution, the district was able to also add the Message Discovery add-on, which costs only a few dollars per user per year, allowing authorized users to locate e-mail messages within minutes. With the success of this cloud computing experience the school district is also considering phasing in a cloud-based solution for use by students throughout the school district. [46,47]

State of Colorado

Announced Project: Launching an Enterprise Cloud
(Office of Information Technology)

In 2008, Colorado's Governor's Office of Information Technology (OIT) began to consolidate the IT systems from 17 Executive Branch agencies. Prior to consolidation, the State was responsible for 40 data centers consisting of 1,800 servers, of which 122 alone powered different versions of Lotus Notes, Microsoft Exchange, and Novell GroupWise for e-mail. The goal of consolidation was to achieve cost savings through standardization while reducing the complexity of administering multiple platforms, and improving service delivery. OIT also envisioned gaining the ability to share resources with local jurisdictions and schools across the State.

Implementing a hybrid cloud strategy to increase offerings and reduce costs while meeting the diverse security needs of 17 agencies

Colorado decided to implement a hybrid cloud solution to meet the diverse needs of its 17 state agencies. Each agency has its own applications which required different levels of security, so the State's plan includes three elements: a private cloud for line-of-business/highly secure data and systems, a virtual private cloud for archival storage/disaster recovery, and a public cloud for e-mail office productivity applications and websites.

For Colorado's private cloud, the State will use an existing data center and begin to leverage server virtualization. All production data will remaion-site while virtualized instances of the production server can be stored off-site, increasing disaster recovery capabilities at reduced cost. Colorado's virtual private cloud allows for additional scalability on a pay-as-you-go model for large systems. Colorado has recently started transitioning systems to the virtual private cloud.

Colorado's usage of the public cloud will initially be a pilot of Google Apps for e-mail and office productivity. Using cloud-based e-mail provides Colorado with increased mobility, disaster recovery, storage, better document sharing, and collaboration. The pilot will test the migration of e-mail from three different agencies, focusing on security and workflow processing. If the pilot is successful and the cost-benefit analysis proves positive, the State plans to transition all 27,600 Executive Branch employees to the new system.

By shifting e-mail to the cloud, Colorado will be able to take all 122 existing e-mail servers out of production and experience significant operational cost savings. An initial cost-benefit analysis of the migration to cloud-based e-mail estimates annual savings of $8 million. In addition, Colorado will avoid additional expenses of up to $20 million over the next three years.[48]

State of Michigan

Announced Project: MiCloud
(Department of Technology Management and Budget)

In March 2010, Michigan's Department of Information Technology consolidated with the State's Department of Management and Budget. The new Department of Technology, Management & Budget (DTMB) is now building a full array of services to provide across governments and the private sector. Michigan is moving toward leveraging cloud-based solutions to provide clients with rapid, secure, and lower cost services though a program dubbed "MiCloud."

One key area of current action is the State's strategic investment in storage virtualization technologies, expected to go live in October 2010. Michigan is actively piloting MiCloud "Storage for Users" and "Storage for Servers" as internal government cloud functions delivered by DTMB. The consumption expectation is more than 250 terabytes in the first year of operation at a projected storage cost that is 90 percent lower than today's lowest-cost storage tier. MiCloud provides self-service and automated delivery within 10 minutes of submitting an online request. The following table expresses projected savings based on migration rates. It is important to note that this low-cost option represents a service alternative that is only appropriate for data that do not require 24x7 availability or real-time, block-level replication.

The State of Michigan's 2010-2014 strategic plan also outlines critical future investments in virtual server hosting and process automation. The State is in the proof-of-concept phase for the MiCloud "Hosting for Development" and "Process Orchestrator" functions in the internal government cloud. The hosting for development function automates the delivery of virtual servers within 30 minutes of submitting an online request. Michigan will also explore a hybrid cloud to deliver a more complex Application Platform as a Service (APaaS). The process orchestrator function enables agency business users, regardless of IT skill level, to create and test simple process definitions. Business users will be able to publish processes and related forms to the service catalog and over time analyze related metrics. Ultimately, the shift to cloud computing will allow Michigan to improve services to citizens and business while freeing up scarce capital, staff resources, and IT assets for critical investments.[49]

Making strategic investments in virtualization technologies and developing a cloud platform to support state-wide services

Migration Rate	Potential Annual Savings or Cost Avoidance
10%	$228,000
20%	$456,000
30%	$684,000
40%	$912,000
50%	$1,140,000
60%	$1,368,000

REFERENCES

Air Force Office of the Chief Information Officer. May 2010.
City of Canton. May 2010.
City of Carlsbad. May 2010.
City of Los Angeles. May 2010.
City of Los Angeles Information Technology Agency. "Los Angeles Google Enterprise Email & Collaboration System." presentation, 2010.
City of Miami. May 2010.
City of Orlando. "Orlando Goes Google." government document, 2010.
Defense Information Systems Agency. May 2010.
Defense Information Systems Agency. May 2010.
Department of Energy Office of the Chief Information Officer. May 2010.
Department of Health and Human Services. May 2010.
Department of the Interior Office of the Chief Technology Officer. April 2010.
Erlichman, Jeff. "Cloud Recruiting." *On the Frontlines: Shaping Government Clouds*, (Winter 2010). http://www.mygazines.com/issue/5865.
Federal Labor Relations Authority. April 2010.

Feeney, Tom C. (2010). "NJ Transit to test online suggestion box for riders." *Nj.com*, (May 14). http://www.nj.com/news/index.ssf/2008/05/nj_transit_to_test_ online_ sugg.html.

General Services Administration. May 2010.

General Services Administration. "Cloud Sourcing Models." government document, 2010.

General Services Administration. "FDCCI – Initial Data Center Inventory." government document, 2010.CIO Council. http://www.cio.gov/documents_details. cfm/uid/ 25A781B7 -BDBE-6B59-F86D3F2751E5CB43/structure/ OMB%20Documents %20 and %20 Guidance/category/Policy%20Letters%20and%20Memos.

Google Enterprise Blog, The. http://googleenterprise.blogspot.com/2009/11/microsoft-exchange-or-google.

Klamath County Oregon. May 2010.

LA GEECS Google Site, The. https://sites.google.

Lawrence Berkeley National Labs Office of the Chief Information Officer. May 2010.

National Aeronautics and Space Administration. March 2010.

National Aeronautics and Space Administration Jet Propulsion Laboratory Office of the Chief Technology Officer. May 2010.

National Aeronautics and Space Administration Office of the Chief Technology Officer. "WWT Case Study." government document, 2010.

National Aeronautics and Space Administration Office of Legislative and Intergovernmental Affairs. May 2010.

National Institute of Standards and Technology. http://csrc.nist.gov/groups/SNS.

National Institute of Standards and Technology. "Summary of NIST Cloud Computing Standards Development Efforts." government document, 2010.

New Jersey Transit. May 2010.

New Mexico Attorney General's Office of the Chief Information Officer. May 2010.

Prince George's County Public Schools. May 2010.

Prince George's County Public Schools. "Googlizing the Masses." presentation, School Board of Prince George's County Public Schools, MD, 2010. http://docs.google.

Recovery Accountability and Transparency Board. "Recovery.gov Moves to Cloud Computing Infrastructure." May 2010. http://www.recovery.gov/ News/mediakit/Pages /PressRelease05132010.aspx.

Schlueb, Mark. "Orlando goes Google for cheaper e-mail." *Orlando Sentinel*, (January 2010). http://articles.orlandosentinel.com/2010-01-09/news/1001080262_1_google.

Securities and Exchange Commission Office of Investor Education and Advocacy. April 2010.

Social Security Administration. May 2010.

State of Colorado Government Office of Information Technology. "Moving Colorado to the cloud: A business case." government document, 2010.

State of Michigan Department of Technology, Management & Budget. "Governing in the cloud – a government case study from Michigan." government document, 2010.

State of Utah. May 2010.

State of Utah Department of Technology Services. "Implementing Utah's cloud computing strategy: A case study on bringing cloud-based IT services to government."government document, 2010.

State of Wisconsin. May 2010.

United States Army G-1. May 2010.

U.S. Congress. *American Recovery and Reinvestment Act of 2009.* H.R. 1. 111th Cong., 1st sess. (January 2009). http://frwebgate.access.gpo.gov/cgi-bin/getdoc.cgi? dbname= 111_cong_bills&docid=f:h1enr.pdf.

U.S. Congress. *Energy Independence and Security Act of 2007.* H.R. 6. 110th Cong., 1st sess. (January 2007). http://frwebgate.access.gpo.gov/cgi-bin/getdoc.cgi?dbname= 110_cong_bills&docid=f:h6enr.txt.pdf.

Virginia Information Technologies Agency. "Cloud computing: Commonwealth of Virginia." government document, 2010.

Yasin, Rutrell. "City of Miami takes citizen services to cloud." *Government Computer News,* (March 2010). http://gcn.com/articles/2010/03/10/city-of-miami-microsoft-azure.aspx.

End Notes

[1] National Institute of Standards and Technology, "The NIST Definition of Cloud Computing," document posted October 2009, http://csrc.nist.gov/groups/SNS.

[2] General Services Administration, "Cloud Sourcing Models" (government document, 2010).

[3] U.S. Congress. *Energy Independence and Security Act of 2007.* H.R. 6. 110th Cong., 1st sess. (January 2007). http://frwebgate.access.gpo.gov/cgi-bin/getdoc.cgi?dbname=110_cong_bills&docid=f:h6enr.txt.pdf.

[4] Office of Management and Budget. "Federal Data Center Consolidation Initiative," CIO Council, government document posted February 2010, http://www.cio.gov/documents_details.cfm/uid/25A781B7-BDBE-6B59-F86D3F2751E5CB43/structure/OMB%20Documents%20and%20Guidance/category/Policy%20Letters%20and%20Memos.

[5] National Institute of Standards and Technology, "Summary of NIST Cloud Computing Standards Development Efforts" (government document, 2010).

[6] National Institute of Standards and Technology, "Summary of NIST Cloud Computing Standards Development Efforts" (government document, 2010).

[7] National Institute of Standards and Technology, "Summary of NIST Cloud Computing Standards Development Efforts" (government document, 2010).

[8] Jeff Erlichman, "Cloud Recruiting," *On the Frontlines: Shaping Government Clouds*, Winter 2010. http://www.mygazines.com/issue/5865.

[9] United States Army G-1, May 2010.

[10] Defense Information Systems Agency, May 2010.

[11] Defense Information Systems Agency, May 2010.

[12] Air Force Office of the Chief Information Officer, May 2010.

[13] Department of Energy Office of the Chief Information Officer, May 2010.

[14] Lawrence Berkeley National Labs Office of the Chief Information Officer, May 2010.

[15] Department of Health and Human Services, May 2010.

[16] Department of the Interior Office of the Chief Technology Officer, April 2010.

[17] General Services Administration, May 2010.

[18] General Services Administration, May 2010.

[19] National Aeronautics and Space Administration, May 2010.

[20] National Aeronautics and Space Administration Office of the Chief Technology Officer, "WWT Case Study" (government document, 2010).

[21] National Aeronautics and Space Administration Jet Propulsion Laboratory Office of the Chief Technology Officer, May 2010.

[22] National Aeronautics and Space Administration Office of Legislative and Intergovernmental Affairs, May 2010.

[23] Social Security Administration, May 2010.

[24] Federal Labor Relations Authority, April 2010.

[25] U.S. Congress. *American Recovery and Reinvestment Act of 2009.* H.R. 1. 111th Cong., 1st sess. (January 2009). http://frwebgate.access.gpo.gov/cgi-bin/getdoc.cgi?dbname=111_cong_bills&docid=f:h1enr.pdf.

[26] Recovery Accountability and Transparency Board, "Recovery.gov Moves to Cloud Computing Infrastructure," May 2010. http://www.recovery.gov/News/mediakit/Pages/PressRelease05132010.aspx.

[27] Securities and Exchange Commission Office of Investor Education and Advocacy, May 2010.

[28] Tom C. Feeney, "NJ Transit to test online suggestion box for riders," *Nj.com*, May 2008. http://www.nj.com/news/index.ssf/2008/05/nj_transit_to_test_online_sugg.html.

[29]New Jersey Transit, May 2010.

[30] James Ferreira, message entitled "Microsoft Exchange or Google Apps? One government agency goes Google," the Google Enterprise Blog, message posted November 2009. http://googleenterprise.blogspot.com/2009/11/microsoft-exchange-or-google.

[31] New Mexico Attorney General's Office of the Chief Information Officer, May 2010.

[32] Virginia Information Technologies Agency, "Cloud computing: Commonwealth of Virginia" (government document, 2010).

[33] State of Wisconsin, May 2010.

[34] State of Utah Department of Technology Services, "Implementing Utah's cloud computing strategy: A case study on bringing cloud-based IT services to government" (government document, 2010).

[35] State of Utah, May 2010.

[36] City of Canton, May 2010.

[37] City of Carlsbad, May 2010.

[38] City of Los Angeles Information Technology Agency, "Los Angeles Google Enterprise Email & Collaboration System" (presentation, 2010).

[39]City of Los Angeles, May 2010.

[40] City of Los Angeles, "City of L.A. CSC/Google Project Highlights – as of 12/18/09," the LA GEECS Google Site, document posted February 2010, https://sites.google.

[41]RutrellYasin, "City of Miami takes citizen services to cloud," Government Computer News, March 2010. http://gcn.com/articles/2010/03/10/city-of-miami-microsoft-azure.aspx.

[42] City of Miami, May 2010.

[43]Mark Schlueb, "Orlando goes Google for cheaper e-mail," Orlando Sentinel, January 2010. http://articles.orlandosentinel.com/2010-01-09/news/1001080262_1_google.

[44]City of Orlando, "Orlando Goes Google" (government document, 2010).

[45] Klamath County Oregon, May 2010.

[46]Prince George's County Public Schools. "Googlizing the Masses" (presentation, School Board of Prince George's County Public Schools, MD, 2010). http://docs.google.

[47]Prince George's County Public Schools, May 2010.

[48] State of Colorado Government Office of Information Technology, "Moving Colorado to the cloud: A business case" (government document, 2010).

[49] State of Michigan Department of Technology, Management & Budget, "Governing in the cloud – a government case study from Michigan" (government document, 2010).

In: Cloud Computing and Government: Background, Benefits...   ISBN: 978-1-61761-784-3
Editor: George I. Nikolov   © 2011 Nova Science Publishers, Inc.

Chapter 3

OPENING STATEMENT OF CHAIRMAN EDOLPHUS TOWNS, COMMITTEE ON OVERSIGHT AND GOVERNMENT REFORM, HEARING ON "CLOUD COMPUTING: BENEFITS AND RISKS OF MOVING FEDERAL IT INTO THE CLOUD"

Good morning. Thank you all for being here today.

The purpose of today's hearing is to examine the benefits and risks of cloud computing for the federal government. At the most basic level, cloud computing is web-based computing whereby computing resources are shared and accessible over the Internet on demand. In this way, cloud computing is like most utility services.

Before the electric grid was developed, business owners who wanted to use machinery also needed to produce enough energy to run that machinery. That meant investing heavily to build and maintain a power source. The electric grid revolutionized the country by centralizing the resource and allowing businesses to simply purchase electricity.

Cloud computing promises the same for computing power. Instead of building and maintaining an entire IT system in house, businesses can purchase computing power and tap into that resource over the Internet.

While the concept might sound like something out of a science fiction novel, when you think about it, most Americans already use some form of cloud computing. I'm sure most of the people in this room have used some web-based email service, social networking site like Facebook or Twitter, or photo and video-sharing site like Flickr and YouTube. Indeed, many of us in Congress are using those tools to communicate with our constituents.

Cloud computing is a very real technology that the federal government has already begun to embrace. The Federal Cloud Computing Initiative and an online cloud computing storefront were launched in September 2009.

I've read that the government-wide implementation of cloud computing will be a decade-long journey. It's the job of this Committee to ensure that journey is well thought out, that the benefits and risks are fully examined, and that there are comprehensive plans in place to ensure that we do this the right way, the first time.

In the same way that common standards improved efficiency and safety for the electric grid, standards are needed for cloud computing to ensure security, promote interoperability, and support data portability. I believe strongly that doing this right the first time will require strong public-private collaboration, particularly on standards development.

The shift to cloud computing offers the federal government tremendous promise, but it is not without risk. The balance between risk and reward is an important one and I hope to get a better understanding of that balance today.

It is clear to me that security and privacy are real concerns. Our natural impulse is to hold the things we value close to us, but cloud computing requires entrusting data to others. The law's current focus on the physical location of data also presents unique privacy and legal challenges.

A major benefit of cloud computing is the potential for significant cost savings. It makes sense – cloud computing allows agencies to pool resources and pay only for the computing power that they actually use. Cost savings estimates vary widely from 25-99% of IT operating costs. I'd like to know why those figures vary so widely and what can we really expect to save?

I look forward to today's hearing, to a thorough examination of the Federal Cloud Computing Initiative, and to addressing the emerging legal and policy issues that federal cloud computing presents. I want to thank all of our witnesses for appearing here today and I look forward to hearing their testimony.

In: Cloud Computing and Government: Background, Benefits...   ISBN: 978-1-61761-784-3
Editor: George I. Nikolov   © 2011 Nova Science Publishers, Inc.

Chapter 4

OPENING STATEMENT OF CHAIRWOMAN DIANE E. WATSON, HEARING ON "CLOUD COMPUTING: BENEFITS AND RISKS OF MOVING FEDERAL IT INTO THE CLOUD"

Thank you Mr. Chairman for agreeing to hold today's hearing in conjunction with the Subcommittee on Government Management, Organization and Procurement on the benefits and risks of the federal government's use of cloud computing services.

At its most basic level the term "cloud computing" is a metaphor for internet-based computing. Some have described it as a new name for an old concept: the delivery of computing services from a remote location, similar to the way electricity and other utilities are provided to most customers. A preponderance of technology experts believe that by 2020 most people will access software applications online and share and retrieve information through the use of remote server networks. This is a dramatic departure from today's environment where we depend on software housed on individual computers.

The use of cloud computing by federal agencies has significant benefits for collaboration across a broad information infrastructure, as well as for reducing costs associated with long-term information technology investments. It holds out the promise of enabling IT assets to remain on the technological cutting edge over their life cycle at reduced costs. It is therefore appropriate that President Obama has targeted the federal government's IT infrastructure as part of his mandate to cut agency budgets by 5 percent in 2011, particularly when we consider that the federal government spends $76 billion annually on IT investments and that the majority of those investments are for software and IT services.

Despite these benefits, I remain concerned with potential or unknown security risks associated with cloud computing across the federal agency community. For example, federal customers may become dependent on their cloud computing vendor's effective implementation of security practices or protocols for ensuring the integrity and reliability of agency data and applications. The cloud computing model also raises privacy issues as well as the level of control over data due to issues of portability across different platforms or the fact that vendors may not be willing to divulge proprietary information.

Due to these concerns, in July 2009, I requested that the GAO evaluate the technical and security risks associated with cloud computing across the federal government. I am pleased to announce that GAO is releasing the report at today's hearing and that Mr. Greg Wilshusen (pronounced Wil-shoe-sen) will be reporting on GAO's findings.

The GAO report notes that while individual agencies have identified security measures needed when using cloud computing, they have not always developed corresponding guidance, and that OMB and GSA have yet to complete government-wide cloud computing security initiatives. Overall, I believe the report makes the point that cloud computing has both advantages as well as disadvantages with respect to cybersecurity and that the Administration should move deliberatively and with caution in considering when or when not to use cloud computing platforms.

Concerns involving vendor cybersecurity have not arisen in a vacuum or in an ad hoc manner. Specifically, we know through reporting done in *The Wall Street Journal* and other publications that multiple technology and industrial base companies, including Google, have been compromised by cyberattacks believed to be sourced from the People's Republic of China. It has subsequently been reported that both the Federal Bureau of Investigation and the National Security Agency have examined these episodes to determine their origins and the extent of damages sustained by all parties.

Cyberattacks place personal data, intellectual property, and our national security at grave risk, and require our partners in the government contractor community to be ever- vigilant in securing those systems and infrastructures used to service both federal agencies and private citizens alike. While I understand the aforementioned incidents may not be appropriate for discussion in an open hearing, I believe our vendor panelists need to address the broader issue of how they plan on meeting federal information security standards for protecting those programs and federal data that may be hosted through their cloud services. I look forward to hearing their specific plans of actions to do so.

Mr. Chairman, once again I thank you for holding this hearing. I look forward to the testimony of our distinguished panels of witnesses and learning more about this important strategy to achieve efficient and effective IT.

In: Cloud Computing and Government: Background, Benefits...   ISBN: 978-1-61761-784-3
Editor: George I. Nikolov   © 2011 Nova Science Publishers, Inc.

Chapter 5

STATEMENT OF VIVEKKUNDRA, FEDERAL CHIEF INFORMATION OFFICER, ADMINISTRATOR FOR ELECTRONIC GOVERNMENT AND INFORMATION TECHNOLOGY, OFFICE OF MANAGEMENT AND BUDGET, BEFORE THE HOUSE COMMITTEE ON OVERSIGHT AND GOVERNMENT REFORM, HEARING ON "CLOUD COMPUTING: BENEFITS AND RISKS OF MOVING FEDERAL IT INTO THE CLOUD"

Good morning Chairman Towns, Chairwoman Watson and members of the Committee. Thank you for the opportunity to testify on "Cloud Computing: Benefits and Risks of Moving Federal IT into the Cloud."

Information technology (IT) has transformed how the private sector operates and has revolutionized the efficiency, convenience, and effectiveness with which it serves its customers.In our everyday lives, we can track the status of a shipment, buy goods and services, make travel, hotel and restaurant reservations, and collaborate with friends and colleagues – all online, anytime and anywhere.

Yet, when it comes to dealing with our government, we have to stand in line, hold on the phone, or mail in a paper form. The Federal Government has largely missed out on the transformation in the use of IT due to poor management of its technology investments.Government IT projects all too often cost millions of dollars more than they should, take years longer than necessary to deploy, and deliver technologies that are obsolete by the time they are completed.

To address these persistent problems, in June 2009 we launched the IT Dashboard, which allows the American people to monitor IT investments across the Federal government and shines light into government operations. However, it is not enough to simply shine a light on IT programs and hope that results will follow.

Building on the foundation of the dashboard, we launched TechStat Accountability Sessions in January 2010. A TechStat accountability session is a face- to- face, evidence-based review of an IT program with OMB and agency leadership. TechStat sessions enable the government to turnaround, halt or terminate IT investments that do not produce dividends for the American people.

Earlier this week, we announced three actions in the Administration's continuing effort to reform Federal IT.

- First, we are undertaking detailed reviews of troubled IT projects across the Federal Government. Where serious problems are identified, actions will be taken to correct the problems, including potential adjustments to Fiscal Year 2012 agency budgets.
- Second, we directed executive departments and agencies to refrain from awarding new task orders or contracts for financial system modernization projects – an area of persistent problems – pending review and approval of project improvement plans by OMB. Across the government, there are approximately 30 financial systems projects that are affected by this policy. The total cost expended on these projects is anticipated to be $20 billion over the life of these projects, with an approximate annual spend of $3 billion. OMB expects this new process to result in a significant reduction in these amounts.
- Third, we will develop recommendations for improving the Federal Government's IT procurement and management practices within 120 days and in consultation with agencies. These recommendations will help address the root causes of problems plaguing Federal IT projects by strengthening existing policies and procedures where appropriate, eliminating outdated and cumbersome rules, and focusing on proven best practices from inside and outside the Federal Government.

These actions reflect the Administration's ongoing commitment to closing the IT gap between the public and private sectors and leveraging the power of technology to improve the efficiency of government and deliver better services to the American people. The President has ordered a three year freeze in non- defense and national security programs in the FY 2011 budget and has ordered some agencies to reduce their 2012 budget request by five percent. To do more with less, we need game-changing technologies.

Cloud computing is one such technology.

BENEFITS OF THE CLOUD

As the world's largest consumer of information technology, the Federal Government spends approximately $80 billion annually on more than 12,000 systems at major agencies.[1] Fragmentation of systems, poor project execution, and the drag of legacy technologies in the Federal Government have presented barriers to achieving the productivity and performance gains that can be found in the private sector's more effective use of technology. For example, over the past decade, while the private sector was consolidating data centers, the Federal Government increased its data centers from 432 to over 1,100, leading to redundant investment, reduced energy efficiency, and poor service delivery.

Cloud computing has the potential to greatly reduce inefficiencies, increase data center efficiency and utilization rates, and lower operating costs. It is a model for delivering computing resources – such as networks, servers, storage, or software applications.

There was a time when every household, town, farm or village had its own water well. Today, shared public utilities give us access to clean water by simply turning on the tap; cloud computing works in a similar fashion. Just like water from the tap in your kitchen, cloud computing services can be turned on or off quickly as needed. Like at the water company, there is a team of dedicated professionals making sure the service provided is safe, secure and available on a 24/7 basis. When the tap isn't on, not only are you saving water, but you aren't paying for resources you don't currently need.

The National Institute of Standards and Technology (NIST) defines cloud computing as a model for enabling convenient, on- demand network access to a shared pool of configurable computing resources (e.g., networks, servers, storage, applications, and services) that can be rapidly provisioned and released with minimal management effort or service provider interaction.[2]

Many organizations in the private sector and at state and local governments are already using cloud computing technologies to streamline their operations and improve delivery of services to their customers.

In the private sector, for example, a web-based multimedia production company used the cloud to allow anyone with access to an Internet connection to create their own fully customized, professional-quality, "TV-like" videos. Consumers upload audio, photos, and videos to the web which are then analyzed and processed with advanced post-production techniques as used in television and film. The resulting videos can then be shared with friends and family across the world. The cloud allowed for a rapid response when demand jumped from 25,000 users to over 250,000 users in three days, eventually reaching a peak rate of 20,000 new customers every *hour*. Because of the cloud, the company was able to scale from 50 to 4,000 virtual machines in three days to support increased demand on a real-time basis.[3]

In contrast, the Car Allowance and Rebate System (CARS, more commonly known as "Cash-For-Clunkers"), failed under peak loads. To process the anticipated 250,000 transactions, the National Highway Traffic Safety Administration (NHTSA) deployed a customized commercial application hosted in a traditional data center environment on June 19, 2009. When dealer registrations began on July 24, 2009, demand far outstripped initial projections, and within three days, the system was overwhelmed, leading to numerous unplanned outages and service disruptions. Ultimately, approximately 690,000 CARS transactions were processed. However, lacking the ability to scale rapidly, system stability was not achieved until August 28, over a month after registrations started coming in.[4]

By using cloud computing services, the Federal Government can gain access to powerful technology resources faster and at lower costs. Ultimately, this will allow the Government to better serve the American people and focus on mission-critical tasks instead of on purchasing, configuring and maintaining redundant infrastructure.

MOVING TO THE CLOUD

We recognize that the shift to cloud computing will not take place overnight. While cloud computing has the potential to provide tremendous benefits, we are still in the early stages of a decade- long journey. As we move to the cloud, we must be vigilant in our efforts to ensure the security of government information, protect the privacy of our citizens, and safeguard our national security interests. The American people must be confident that their information is safe in the cloud. Therefore, we are being deliberate in making sure the Federal Government's journey to the cloud fully considers the advantages and risks associated with cloud technologies, by defining standards and security requirements. The following represent key milestones in the Administration's deliberate approach:

- **April 2009** – Cloud Computing Program Management Office (PMO) established at the General Services Administration (GSA). The Cloud Computing PMO is responsible for coordinating the Federal Government's cloud computing efforts in key areas, such as security, standards, acquisition, and is developing the governance approaches necessary to effectively engage with Federal agencies for the safe and secure adoption of cloud technology.
- **May 2009** – Industry Summit conducted with the private sector to explore the risks and benefits associated with cloud computing.
- **November 2009** – Security and Standards Working Groups convened to better enable agencies to collaborate on these topics. The Security Working Group serves as the central organization for identifying, aggregating, and disseminating security and standards concerns, solutions, and processes impacting the implementation and adoption of available cloud computing. The Standards Working Group is charged with establishing a framework and roadmap to drive standards to facilitate interoperability, portability, and management for cloud computing services.
- **February 2010** – Initiated development of a government- wide security certification and accreditation process for cloud computing solutions.
- **May 2010** – "Cloud Computing Forum and Workshop" hosted by NIST to initiate engagement with industry to collaboratively develop standards and explore solutions for cloud interoperability, portability, and security. Attendees included a broad range of participants from standards bodies, state and local governments, academia, and leading security, hardware, software, and cloud services providers.

SECURITY & PRIVACY

As we increasingly leverage technology to deliver services to the American people, we cannot lose sight of the fact that we operate in an inter-connected environment, in which new threats arise daily. To realize the full benefits of the digital revolution, the American people must have confidence that sensitive information is not compromised, their communications with the government are secure, their privacy and civil liberties are protected, and that the Federal infrastructure is not compromised.

To advance the security posture of the Federal Government, the Administration is taking a number of actions. Shifting from an outdated, compliance-based process to a performance-based approach and automated tools will enable agencies to continuously monitor security-related information from across the enterprise in a manageable and actionable way. Efforts such as the National Cybersecurity Education Initiative will improve the effectiveness of the cybersecurity workforce. Developing an integrated plan for research and development will encourage innovation in game-changing technologies in coordination with industry and academia.

Cloud computing, like any technology, has inherent benefits and risks. Some of the challenges we face as the government moves towards greater adoption of cloud computing include ensuring clarity of data ownership, meeting the requirements of privacy regulations such as those for health records, data recovery following a disaster or cyber attack, long- term storage, records management and data viability. Additionally, vendor dependence, sharing of computing resources, and concerns related to multi-tenancy are all risks often associated with cloud computing. There is a common misperception that these are all new risks, brought on by the use of third- party resources to operate government systems.

However, the Federal Government currently uses a wide array of external providers and shared services to support its employees and to deliver services to the American people. From public telecommunications networks to agency data centers, Federal agencies make use of commercially operated facilities and networks every day. And many agencies currently make use of systems that are contractor owned and/or operated on behalf of the Federal Government. In fact, agencies reported the use of 4,186 contractor systems in FY 2009.[5]

The adoption of new technologies in the Federal government takes place within a framework of risk management at the Department and Agency level. The Federal Information Security Management Act of 2002 (FISMA) requires agency heads to implement security controls commensurate with risk, after a cost- benefit analysis. Once a possible business use is identified for a given technology, agency Chief Information Officers and Chief Information Security Officers assess risk using a framework of Federal laws and guidance that includes FISMA, Federal Information Processing Standards (FIPS), and NIST guidance as reflected in NIST Special Publications (SP) 800 series.

In April 2010, OMB issued memorandum M-10-15, *FY 2010 Reporting Instructions for the Federal Information Security Management Act and Agency Privacy Management*[6], which instructs agencies to develop automated risk models and apply them to the vulnerabilities and threats identified by security management tools. In the case of cloud computing, we expect these risk models to vary based on the specific cloud deployment model used (e.g., private cloud versus public cloud). Agencies will incorporate these risk models into their business decision-making processes and use them to inform the development of comprehensive agency risk management plans that address issues such as continuity of service, quality control, and long-term preservation of data to support Federal records requirements.

While the decisions to use cloud computing are made at the agency level by agency Chief Information Officers and Chief Information Security Officers, the potential benefits of cloud computing won't be fully realized if every agency independently reviews and certifies solutions. The current fragmented certification process – where agencies independently conduct certifications and accreditations on the same products – is redundant, and adds both time and cost to an already complex procurement process.

This is why we directed NIST to establish a technical process for centralized certification to provide common security management services to Federal agencies. The process supports the development of common security requirements and performs authorization and continuous monitoring services for government-wide use, enabling Federal agencies to rapidly, securely and cost-effectively procure technologies. Agencies can realize these benefits by leveraging the security authorizations provided through a joint authorization board. The board will provide both initial and ongoing assessment of risk on behalf of the government as systems are continuously monitored throughout their lifecycle.

Additionally, GSA is working to streamline acquisition processes for cloud computing technologies. The goal is to provide an efficient acquisition process that minimizes redundancy, delay, and administrative burden and supports agencies in the safe, secure and timely adoption of cloud computing technologies.

CLOSING THE IT GAP

We have been deliberate in engaging government, industry, and academia to ensure a broad range of views are considered as we develop a comprehensive approach to cloud computing.

The Federal Chief Information Officers Council, in partnership with the GSA and NIST, is working on a government- wide strategy for the safe and secure use of cloud computing services for release by the end of calendar year 2010.

We are also working closely with the National Association of State Chief Information Officers (NASCIO) to streamline procurement processes, develop standards, and ensure the safe and secure adoption of cloud computing technologies.

Additionally, we are asking agencies to reflect their data center consolidation plans and analysis of cloud computing alternatives in their FY 2012 budget submissions.[7]

Cloud computing reflects the commoditization of IT services and follows naturally from the combination of cheaper and more powerful processors with faster and more ubiquitous networks.

Investments in the private sector have led to historic productivity gains. In their daily lives, the American people can receive services on line rather than in line. They expect the same from their Government. Unfortunately, the IT gap contributes to a vastly different experience. When the American people deal with their Government, they are confronted by a culture that says "there's a paper form that" versus one that says "there's an app for that" when dealing with the private- sector.

Cloud computing is not a silver bullet, but offers a transformational opportunity to fundamentally reshape the operations of government and close the IT gap. The Obama Administration is committed to leveraging the power of cloud computing in a safe and secure manner to help close the technology gap and deliver results for the American people. Thank you again for the opportunity to appear today and I look forward to answering your questions.

APPENDIX – CHARACTERISTIC OF CLOUD COMPUTING

Below is from NIST's Cloud Computing Definition (Version 15), available via: csrc.nist.gov/groups/SNS/cloud- computing/cloud-def- v15.doc
Essential Characteristics:

- **On-demand self-service.** A consumer can unilaterally provision computing capabilities, such as server time and network storage, as needed automatically without requiring human interaction with each service's provider.
- **Broad network access.** Capabilities are available over the network and accessed through standard mechanisms that promote use by heterogeneous thin or thick client platforms (e.g., mobile phones, laptops, and PDAs).
- **Resource pooling.** The provider's computing resources are pooled to serve multiple consumers using a multi-tenant model, with different physical and virtual resources dynamically assigned and reassigned according to consumer demand. There is a sense of location independence in that the customer generally has no control or knowledge over the exact location of the provided resources but may be able to specify location at a higher level of abstraction (e.g., country, state, or datacenter). Examples of resources include storage, processing, memory, network bandwidth, and virtual machines.
- **Rapid elasticity.** Capabilities can be rapidly and elastically provisioned, in some cases automatically, to quickly scale out and rapidly released to quickly scale in. To the consumer, the capabilities available for provisioning often appear to be unlimited and can be purchased in any quantity at any time.
- **Measured Service.** Cloud systems automatically control and optimize resource use by leveraging a metering capability at some level of abstraction appropriate to the type of service (e.g., storage, processing, bandwidth, and active user accounts). Resource usage can be monitored, controlled, and reported providing transparency for both the provider and consumer of the utilized service.

Deployment Models:

- **Private cloud.** The cloud infrastructure is operated solely for one organization. It may be managed by the organization or a third party and may exist on premises or off premises.
- **Community cloud.** The cloud infrastructure is shared by several organizations and supports a specific community that has shared concerns (e.g., mission, security requirements, policy, and compliance considerations). It may be managed by the organizations or a third party and may exist on premises or off premises.
- **Public cloud.** The cloud infrastructure is made available to the general public or a large industry group and is owned by an organization selling cloud services.
- **Hybrid cloud.** The cloud infrastructure is a composition of two or more clouds (private, community, or public) that remain unique entities but are bound together by standardized or proprietary technology that enables data and application portability (e.g., cloud bursting for load-balancing between clouds).

Service Models:

- **Cloud Software as a Service (SaaS).** The capability provided to the consumer is to use the provider's applications running on a cloud infrastructure. The applications are accessible from various client devices through a thin client interface such as a web browser (e.g., web-based email). The consumer does not manage or control the underlying cloud infrastructure including network, servers, operating systems, storage, or even individual application capabilities, with the possible exception of limited user- specific application configuration settings.

- **Cloud Platform as a Service (PaaS).** The capability provided to the consumer is to deploy onto the cloud infrastructure consumer- created or acquired applications created using programming languages and tools supported by the provider. The consumer does not manage or control the underlying cloud infrastructure including network, servers, operating systems, or storage, but has control over the deployed applications and possibly application hosting environment configurations.
- **Cloud Infrastructure as a Service (IaaS).** The capability provided to the consumer is to provision processing, storage, networks, and other fundamental computing resources where the consumer is able to deploy and run arbitrary software, which can include operating systems and applications. The consumer does not manage or control the underlying cloud infrastructure but has control over operating systems, storage, deployed applications, and possibly limited control of select networking components (e.g., host firewalls).

End Notes

[1] http://www.whitehouse.gov/omb/assets/egov_docs/FY09_FISMA.pdf (Appendix 1, Table 1)
[2] http://csrc.nist.gov/groups/SNS/cloud- computing/cloud-def-v15.doc; see Appendix for further details
[3] http://blog.rightscale.com/2008/04/23/animoto-facebook-scale-up/
[4] http://www.cars.gov/files/official-information/CARS-Report-to-Congress.pdf, pg.10-12
[5] http://www.whitehouse.gov/omb/assets/egov_docs/FY09_FISMA.pdf; Appendix 1, Table 2
[6] http://www.whitehouse.gov/omb/assets/memoranda_2010/m10-15.pdf
[7] http://www.whitehouse.gov/omb/assets/memoranda_2010/m10-19.pdf

In: Cloud Computing and Government: Background, Benefits...   ISBN: 978-1-61761-784-3
Editor: George I. Nikolov

Chapter 6

STATEMENT OF DR. DAVID MCCLURE, ASSOCIATE ADMINISTRATOR, OFFICE OF CITIZEN SERVICES AND INNOVATIVE TECHNOLOGIES, GENERAL SERVICES ADMINISTRATION, BEFORE THE HOUSE COMMITTEE ON OVERSIGHT AND GOVERNMENT REFORM, HEARING ON "CLOUD COMPUTING: BENEFITS AND RISKS OF MOVING FEDERAL IT INTO THE CLOUD"

Chairman Towns, Chairwoman Watson, and Members of the Committee, I am David McClure, Deputy Administrator, Office of Citizen Services and Innovative Technologies at the General Services Administration (GSA). Thank you for the opportunity to appear before you today to discuss GSA's role in supporting development and deployment of cloud computing technology.

Cloud computing enables convenient, rapid, and on-demand computer network access—most often via the Internet--to a shared pool of configurable computing resources (in the form of servers, networks, storage, applications, and services). Quite simply, it is the way computing services are delivered that is revolutionary. Cloud computing allows users to provision computing capabilities rapidly and as needed; that is, to scale out and scale back as required, and to pay only for services used. Users can provision software and infrastructure cloud services on demand with minimal, if any, human intervention. Because cloud computing is based on resource pooling and broad network access there is a natural economy of scale that can result in lower costs to agencies. In addition, cloud computing offers a varied menu of service models from a private cloud operated solely for one organization to a public cloud that is available to a large industry group and the general public and owned by an organization that is selling cloud computing services.

At GSA, we think the adoption of safe and secure cloud computing by the Federal government presents an opportunity to close the IT performance gap. Various forms of cloud computing solutions are already being used in the federal government today to save money and improve services. Let me illustrate with just a few examples:

- The Department of the Army Experience Center in Philadelphia is piloting the use of a customer relationship management (CRM) tool. The Center is a recruiting center that reaches out to young people who are interested in joining our armed forces. The Center wants to move to real time recruiting and to use tools and techniques that are familiar and appeal to its young demographic. They are using a CRM provided by SalesForce to track recruits as they work with the Center. Since the tool integrates directly with e-mail, Twitter and Facebook, recruiters can maintain connections with potential candidates directly after they leave the Center. The Army estimated that to implement a traditional CRM would have cost $500,000. The cloud-based solution has been implemented at the cost of $54,000.
- The Department of Energy is evaluating the cost and efficiencies resulting from leveraging cloud computing solution across the enterprise to support business and scientific services. The Lawrence Berkeley Lab has deployed over 5,000 mailboxes on Google Federal Premiere Apps and they are now evaluating the use of Amazon Elastic Compute Cloud (EC2) to handle excess capacity for computers during peak demand. The Lab estimates that they will save $1.5 million over the next five year in hardware, software and labor costs from the deployments they have made.
- Finally, my own agency – GSA has moved the primary information portal, USA.gov, to a cloud-based host. This enabled the site to deliver a consistent level of access to information as new data bases are added, as peak usage periods are encountered, and as the site evolves to encompass more services. By moving to a cloud, GSA was able to reduce site upgrade time from nine months to one day; monthly downtime improved from two hours to 99.9% availability; and GSA realized savings of $1.7M in hosting services.

In addition to improved services, GSA anticipates that cloud computing will be a major factor in reducing the environmental impact of technology and help achieve important sustainability goals. Effective use of cloud computing can be part of an overall strategy to reduce the need for multiple data centers and the energy they consume. Currently, GSA is supporting OMB in working with agencies to develop plans to consolidate their data centers. Using the right deployment model – private cloud, community cloud, public cloud, or a hybrid model – can help agencies buy improved services at a lower cost within acceptable risk levels, without having to maintain expensive, separate, independent and often needlessly redundant brick and mortar data centers.

In February 2010, the Federal CIO announced the Federal Data Center Consolidation Initiative. In it, he designated two Federal agency CIOs -- Richard Spires (DHS) and Michael Duffy (Treasury) – to lead the effort inside the Federal CIO Council. It also highlighted the following goals:

- Reduce the cost of data center hardware, software and operations
- Increase the overall IT security posture of the government
- Shift IT investments to more efficient computing platforms and technologies
- Promote the use of Green IT by reducing the overall energy and real estate footprint of government data centers

GSA has a significant leadership role in supporting the adoption of cloud computing in the federal government. We have concentrated our efforts on facilitating easy access to cloud based solutions from commercial providers that meet federal requirements, enhancing agencies' capacity to analyze viable cloud computing options that meet their business and technology modernization needs, and addressing obstacles to safe and secure cloud computing. In particular, GSA facilitates innovative cloud computing procurement options, ensures effective cloud security and standards are in place, and identifies potential multi-agency or government-wide uses of cloud computing solutions. GSA is also the information "hub" for cloud use case examples, decisional and implementation best practices, and sharing exposed risks and lessons learned. We have set up the Info.Apps.Gov site as an evolving knowledge repository for all government agencies to use and contribute their expertise.

Let me briefly highlight how GSA is specifically providing execution capabilities to empower sensible cloud computing adoption in the federal government.

Federal Cloud Computing Project Management Office

In March of 2009, the Federal Chief Information Officer (CIO) Council identified cloud computing as a priority for meeting the growing need for effective and efficient use of information technology to meet the performance and mission needs of the government. To assist in fostering cloud computing adoption, the Federal Cloud Computing Program Management Office (PMO) was created in April of 2009 at GSA. The PMO resides in the Office of Citizen Service and Innovation Technologies and is directed by Ms. Katie Lewin who directly reports to the Deputy Administrator for Innovative Technology, Mr. Sonny Bhagowalia. The Director of the PMO also meets weekly with the Federal CIO to report on progress, discuss risks and mitigations, identify promising cloud projects across the government and refine direction. The PMO also reports on its activities and results to the CIO Council Cloud Computing Executive Steering Committee (ESC). The ESC provides oversight for the Federal Cloud Computing Initiative and fosters communications among agencies on cloud computing. ESC Membership includes senior IT executives from across the entire Federal government.

The PMO provides technical and administrative leadership to cloud computing initiatives. PMO staff is drawn from GSA technical experts with some additional contractor support. The primary focus of the PMO is on the following activities:

- Support for the design and operation of the Apps.Gov cloud computing storefront and related cloud procurement initiatives
- Facilitating identification of key cloud security requirements (certification, accreditation, and authorization), particularly on a government-wide basis through a new FedRAMP initiative
- Promotion of current and planned cloud projects across the government
- Data center consolidation analysis, planning, and strategy support
- Development and open dissemination of relevant cloud computing information.

To augment their skill base, the PMO has formed working groups to address specific areas including security, standards and specific cloud-based solutions with government or multi-agency use, such as cloud based e-mail services. The working groups are composed of staff from across the government who bring expertise and interest to address specific obstacles or define paths to adoption. Each group is chaired by a government expert. The National Institute of Standards and Technology (NIST) led both the security and the standards groups. The e-mail group is chaired by an expert from Department of the Interior.

Cloud Procurement

Cloud services are usually offered and purchased as commodities. This is a new way of buying IT services and requires careful research on both government requirements and industry capability to meet demand. To assist agencies in buying new commercially provided cloud services, GSA established a website -- Apps.Gov -- modeled on other GSA product and service acquisition "storefronts." The purpose of Apps.Gov is to provide easy, simple ways to find, research, and procure commercial cloud products and services. Agencies can search for software as a service (SaaS) products categorized under 33 business purpose headings and get product descriptions, price quotes, and links to more information on specific products. Usage patterns to date indicate that agencies use this information to either directly buy SaaS products or, alternatively, as a source of marketplace research that is used to support cloud procurements using other vehicles such as GSA Schedule or GSA Advantage.

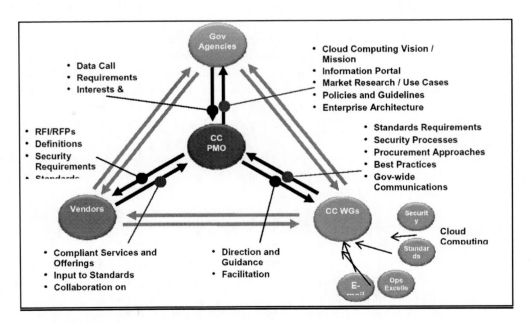

Cloud Computing PMO Operations

Apps.Gov also has information on no-cost social media applications that have agreed to "government-friendly" Terms of Service. When a user hits the SEND REQUEST button, they are linked to their agency's social media coordinator to complete the request for use of the tool in compliance with their agency's social media policy.

To support access to cloud-based Infrastructure as a Service (IaaS), the Cloud PMO works with the Federal Acquisition Service (FAS) at GSA. FAS has primary responsibility for operating on-line acquisition services that are available for government-wide use. In May 2009, the PMO issued a Request for Information (RFI) asking the marketplace how they would address cloud computing business models, pricing, service level agreements, operational support, data management, security and standards. The responses to this RFI were incorporated into a Request for Quote (RFQ) for Infrastructure as a Service capabilities and pricing. The result will be a multiple award blanket purchase agreement that agencies can use to procure cloud based web hosting, virtual machine, and storage services within a moderate security environment as defined by the Federal Information Security Act (FISMA). That RFQ closed yesterday and is currently in an evaluation stage.

Cloud Computing Security

One of the most significant obstacles to the adoption of cloud computing is security. Agencies are concerned about the risks of housing data off-site in a cloud if FISMA security controls and accountabilities are not in place. In other words, agencies need to have valid certification and accreditation (C&A) process and a signed Authority to Operate (ATO) in place for each cloud-based product they use. While vendors are willing to meet security requirements, they would prefer not to go through the expense and effort of obtaining a C&A and ATO for each use of that product in all the federal departments and agencies. The PMO formed a security working group, initially chaired by NIST to address this problem. The group developed a process and corresponding security controls that were agreed to by multiple agencies – which we have termed as the Federal Risk and Authorization Management Program (FedRAMP).

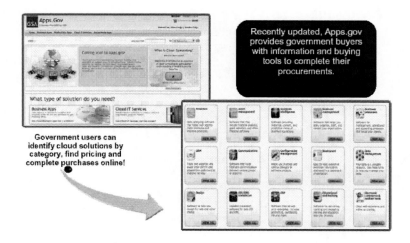

Apps.Gov Storefront Screen Shot

FedRAMP is a government-wide initiative to provide joint authorizations and continuous security monitoring services for all federal agencies with an initial focus on cloud computing. By providing a unified government-wide risk management for enterprise level IT systems, FedRAMP will enable agencies to either use or leverage authorizations with:

- Vetted interagency approach;
- Consistent application of Federal security requirements;
- Improved community-wide risk management posture; and
- Increased effectiveness and management cost savings.

FedRAMP allows agencies to use or leverage authorizations. Under this program, agencies will be able to rely upon review security details, leverage the existing authorization, and secure agency usage of system. This should greatly reduce cost, enable rapid acquisition, and reduce effort.

FedRAMP has three components:

1. Security Requirement Authorities which create government-wide baseline security requirements that are interagency developed and approved. This will initially be the Federal Cloud Computing Initiative and ultimately live with the ISIMC Working Group.
2. The FedRAMP Office which will coordinate authorization packages, manage authorized system list, and provide continuous monitoring oversight. This will be managed by GSA.
3. A Joint Authorization Board which will perform authorizations and on-going risk determinations to be leveraged government-wide. The board will consist of representatives from GSA, DoD, DHS and the sponsoring agency of the authorized system.

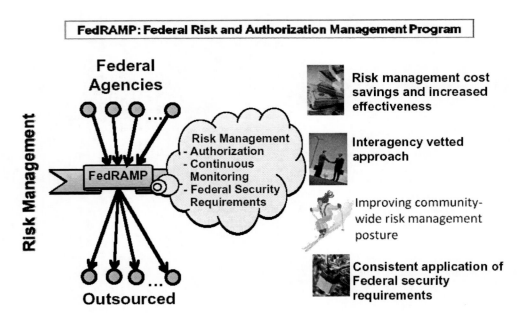

FedRAMP: Federal Risk and Authorization Management Program

GSA is working with OMB, security groups including the Federal CIO Council's Information Security and Identity Management Committee, and the marketplace to vet this program and ensure that it will meet the security requirements of the government while streamlining the process for industry.

Cloud Computing and Open Government

In the past decade, vast increases in the ubiquity and availability of storage space, bandwidth, and computing power have enabled a new class of Internet-based applications—broadly called "web 2.0"—that focus less on one-way delivery of information and more on enabling large, diverse communities to come together, share their wisdom, and take action. Increasingly, citizens—government's customers—simply expect to find the information they want and need through the use of the on-line social networks and platforms they are rapidly adopting and use as part of their everyday lives.

As our Administrator, Martha Johnson, noted upon being sworn in February 2010:

> *Hoarding and hiding information prevents citizens and civil servants from understanding and participating in the public process effectively...We at GSA can help change that. We can make the information more available, as a first step. And we can do much more. We can, and will, take advantage of emerging technologies for sorting, sharing, networking, collective intelligence, and using that information. Our goal is nothing short of a nation that relies not on select data and statistical boxing matches, but on accurate evidence that supports knowledge and wisdom.* [1]

Most of these new web 2.0 technologies and tools are available as cloud-based SaaS solutions and/or are hosted in cloud computing infrastructure environments. This allows the government to offer these tools and services in a very cost-efficient manner. Let me highlight a few examples:

- The **Common Open Government Dialogue Platform** is a project undertaken by GSA in response to the Open Government Directive's mandate that agencies "incorporate a mechanism for the public to provide input on the agency's Open Government Plan." Over the course of six weeks, GSA provided interested agencies with a no-cost, law- and policy-compliant, public-facing online engagement tool, as well as training and technical support to enable them to immediately begin collecting public and employee input on their forthcoming open government plans. Since then, GSA has worked to transfer ownership of the open government public engagement tool, powered by a cloud SaaS platform called IdeaScale, to interested agencies, in a manner that provided both policy and legal compliance, as well as support for sustained engagement. The tool was launched in February 2010 across 22 federal agencies and the White House Office of Science and Technology Policy; overall resource investment was less than $10,000 – far less than the hundreds of thousands or millions of dollars that would have resulted from agencies independently pursuing and procuring IT solutions. The agencies' dialogue sites garnered over 2,100 ideas, over 3,400 comments, and over 21,000 votes during a six-week "live" period and the tool continues to be used by several agencies for a variety of other open government purposes.

- **USASpending.gov** is a source for information collected from agencies in accordance with the Federal Funding Accountability and Transparency Act of 2006. This public facing web site is a cornerstone of the Administration's efforts to make government open and transparent. Using USAspending.gov, the public can determine how their tax dollars are spent and gain insight into the Federal spending processes across agencies. It also houses the Federal IT Dashboard, which displays details on the nearly 800 major federal IT investments based on data reported to the Office of Management and Budget. This data is also now housed in a cloud infrastructure environment maintained by NASA.

- **Data.gov** is the central portal for citizens to find, download, and assess government data. It now hosts over 270,000 data sets covering topics ranging from healthcare to commerce to education. Data.gov was one of the first public facing government websites to deploy cloud computing successfully in government. It empowers citizens by allowing them to create personalized mash-ups of information from diverse sources (e.g., local school academic scores arrayed by education spending levels), solve problems (e.g., FAA flight time arrival information), and build awareness of government's role in activities affecting daily activities (e.g., food safety, weather, and the like).

- **Challenge.gov** is a government-wide challenge platform that will be hosted in a cloud computing infrastructure service to facilitate government innovation through challenges and prizes. This tool provides forums for seekers (the federal agency challenger looking for solutions) and solvers (those with potential solutions) to suggest, collaborate on, and deliver solutions. It will also allow the public to easily find and interact with federal government challenges. The platform responds to requirements defined in a March 8, 2010, OMB Memo, "Guidance on the Use of Challenges and Prizes to Promote Open Government" which included a requirement to provide a web-based challenge platform within 120 days. GSA is also exploring acquisition options to make it easier for agencies to procure products and services related to challenges.

- **Citizen Engagement Platform** will provide a variety of blog, challenge and other engagement tools to make it easy for government to engage with citizens, and easy for citizens to engage with government. The platform addresses agencies' need for easy-to-use, easy-to-deploy, secure and policy-compliant tools. This "build once, use many" approach adds lightweight, no-cost options for agencies to create a more open, transparent and collaborative government with tools either hosted or directly managed by GSA.

Conclusion

Mr. Chairman, cloud computing has a promising future in transforming the federal government because of its ability to fundamentally reshape government IT operations used for critical government business process and citizen service delivery support. It can help shift our focus to value added use of the information we collect and provide cost effective services in a digitally and networked enabled world. Additionally, it has the potential to free up resources that have gone to support data centers and capabilities that are better leveraged across the community – at bureau, agency or cross-agency level. At GSA, we are supporting this transformation by leveraging cloud solutions and acquisitions on a government-wide basis wherever possible to maximize economies of scale.

Thank you for the opportunity to appear today and I look forward to answering questions from you and members of the Subcommittee.

End Notes

[1]http://www.gsa.gov/Portal/gsa/ep/contentView.do?pageTypeId=10430&channelId=-24827&P=&contentId=29129&contentType=GSA_BASIC

In: Cloud Computing and Government: Background, Benefits...   ISBN: 978-1-61761-784-3
Editor: George I. Nikolov   © 2011 Nova Science Publishers, Inc.

Chapter 7

Testimony of Cita M. Furlani, Director, Information Technology Laboratory, National Institute of Standards and Technology, U.S. Dept. of Commerce, before the House Committee on Oversight and Government Reform, Hearing on "Cloud Computing: Benefits and Risks of Moving Federal IT into the Cloud"

Chairman Towns, Chairwoman Watson, and Members of the Committee, I am CitaFurlani, the Director of the Information Technology Laboratory (ITL) at the Department of Commerce's National Institute of Standards and Technology (NIST). Thank you for the opportunity to appear before you today to discuss our role in the development and deployment of cloud computing technology.

NIST's mission is to promote U.S. innovation and industrial competitiveness by advancing measurement science, standards, and technology in ways that enhance economic security and improve our quality of life.

As one of the major research components within NIST, the ITL accelerates the development and deployment of information and communication systems that are reliable, usable, interoperable, and secure; advances measurement science through innovations in mathematics, statistics, and computer science; and conducts research to develop the measurements and standards infrastructure for emerging information technologies and applications.

NIST works with federal agencies, industry, and academia to research, develop and deploy information security standards and technology to protect information systems against threats to their confidentiality, integrity and availability. NIST researches technologies such as identity management and verification, metrics for complex systems, automation of discovery and maintenance of system security configurations and status, and techniques for specification and automation of access authorization in support of many different kinds of access policies.

In addition to IT-related technology research, ITL is responsible for the development of, publishing, and providing explanatory support for Federal standards, guidelines, and best practices related to cybersecurity.

NIST's role in cloud computing is to promote the effective and secure use of the technology within government by providing technical guidance and promoting standards. The three cybersecurity objectives, ensuring the confidentiality, integrity, and availability of information technology systems, are particularly relevant as these are the high priority concerns and perceived risks related to cloud computing.

Although the power of modern cloud computing systems is new, the ideas behind cloud computing reach back through decades. In the early 1960s, researchers proposed the idea of computing as a utility, similar to other services such as gas or electricity. Around the same time, techniques to make a single computer appear to be many separate "virtual" computers were developed and implemented on mainframe computers. Some of the building blocks for cloud computing were in place, but performance and costs were barriers, and networking was inadequate. Years of hardware advances were needed to close the gap. By the 1990s, the Internet had made grid computing possible: many computers working together on a single problem over a network. By the 2000s, the term cloud computing was being used to describe computing services delivered over a network, and, in 2010, a substantial and growing number of vendors are developing cloud computing offerings for government, industry, and the general public.

Before discussing ongoing NIST efforts which are directed toward promoting secure and effective use of cloud computing, I refer to the widely-cited NIST definition of cloud computing[1]. Computer scientists at NIST developed this definition in collaboration with industry, academia and government and we expect it to evolve over time as the cloud industry and cloud technology matures:

Cloud computing is a model for enabling convenient, on-demand network access to a shared pool of configurable computing resources (e.g., networks, servers, storage, applications, and services) that can be rapidly provisioned and released with minimal management effort or service provider interaction.

This cloud model promotes availability and is composed of five essential characteristics, three service models, and four deployment models.

Essential Characteristics:

- *On-demand self-service.* A consumer can unilaterally provision computing capabilities, such as server time and network storage, as needed automatically without requiring human interaction with each service's provider.
- *Broad network access.* Capabilities are available over the network and accessed through standard mechanisms that promote use by heterogeneous thin or thick client platforms (e.g., mobile phones, laptops, and PDAs).
- *Resource pooling.* The provider's computing resources are pooled to serve multiple consumers using a multi-tenant model, with different physical and virtual resources dynamically assigned and reassigned according to consumer demand. There is a sense of location independence in that the customer generally has no control or knowledge over the exact location of the provided resources but may be able to specify location at a higher level of abstraction (e.g., country, state, or datacenter).

Examples of resources include storage, processing, memory, network bandwidth, and virtual machines.

- *Rapid elasticity.* Capabilities can be rapidly and elastically provisioned, in some cases automatically, to quickly scale out and rapidly released to quickly scale in. To the consumer, the capabilities available for provisioning often appear to be unlimited and can be purchased in any quantity at any time.
- *Measured Service.* Cloud systems automatically control and optimize resource use by leveraging a metering capability at some level of abstraction appropriate to the type of service (e.g., storage, processing, bandwidth, and active user accounts). Resource usage can be monitored, controlled, and reported providing transparency for both the provider and consumer of the utilized service.

Service Models:

- *Cloud Software as a Service (SaaS).* The capability provided to the consumer is to use the provider's applications running on a cloud infrastructure. The applications are accessible from various client devices through a thin client interface such as a web browser (e.g., web-based email). The consumer does not manage or control the underlying cloud infrastructure including network, servers, operating systems, storage, or even individual application capabilities, with the possible exception of limited user-specific application configuration settings.
- *Cloud Platform as a Service (PaaS).* The capability provided to the consumer is to deploy onto the cloud infrastructure consumer-created or acquired applications created using programming languages and tools supported by the provider. The consumer does not manage or control the underlying cloud infrastructure including network, servers, operating systems, or storage, but has control over the deployed applications and possibly application hosting environment configurations.
- *Cloud Infrastructure as a Service (IaaS).* The capability provided to the consumer is to provision processing, storage, networks, and other fundamental computing resources where the consumer is able to deploy and run arbitrary software, which can include operating systems and applications. The consumer does not manage or control the underlying cloud infrastructure but has control over operating systems, storage, deployed applications, and possibly limited control of select networking components (e.g., host firewalls).

Deployment Models:

- *Private cloud.* The cloud infrastructure is operated solely for an organization. It may be managed by the organization or a third party and may exist on premise or off premise.
- *Community cloud.* The cloud infrastructure is shared by several organizations and supports a specific community that has shared concerns (e.g., mission, security requirements, policy, and compliance considerations). It may be managed by the organizations or a third party and may exist on premises or off premises.

- *Public cloud.* The cloud infrastructure is made available to the general public or a large industry group and is owned by an organization selling cloud services.
- *Hybrid cloud.* The cloud infrastructure is a composition of two or more clouds (private, community, or public) that remain unique entities but are bound together by standardized or proprietary technology that enables data and application portability (e.g., cloud bursting for load-balancing between clouds).

  Note: Cloud software takes full advantage of the cloud paradigm by being service oriented with a focus on statelessness, low coupling, modularity, and semantic interoperability.

This NIST cloud computing definition, most recently revised in October 2009, has been broadly recognized and helps to clarify a complex emerging information technology paradigm. However, there is still much work to be done.

NIST has initiated focused activities to develop federal cloud computing security guidance as well as to facilitate the development of cloud computing standards. Both are essential and must be considered in parallel in order to effectively support the secure implementation of cloud computing technology. NIST efforts respond not only to high priority security requirements, but to interoperability and portability requirements, which are interrelated with and essential to effectively address cloud computing security.

Following are specific NIST efforts which promote the effective and secure use of cloud computing technology within government by providing technical guidance and promoting the development of standards.

NIST recently held a Cloud Computing Forum and Workshop. The goal was to engage with stakeholders on ways to accelerate the federal government's secure adoption of cloud computing. Over 500 stakeholders registered for the event – which included representatives from industry, federal government, state governments, academia, and standards development organizations.

NIST is developing a cloud computing Special Publication which will use the definition of cloud computing as a frame of reference to organize and present analysis, recommendations and guidance. The document will provide insight into the technical benefits, risks, and considerations related to the secure and effective uses of cloud computing and guidance in the context of cloud computing: interoperability, portability, and security. The publication will also outline typical terms of use for cloud systems and will identify future research areas in cloud computing as well as recommendations. NIST will develop additional cloud computing Special Publications as research and analysis are completed.

As requested by OMB, NIST serves as the government lead, working with other government agencies, industry, academia, and standards development organizations to leverage appropriate existing standards and to accelerate the development of cloud computing standards where gaps exist. The expectation is that standards will shorten the adoption cycle, support cost savings and the ability to more quickly create and deploy enterprise applications.

Under the provisions of the National Technology Transfer and Advancement Act (PL 104-113) and OMB Circular A-119, NIST is tasked with the role of encouraging and coordinating federal agency use of voluntary consensus standards and participation in the development of relevant standards, as well as promoting coordination between the public and private sectors in the development of standards and in conformity assessment activities. NIST works with other agencies to coordinate standards issues and priorities with the private sector through consensus standards organizations such as the American National Standards Institute (ANSI), the International Organization for Standardization (ISO), the Institute of Electrical and Electronic Engineers (IEEE), the Internet Engineering Task Force (IETF), and the International Telecommunication Union (ITU). NIST leads national and international consensus standards activities in cryptography, biometrics, electronic credentialing, secure network protocols, software and systems reliability, and security conformance testing – all essential for secure cloud computing implementation.

NIST has initiated the Standards Acceleration to Jumpstart Cloud Computing (SAJACC) project.The SAJAAC goal is to facilitate the development of cloud computing standards. The analysis and results completed under SAJACC will be used to inform the cloud computing Special Publications described above. SAJACC refers to a strategy, a process, and a portal.

SAJACC was initiated to address a widely acknowledged need in the development and implementation of new complex technologies. Historically, a gap has existed between the time when standards are needed and the time when they become formalized. Complex standards such as the Portable Operating System Interface [for Unix] and current Internet standards have taken years to develop. This has occurred because the development of standards is dependent on the inherently time consuming process of broad participation and consensus building, is driven by technical innovation, and requires due diligence in order to produce a standard of quality and completeness such that it will be effective and broadly adopted.

The SAJAAC strategy is two-fold: 1) to accelerate the development of high-quality standards and 2) to reduce technical uncertainty during the interim adoption period before many cloud computing standards are formalized.

The heart of the SAJACC concept is the process of identifying and validating interim candidate interface specifications by testing against requirements which demonstrate portability, interoperability, and security for users of cloud systems. SAJACC is applying the use case development method to define, refine, and interpret requirements in the form of behavioral scenarios which describe the interaction between people and computer systems. The project is currently formulating an initial set of twenty five use cases, and vetting these with cloud computing stakeholders in academia, government, and industry. After the use cases have been refined, they will be made available through a public website. In order to verify and demonstrate the test plan and execution process, NIST will conduct an initial set of validation tests against an initial set of legacy interfaces, and publish the results as an example of how future collaborative efforts could be accomplished.

Information exchange and visibility will be accomplished through a SAJACC website. This portal is planned as a public Internet-accessible repository of cloud computing use cases, documented cloud system interfaces (i.e., specifications which have not yet evolved to become formal standards), pointers to cloud system reference implementations (i.e., cloud computing systems where these specifications were incorporated as part of the implementation), and test results which show the extent to which different interfaces can support individual use cases (i.e., satisfy security, portability, and interoperability requirements.)

SAJACC by definition leverages, coordinates, and is heavily dependent on contributions from external stakeholders with an interest in cloud computing standards. The process of identifying new interfaces (with corresponding reference implementations) and new use cases will be ongoing.

NIST has developed standards to support federal agencies' information security requirements for many years, beginning in the early 1970s with enactment of the Brooks Act. Through the Federal Information Security Management Act (FISMA), Congress again reaffirmed NIST's leadership role in developing standards for cyber security. FISMA provides for the development and promulgation of Federal Information Processing Standards (FIPS) that are "compulsory and binding" for Federal computer systems. The responsibility for the development of FIPS rests with NIST, and the authority to promulgate mandatory FIPS is given to the Secretary of Commerce. Section 303 of FISMA states that NIST shall:

- have the mission of developing standards, guidelines, and associated methods and techniques for information systems;
- develop standards and guidelines, including minimum requirements, for information systems used or operated by an agency or by a contractor of an agency or other organization on behalf of an agency, other than national security systems; and
- develop standards and guidelines, including minimum requirements, for providing adequate information security for all agency operations and assets, but such standards and guidelines shall not apply to national security systems.

These activities include, for systems other than national security systems, standards and guidelines that must include, at a minimum (1) standards to be used by all agencies to categorize all their information and information systems based on the objectives of providing appropriate levels of information security, according to a range of risk levels; (2) guidelines recommending the types of information and information systems to be included in each category; and (3) minimum information security requirements for information and information systems in each category.

NIST addresses cyber security challenges, which are directly applicable to cloud computing throughout the information and communications infrastructure, through its cross-community engagements. NIST employs collaborative partnerships with our customers and stakeholders in industry, government, academia, and consortia to take advantages of technical and operational insights and to leverage the resources of a global community. NIST is responsible for establishing and updating, on a recurring basis, the federal government's risk management framework, cybersecurity controls, and assessment procedures to determine control effectiveness. NIST engages government and industry to harmonize information security requirements to align with industry business models and best practices.

An example is the release of Special Publication 800-53, Revision 3, *Recommended Security Controls for Federal Information Systems and Organizations* in August 2009 which was developed by the Joint Task Force Transformation Initiative consisting of members from NIST, the Department of Defense, Office of the Director of National Intelligence, and the Committee on National Security Systems. This unified set of security controls provides a standardized method for expressing security at all levels, from system development and acquisition to operational implementation. This allows for an environment of information sharing and interconnections among these communities and significantly reduces costs, time, and resources needed to secure information systems.

In close collaboration with the Department of Defense, the Committee on National Security Systems and the Intelligence Community, NIST revised its Certification and Accreditation (C&A) guideline, Special Publication 800-37, Revision 1, *Guide for Applying the Risk Management Framework to Federal Information Systems: A Security Life Cycle Approach* to fundamentally change the focus of the information system authorization process from a static (a point in time) approach to a continuous monitoring approach. This continuous monitoring approach, implemented with automated tools whenever possible, will provide authorizing officials and senior leaders within federal agencies with critical and timely information on the ongoing security state of their information systems, thus allowing them to make more informed, risk-based decisions when authorizing federal information systems for operation.

The current version of Special Publication 800-37 was also updated to allow certification and accreditation efforts to be leveraged among federal agencies. This is an important building block needed to support government adoption of cloud computing.

In 2009 and 2010,NIST, in a technical advisory role, supported the interagency Federal Cloud Computing Advisory Council (CCAC) Security Working Group in the development of a concept for a federal approach to coordinate and apply consistent security authorization requirements for cloud computing systems.

The overall approach is being defined under the governance and implementation auspices of the Federal CIO Council. The NIST role is to provide guidance for a technical approach and process which is consistent with NIST security guidance in the context of FISMA. More specifically, NIST is supporting the definition of a technical process in the context of and to be consistent with Special Publication 800-37, Revision 1, *Guide for Applying the Risk Management Framework to Federal Information Systems: A Security Life Cycle Approach*, referenced earlier.

Cybersecurity is a vital, central mission of our laboratory and is a key concern and risk factor related to cloud computing adoption. In a public cloud computing deployment model the customer generally does not have control or knowledge over the exact location of the provided resources such as storage, processing, memory, network bandwidth, and virtual machines.

NIST recognizes that effective cybersecurity guidance is holistic and must be considered in the context of broad and comprehensive information security guidance for federal agencies as well as the interoperability, portability and security technical standards development efforts described previously. The NIST cloud computing security guidance recognizes the need to consider the security requirements of the foundation technologies which are applied to implement cloud computing and to leverage the existing computer security capabilities and knowledge base.

NIST will continue to conduct the research necessary to enable and to provide cloud computing and cybersecurity specifications, standards, assurance processes, guidance and technical expertise needed for effective and secure U.S. government and critical infrastructure information systems.

NIST is actively engaged with private industry, academia, non-national security federal departments and agencies, the intelligence community, and other elements of the law enforcement and national security communities in coordination and prioritization of cyber security research, standards development, standards conformance demonstration, and cyber security education and outreach activities.

NIST has initiated a strategic Virtualization Laboratory effort to research and evaluate the security of virtualization techniques and the cloud computing systems that employ them. The lab will serve as a resource for the development of ideas to mitigate security vulnerabilities in virtualized and cloud systems, and to gain hands-on experience that will inform NIST cloud and virtualizations guidelines. The lab plans include two research tasks. The first is to conduct research on the integration of advanced access control mechanisms into virtualized systems. The second task is to conduct research of metrics to evaluate hypervisor security vulnerability and quality. This task will conduct a study of hypervisor architectural principles and will measure the complexity of hypervisor implementations.

NIST has also initiated the Modeling and Analyzing Complex Behaviors in Cloud Computing project. This project seeks to understand and predict behavior in large distributed information systems by using mathematical and statistical techniques applied by scientists to study physical systems. NIST is evaluating various modeling and analysis methods. NIST is conducting its evaluation in the context of communication networks, computational grids and computational clouds. NIST has conducted several studies related to networks and grids. In cloud computing, NIST is initiating a study of the applicability of our modeling and analysis techniques to computational clouds. As a challenge problem, NIST intends to use the model to study various resource allocation algorithms that might be employed to assign virtual machines to clusters and nodes within a cloud.

Thank you for the opportunity to testify today on NIST's role in the development and deployment of cloud computing technology. I would be happy to answer any questions you may have.

End Notes

[1]*The NIST Definition of Cloud Computing*, Version 15, Peter Mell and Tim Grance, October 7, 2009.

In: Cloud Computing and Government: Background, Benefits...   ISBN: 978-1-61761-784-3
Editor: George I. Nikolov   © 2011 Nova Science Publishers, Inc.

Chapter 8

INFORMATION SECURITY: GOVERNMENTWIDE GUIDANCE NEEDED TO ASSIST AGENCIES IN IMPLEMENTING CLOUD COMPUTING

Gregory C. Wilshusen

WHY GAO DID THIS STUDY

Cloud computing, an emerging form of computing where users have access to scalable, on-demand capabilities that are provided through Internet-based technologies, reportedly has the potential to provide information technology services more quickly and at a lower cost, but also to introduce information security risks. Accordingly, GAO was asked to testify on the benefits and risks of moving federal information technology into the cloud. This testimony summarizes the contents of a separate report that is being released today which describes (1) the models of cloud computing, (2) the information security implications of using cloud computing services in the federal government, and (3) federal guidance and efforts to address information security when using cloud computing. In preparing that report, GAO collected and analyzed information from industry groups, private-sector organizations, and 24 major federal agencies.

WHAT GAO RECOMMENDS

In the report being released today, GAO recommended that the Office of Management and Budget, the General Services Administration, and the Department of Commerce take steps to address cloud computing security, including completion of a strategy, consideration of security in a planned procurement of cloud computing services, and issuance of guidance related to cloud computing security. These agencies generally agreed with GAO's recommendations.

WHAT GAO FOUND

Cloud computing has several service and deployment models. The service models include the provision of infrastructure, computing platforms, and software as a service. The deployment models relate to how the cloud service is provided. They include a private cloud, operated solely for an organization; a community cloud, shared by several organizations; a public cloud, available to any paying customer; and a hybrid cloud, a composite of deployment models.

Cloud computing can both increase and decrease the security of information systems in federal agencies. Potential information security benefits include those related to the use of virtualization and automation, broad network access, potential economies of scale, and use of self-service technologies. In addition to benefits, the use of cloud computing can create numerous information security risks for federal agencies. Specifically, 22 of 24 major federal agencies reported that they are either concerned or very concerned about the potential information security risks associated with cloud computing. Risks include dependence on the security practices and assurances of a vendor, and the sharing of computing resources. However, these risks may vary based on the cloud deployment model. Private clouds may have a lower threat exposure than public clouds, but evaluating this risk requires an examination of the specific security controls in place for the cloud's implementation.

Federal agencies have begun efforts to address information security issues for cloud computing, but key guidance is lacking and efforts remain incomplete. Although individual agencies have identified security measures needed when using cloud computing, they have not always developed corresponding guidance. Agencies have also identified challenges in assessing vendor compliance with government information security requirements and clarifying the division of information security responsibilities between the customer and vendor. Furthermore, while several governmentwide cloud computing security initiatives are under way by organizations such as the Office of Management and Budget and the General Services Administration, significant work needs to be completed. For example, the Office of Management and Budget has not yet finished a cloud computing strategy, or defined how information security issues will be addressed in this strategy. The General Services Administration has begun a procurement for expanding cloud computing services, but has not yet developed specific plans for establishing a shared information security assessment and authorization process. In addition, while the National Institute of Standards and Technology has begun efforts to address cloud computing information security, it has not yet issued cloud-specific security guidance. Until specific guidance and processes are developed to guide the agencies in planning for and establishing information security for cloud computing, they may not have effective information security controls in place for cloud computing programs.

Chairman Towns, Chairwoman Watson, and Members of the Committee and Subcommittee:

Thank you for the opportunity to participate in today's hearing on federal guidance and efforts to address information security when using cloud computing. My statement today is based on our report titled *Information Security: Federal Guidance Needed to Address Control Issues with Implementing Cloud Computing* (GAO-10-513), which provides a fuller discussion of our results and is being released at this hearing.[1]

Cloud computing is an emerging form of computing that relies on Internet-based services and resources to provide computing services to customers. Examples of cloud computing include Web-based e-mail applications and common business applications that are accessed online through a browser, instead of through a local computer. The current administration has highlighted cloud computing as having the potential to provide information technology (IT) services more quickly and at a lower cost than traditional methods.

We have previously reported that cyber threats to federal information systems and cyber-based critical infrastructures are evolving and growing.[2] Without proper safeguards, computer systems are vulnerable to individuals and groups with malicious intentions who can intrude and use their access to obtain and manipulate sensitive information, commit fraud, disrupt operations, or launch attacks against other computer systems and networks. Further, the increasing interconnectivity among information systems, the Internet, and other infrastructure presents increasing opportunities for attacks. For example, in 2009, several media reports described incidents that affected cloud service providers such as Amazon and Google.

Given the potential risks, you requested that we examine the security implications of cloud computing. In response to your request, our report and my statement provide (1) a description of the models of cloud computing, (2) a description of the information security implications of using cloud computing services in the federal government, and (3) an assessment of federal guidance and efforts to address information security when using cloud computing. In conducting the work for our report, we collected and analyzed information from industry groups, private-sector organizations, the National Institute of Standards and Technology (NIST), and 24 major federal agencies.[3] Our work for the report was performed in accordance with generally accepted government auditing standards.

Cloud Computing Is a Form of Shared Computing with Several Service and Deployment Models

Cloud computing is a new form of delivering IT services that takes advantage of several broad evolutionary trends in information technology, including the use of virtualization.[4] According to NIST, cloud computing is a means "for enabling convenient, on-demand network access to a shared pool of configurable computing resources that can be rapidly provisioned and released with minimal management effort or service provider interaction." NIST also states that an application should possess five essential characteristics to be considered cloud computing; on-demand self service, broad network access, resource pooling, rapid elasticity, and measured service.

Cloud computing offers three service models: infrastructure as a service, where a vendor offers various infrastructure components; platform as a service, where a vendor offers a ready-to-use platform on which customers can build applications; and software as a service, which provides a self-contained operating environment used to deliver a complete application such as Web-based e-mail.

In addition, four deployment models for providing cloud services have been developed: private, community, public, and hybrid cloud. In a private cloud, the service is set up specifically for one organization, although there may be multiple customers within that organization and the cloud may exist on or off the premises. In a community cloud, the service is set up for related organizations that have similar requirements. A public cloud is available to any paying customer and is owned and operated by the service provider. A hybrid cloud is a composite of the deployment models.

Cloud Computing Has Both Positive and Negative Information Security Implications

The adoption of cloud computing has the potential to provide benefitsrelated to information security. The use of virtualization and automation in cloud computing can expedite the implementation of secure configurations for virtual machine images. Other advantages relate to cloud computing's broad network access and use of Internet-based technologies. For example, several agencies stated that cloud computing provides a reduced need to carry data in removable media because of the ability to access the data through the Internet, regardless of location. Additional advantages relate to the potential economies of scale and distributed nature of cloud computing. In response to our survey, 22 of the 24 major agencies identified low-cost disaster recovery and data storage as a potential benefit. The self-service aspect of cloud computing may also provide benefits. For example, 20 of 24 major agencies identified the ability to apply security controls on demand as a potential benefit.

In addition to benefits, the use of cloud computing can create numerous information security risks for federal agencies. In response to our survey, 22 of 24 major agencies reported that they are either concerned or very concerned about the potential information security risks associated with cloud computing. Several of these risks relate to being dependent on a vendor's security assurances and practices. Specifically, several agencies stated concerns about:

- the possibility that ineffective or non-compliant service provider security controls could lead to vulnerabilities affecting the confidentiality, integrity, and availability of agency information;
- the potential loss of governance and physical control over agency data and information when an agency cedes control to the provider for the performance of certain security controls and practices;
- the insecure or ineffective deletion of agency data by cloud providers once services have been provided and are complete; and
- potentially inadequate background security investigations for service provider employees that could lead to an increased risk of wrongful activities by malicious insiders.

Multitenancy, or the sharing of computing resources by different organizations, can also increase risk. Twenty-three of 24 major agencies identified multitenancy as a potential information security risk because one customer could intentionally or unintentionally gain access to another customer's data, causing a release of sensitive information. Another concern is the increased volume of data transmitted across agency and public networks. This could lead to an increased risk of the data being intercepted in transit and then disclosed.

Although there are numerous potential information security risks related to cloud computing, these risks may vary based on the particular deployment model. For example, NIST states that private clouds may have a lower threat exposure than community clouds, which may have a lower threat exposure than public clouds. Several industry representatives stated that an agency would need to examine the specific security controls of the vendor the agency was evaluating when considering the use of cloud computing.

Federal Agencies Have Begun Efforts to Address Information Security Issues for Cloud Computing, but Specific Guidance Is Lacking and Efforts Remain Incomplete

Federal agencies have begun to address information security for cloud computing; however, they have not developed the corresponding guidance. About half of the 24 major agencies we asked reported using some form of public or private cloud computing for obtaining infrastructure, platform, or software services. These agencies identified measures they are taking or plan to take when using cloud computing. These actions, however, have not always been accompanied by development of related policies or procedures to secure their information and systems.

Most agencies have concerns about ensuring vendor compliance and implementation of government information security requirements. In addition, agencies expressed concerns about limitations on their ability to conduct independent audits and assessments of security controls of cloud computing service providers. Several industry representatives agreed that compliance and oversight issues are a concern and raised the idea of having a single government entity or other independent entity conduct security oversight and audits of cloud computing service providers on behalf of federal agencies. Agencies also stated that having a cloud service provider that had been precertified as being in compliance with government information security requirements through some type of governmentwide approval process would make it easier for them to consider adopting cloud computing. Other agency concerns related to the division of information security responsibilities between customer and vendor. Until these concerns are addressed, the adoption of cloud computing may be limited.

SeveralGovernmentwide Cloud Computing Information Security Initiatives Have Been Started, but Key Guidance and Efforts Have Not Been Completed

While several governmentwide cloud computing security activities are under way by organizations such as the Office of Management and Budget (OMB) and the General Services Administration (GSA), significant work remains to be completed. For example, OMB stated that it began a federal cloud computing initiative in February 2009; however, it does not yet have an overarching strategy or an implementation plan. According to OMB officials, the initiative includes an online cloud computing storefront managed by GSA and will likely contain several pilot cloud computing projects, each with a lead agency. However, as of March 2010, a date had not been set for the release of the strategy or for any of the pilots. In addition, OMB has not yet defined how information security issues, such as a shared assessment and authorization process, will be addressed in this strategy.

Federal agencies have stated that additional guidance on cloud computing security would be helpful. Addressing information security issues as part of this strategy would provide additional direction to agencies looking to use cloud computing services. Accordingly, we recommended that OMB establish milestones for completing a strategy for implementing the cloud computing initiative and ensure the strategy addresses the information security challenges associated with cloud computing, such as needed agency-specific guidance, controls assessment of cloud computing service providers, division of information security responsibilities between customer and provider, a shared assessment and authorization process, and the possibility for precertification of cloud computing service providers. OMB agreed with our recommendation and noted that it planned to issue a strategy over the next 6 months that covers activities for the next 5 to 10 years based on near term lessons learned. OMB also identified several federal activities planned in the short term to address security issues in cloud computing.

GSA Has Established Program Office and Cloud Computing Storefront, but Has Not Yet Developed Plans for a Shared Assessment and Authorization Process

GSA has established the Cloud Computing Program Management Office that manages several cloud computing activities within GSA and provides administrative support for cloud computing efforts by the Federal Chief Information Officers (CIO) Council. Specifically, the program office manages a storefront, www.apps.gov, established by GSA to provide a central location where federal customers can purchase software as a service cloud computing applications. GSA has also initiated a procurement to expand the storefront by adding infrastructure as a service cloud computing offerings such as storage, virtual machines, and Web hosting.

Establishing both an assessment and authorization process for customers of these services and a clear division of security responsibilities will help ensure that these services, when purchased and effectively implemented, protect sensitive federal information. GSA officials stated that they need to work with vendors after a new procurement has been completed to develop a shared assessment and authorization process, but have not yet developed specific plans to do so. Accordingly, we recommended that GSA ensure that full consideration is given to the information security challenges of cloud computing, including a need for a shared assessment and authorization process as part of their procurement for infrastructure as a service cloud computing technologies. GSA agreed and identified plans for ensuring issues such as a shared assessment and authorization process would be addressed.

Federal CIO Council Has Established Cloud ComputingExecutiveSteeringCommittee but Has Not Finalized Key Process or Guidance

The Federal CIO Council established the Cloud Computing Executive Steering Committee to promote the use of cloud computing in the federal government. Under this committee, the security subgroup has developed the Federal Risk and Authorization Management Program, which is a governmentwide program to provide joint authorizations and continuous security monitoring services for all federal agencies, with an initial focus on cloud computing.

The subgroup is currently working with its members to define interagency security requirements for cloud systems and services and related information security controls. However, a deadline for completing development and implementation of a shared assessment and authorization process has not been established. We recommended that OMB direct the CIO Council Cloud Computing Executive Steering Committee to develop a plan, including milestones, for completing a governmentwide security assessment and authorization process for cloud services. OMB agreed and identified current activities of the CIO Council which are intended to address the recommendation.

NIST Is Coordinating Activities with CIO Council but Has Not Established Cloud-Specific Guidance

NIST is responsible for establishing information security guidance for federal agencies to support FISMA; however, it has not yet established guidance specific to cloud computing or to information security issues specific to cloud computing, such as portability and interoperability, and virtualization.

The NIST official leading the institute's cloud computing activities stated that existing NIST guidance in SP 800-53 and other publications applies to cloud computing and can be tailored to the information security issues specific to cloud computing. However, both federal and private sector officials have made clear that existing guidance is not sufficient. Accordingly, we recommended that NIST issue cloud computing guidance to federal agencies to more fully address key cloud computing domain areas that are lacking in SP 800-53 areas such as virtualization, and portability and interoperability, and include a process for defining roles and responsibilities of cloud computing service providers and customers. NIST officials agreed and stated that the institute is planning to issue guidance on cloud computing and virtualization this year.

In summary, the adoption of cloud computing has the potential to provide benefits to federal agencies; however, it can also create numerous information security risks. Federal agencies have taken steps to address cloud computing security, but many have not developed corresponding guidance. OMB has initiated a federal cloud computing initiative, but has not yet developed a strategy that addresses the information security issues related to cloud computing, and guidance from NIST to ensure information security is insufficient. While the Federal CIO Council is developing a shared assessment and authorization process, which could help foster adoption of cloud computing, this process remains incomplete, and GSA has yet to develop plans for a shared assessment and authorization process for its procurement of cloud computing infrastructure as a service offerings. Until federal guidance and processes that specifically address information security for cloud computing are developed, agencies may be hesitant to implement cloud computing, and those programs that have been implemented may not have effective information security controls in place.

Chairman Towns, Chairwoman Watson, and Members of the Committee and Subcommittee, this concludes my prepared statement. I would be pleased to respond to any questions.

For questions about this statement, please contact Gregory C. Wilshusen at (202) 512-6244 or wilshuseng@gao.gov. Individuals making key contributions to this testimony included Season Dietrich, Vijay D'Souza, Nancy Glover, and Shaunyce Wallace.

End Notes

[1] GAO, *Information Security: Federal Guidance Needed to Address Control Issues with Implementing Cloud Computing*, GAO-10-513 (Washington, D.C. May 27, 2010).
[2] GAO, *Continued Efforts Are Needed to Protect Information Systems From Evolving Threats*, GAO-10-230T (Washington D.C.: Nov. 17, 2009) and *Cyber Threats and Vulnerabilities Place Federal Systems at Risk*, GAO-09-661T (Washington, D.C.: May 5, 2009).
[3] The 24 major federal agencies are the Agency for International Development; the Departments of Agriculture, Commerce, Defense, Education, Energy, Health and Human Services , Homeland Security, Housing and Urban Development, the Interior, Justice, Labor, State, Transportation, the Treasury, and Veterans Affairs; the Environmental Protection Agency; the General Services Administration; the National Aeronautics and Space Administration; the National Science Foundation; the Nuclear Regulatory Commission; the Office of Personnel Management; the Small Business Administration; and the Social Security Administration.
[4] Virtualization is a technology that allows multiple software-based virtual machines with different operating systems to run in isolation, side-by-side on the same physical machine. Virtual machines can be stored as files, making it possible to save a virtual machine and move it from one physical server to another.

In: Cloud Computing and Government: Background, Benefits...   ISBN: 978-1-61761-784-3
Editor: George I. Nikolov   © 2011 Nova Science Publishers, Inc.

Chapter 9

STATEMENT OF SCOTT CHARNEY, CORPORATE VICE PRESIDENT, TRUSTWORTHY COMPUTING, MICROSOFT CORPORATION, BEFORE THE HOUSE COMMITTEE ON OVERSIGHT AND GOVERNMENT REFORM, HEARING ON "CLOUD COMPUTING: BENEFITS AND RISKS OF MOVING FEDERAL IT INTO THE CLOUD"

Chairman Towns, Ranking Member Issa, Chairwoman Watson, Ranking Member Bilbray, Members of the Committee and Subcommittee: Thank you for inviting me here today to discuss the federal government's use of cloud computing.

My name is Scott Charney, and I am the Corporate Vice President for Trustworthy Computing at Microsoft Corporation. I also serve as one of four Co-Chairs of the Center for Strategic and International Studies (CSIS) Commission on Cybersecurity for the 44th Presidency. Prior to joining Microsoft, I was Chief of the Computer Crime and Intellectual Property Section in the Criminal Division of the United States (U.S.) Department of Justice. I was involved in nearly every major hacker prosecution in the U.S. from 1991 to 1999; worked on legislative initiatives, such as the National Information Infrastructure Protection Act that was enacted in 1996; and chaired the G8 Subgroup on High Tech Crime from its inception in 1996 until I left government service in 1999.

I currently lead Microsoft's Trustworthy Computing (TWC) group, which is responsible for ensuring that Microsoft provides a secure, private, and reliable computing experience for every computer user. Among other things, the TWC group oversees the implementation of the Security Development Lifecycle (which also includes privacy standards); investigates vulnerabilities; provides security updates through the Microsoft Security Response Center; and incorporates lessons learned to mitigate future attacks.

Microsoft plays a unique role in the cyber ecosystem by providing the software and services that support hundreds of millions of computer systems worldwide. Windows-based software is the most widely deployed platform in the world, helping consumers, enterprises, and governments to achieve their personal, business, and governance goals. Also, as Steve

Ballmer, our Chief Executive Officer, stated, "we're all in" when it comes to the cloud. We already offer a host of consumer and business cloud services, including a wide array of collaboration and communications software.

We operate one of the largest online e-mail systems, with more than 360 million active Hotmail accounts in more than 30 countries/regions around the world. Microsoft's Windows Update Service provides software updates to over 600 million computers globally, and our Malicious Software Removal Tool cleans more than 450 million computers each month on average. We are a global information technology (IT) leader whose scale and experience shapes technology innovations, helps us recognize and respond to ever changing cyber threats, and allows us to describe the unique challenges facing the government as it moves to the cloud.

Cloud computing creates new opportunities for government, enterprises, and citizens, but also presents new security, privacy, and reliability challenges when assigning functional responsibility (*e.g.*, who must maintain controls) and legal accountability (*e.g.*, who is legally accountable if those controls fail). As a general rule, it is important that responsibility and accountability remain aligned; bifurcation creates a moral hazard and a legal risk because a "responsible" party may not bear the consequences for its own actions (or inaction) and the correct behavior will not be incentivized. With the need for alignment in mind, I will, throughout the rest of my testimony, use the word "responsibility" to reflect both responsibility and legal accountability. It must also be remembered that there is another type of accountability: political accountability. Citizens have certain expectations of governments (much like customers and shareholders have certain expectations of businesses) that may exceed any formally defined legal accountability.

As a cloud provider, Microsoft is responding to security, privacy, and reliability challenges in various ways, including through its software development process, service delivery, operations, and support. In my testimony today, I will (1) characterize the cloud and describe how cloud computing impacts the responsibility of the government and cloud providers; (2) discuss the responsibilities cloud computing providers and government must fulfill individually and together; and (3) examine the importance of trust and identity to cloud computing.

New Computing Models ("The Cloud") Create New Opportunities and Risks

Many people talk about "cloud computing"— what it is, what it does, and why it matters — but it is critically important to have a common understanding of the term before discussing how it changes risk management responsibilities. "Cloud computing" permits all users to leverage Internet-based data storage, processing, and services in new ways, thus complementing the traditional model of running software and storing data on personal devices and servers. There are several key characteristics of the cloud that differ from the traditional client-server model of computing and deliver benefits for customers, including global elasticity, geo-diversity, and cotenancy.

- Global elasticity means that customers, including governments, enterprises, and consumers, can buy the computing power, storage, and resources they need in a fast and flexible manner without committing to long-term and costly technology investments. Global elasticity provides convenient access to, and creates opportunities for, more efficient delivery of services, and it helps control costs.
- Geo-diversity enables data to be stored in multiple locations, generating efficiency and speed benefits and enhancing reliability.
- Co-tenancy means multiple users share cloud infrastructure, which can create tremendous economies of scale and cost savings.

Service Models and Accountability

The benefits of the cloud can be realized through three different service models described below:

1. *Software as a Service (SaaS):* The cloud provider makes available to users a single application, such as Hotmail e-mail, or multiple applications, such as Microsoft's Office Suite online.
2. *Platform as a Service (PaaS):* Users may choose to develop and run their own software applications, while relying on the cloud provider to provide the underlying infrastructure and operating system. Microsoft's Azure is a cloud platform that enables users and developers to write and/or run their own applications.
3. *Infrastructure as a Service (IaaS):* At its most basic, users rent hardware or virtualized instances of hardware — the infrastructure — to deploy and run their own operating systems and software applications.

Customers need to make informed decisions about adoption of the cloud and its various service models because the model that is embraced will entail different allocations of responsibility between the customer and the cloud provider(s). In the traditional IT model, an organization is responsible for all aspects of its data protection, from its actual use of the data to the protection of that data in its IT environment. A complete data protection program will address the physical security of the data center, the trustworthiness of data center personnel, the configuration and management of hardware and software, and the management of IDs and access controls. Cloud computing changes this. While an organization will still control the use of its data, it will need to set limits on the cloud provider's use of that data. Additionally, it may transfer to the cloud provider the responsibility for certain data center operations. For example, the customer using IaaS may transfer responsibility for data center operations, including the trustworthiness of data center personnel, to the cloud provider.

Once this is understood, it becomes clear that the different cloud service models transfer different amounts of responsibility between the customer and the cloud provider. Figure 1 illustrates these shifts for the different cloud service models.

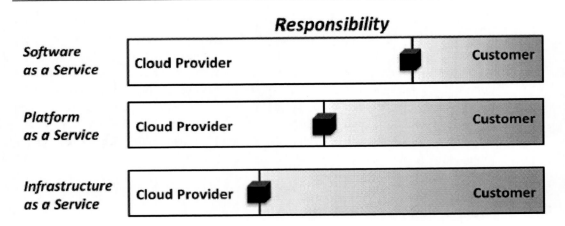

Figure 1. Shifting Responsibility in the Cloud

For example, IaaS customers maintain considerable responsibility for platform, applications, and personnel, but transfer responsibility for the infrastructure (*e.g.*, the physical data center, data center personnel, and hardware) to the cloud provider. At the other end of the spectrum, if customers utilize the entire cloud (from infrastructure to applications), they transfer yet more responsibility to cloud service providers, from physical and personnel security to the secure development and maintenance of applications and the management of identities for access control. Of course, the fact that a customer has transferred these responsibilities to the cloud provider — and may even have transferred legal liability by contract — is not the end of the matter. For example, citizens ultimately may hold a government accountable if data is lost or stolen, or critical data is not available when needed, notwithstanding any cloud provider agreement. Thus, a government may remain "accountable" to its constituents when an incident occurs, notwithstanding any contractual apportionment of responsibility. That said, as the federal government becomes a customer of cloud services, it must be clear about its requirements— and cloud providers must be responsible for meeting those requirements.

Contracts remain, of course, the primary legal documents for aligning responsibilities, but clearly and comprehensively defining requirements for cloud services is an arduous task. As more functions are transferred to cloud providers, requirements become more critical, more challenging, and more complex. The requirements are more critical because of the scale and scope of functions and data being moved to the cloud; they are harder because this is a relatively new domain where reasonable minds may often differ; and they are more complex because specificity is necessary to ensure a common understanding of expectations between customers and providers. While many enterprises have significant experiences with outsourcing services, the integration and adoption of cloud services is an important evolution in technology adoption and integration. Defining how responsibilities for security, privacy, and reliability are allocated — and creating sufficient transparency about this allocation — represent new challenges. Both customers and cloud providers must understand their respective roles and be able to communicate compliance requirements and controls across the spectrum of services available in the cloud.

Types of Clouds

The three basic service models are generally deployed in four different ways: public clouds, private clouds, community clouds, and hybrid clouds.

- In a public cloud, the general public can access the cloud services through a multi-tenant environment.
- In a private cloud, a single organization makes use of a dedicated cloud infrastructure.
- A community cloud is a private cloud shared by a group of organizations or a community with shared concerns, missions, or interests.
- Finally, a hybrid cloud makes use of two or more cloud types, such as a private cloud and a public cloud, where each cloud remains separate, but is linked in a way that can enable data and applications to flow and communicate between the two.

Which cloud model is most appropriate depends on the nature of the IT activity. For highly sensitive information, dedicated on-premises private clouds can provide more control and security, but at a higher cost and with lower scalability, redundancy, and other benefits. In comparison, public clouds offer the greatest cost savings and likely the greatest elasticity, but at the cost of reduced control and increased risk due to co-tenancy. Hybrid clouds may provide the benefits and risks of both types.

SECURITY, PRIVACY AND RELIABILITY RESPONSIBILITIES IN THE CLOUD

Regardless of the service model and type of cloud deployment selected, security, privacy, and reliability challenges must be addressed. Cloud providers and governments each have distinct responsibilities and, in some cases, shared responsibilities, as they work to help the Nation realize the benefits of cloud computing services.

Cloud Providers

The importance of assuring the confidentiality, integrity, and availability of customer data and operations is not new, but cloud computing does have the effect of shifting the responsibility (in whole or in part) for these areas to cloud service providers. Providers must rise to this new reality and provide commensurate levels of assurance for their customers.

Microsoft addresses this challenge through our holistic approach for managing security, privacy, and reliability that is designed to meet or exceed customer requirements. Our approach includes three cross-cutting functions to manage physical, personnel, and IT security: (1) utilizing a risk- based information security program that assesses and prioritizes security and operational threats to the business; (2) maintaining and updating a detailed set of security controls that mitigate risk; and (3) operating a compliance framework that ensures controls are designed appropriately and are operating effectively.

Any analysis of the cloud must start with the technology that powers it. Microsoft has long recognized the importance of building secure and reliable software, and we devote considerable resources to ensuring the quality of our software, including adherence to the Security Development Lifecycle (SDL). The SDL consists of continuously evolving processes and tools designed to reduce the number and severity of vulnerabilities in software products and ensure appropriate and agile response when necessary. Importantly, in the context of discussing providers' responsibilities in the cloud, it should be noted that the SD L considers and accounts for risks related to the environment in which the application will run (*e.g.*, client computers, on- premises services, or the cloud). Thus, the SDL ensures that Microsoft cloud services are developed using secure development practices.

The SDL is not only about improving code quality; it also helps protect people and their personal information. In cases where data from multiple users is stored on the same system, there are implications for managing the transfer, storage, retrieval, and access of that data in a manner that avoids disclosure of the data to unauthorized parties. Users need to know that they can trust the software and hardware to protect their sensitive information and to isolate them from other cotenants.

Online service providers can use a variety of technologies and procedures to help protect personal information from unauthorized access, use, or disclosure. Microsoft's software development teams apply the "PD3+C" principles, defined in the SDL, throughout the company's development and operational practices. The PD3+C principles are:

- **Privacy by Design** – Microsoft uses this principle in multiple ways during the development, release, and maintenance of applications to ensure that data collected from customers is used for specified purposes and that the customer is given appropriate notice in order to enable informed decision-making. When data to be collected is classified as highly sensitive, additional security measures — such as encrypting while in transit, at rest, or both — may be taken.
- **Privacy by Default** – Microsoft offerings ask customers for permission before collecting or transferring sensitive data. Once authorized, such data is protected using multiple means, such as access control lists (ACLs) and identity authentication mechanisms.
- **Privacy in Deployment** – Microsoft discloses privacy mechanisms to organizational customers as appropriate to allow them to establish appropriate privacy and security policies for their users.
- **Communications** – Microsoft actively engages the public through publication of privacy policies, white papers, and other documentations pertaining to privacy.[1]

Finally, cloud providers have a responsibility to provide reliable and trusted services. Reliability can be achieved through geo-diversity and redundancy in applications, data, and data centers, resiliency in communications, and high availability of services (as guaranteed in Service Level Agreements (SLAs)). Microsoft has multiple data centers located in the U.S., Europe, and Asia that meet internationally recognized standards and third party evaluations (*e.g.*, ISO 27001:2005 and SAS 70 Type I and Type II).[2] We are able to provide robust, geo-diverse services with more than 9,000 Microsoft hosting providers and more than 40% of all hosting providers worldwide using Microsoft products to support their hosting services. We also provide customers the ability to geo-locate their data, for example, ensuring that data resides only in U.S.-based servers. The integrity of cloud providers — including their personnel — is increasingly important, because the scale and scope of their actions can be exponentially increased in the cloud. Microsoft engineers are required to complete state-of-the-art training on many technology topics, including security and privacy, to help them keep pace with an ever-changing industry. By building and managing resilient infrastructure with trustworthy people, we can ensure high availability and commit to 99.9% uptime and 24x7 support in our SLAs.

Government

As cloud providers continue to evolve their operations to meet the responsibilities cloud customers transfer to them, so too must government evolve its approach to integrating the cloud into its operations. The Information Age has arrived and the cloud is ready for the government, but in many respects, the government is not yet ready for cloud computing. For example, according to the Government Accountability Office, federal agencies have serious and widespread information security control deficiencies. In their fiscal year 2009 performance and accountability reports, 21 of 24 major federal agencies noted that inadequate information system controls over their financial systems and information were either a material weakness or a significant deficiency. Furthermore, agencies continue to place federal assets at risk of inadvertent or deliberate misuse, financial information at risk of unauthorized modification or destruction, sensitive information at risk of inappropriate disclosure, and critical operations at risk of disruption. Agencies' current struggles to identify, manage, or account for security of data and systems are not immediately solved by integrating cloud services. Agencies must still identify and communicate requirements and expectations before transferring the responsibility of these functions to cloud providers. Once this is done, cloud service providers can then enhance agencies' abilities to meet their compliance challenges.

Progress is being made. The Federal Risk and Authorization Management Program (FedRAMP) is an important initial effort to provide joint security authorization for large outsourced systems. This program creates efficiencies for the government by enabling common assessments of cloud service providers, which allows a cloud provider to certify once and have that certification shared among the agencies. The result is a more efficient process than individual agency evaluations. FedRAM P also creates a process for cloud service providers to provide transparency into their operations and empowers agencies to fulfill their responsibilities for systems. Over time, this program could even begin to help reduce the number of federal systems resulting in further savings. In short, FedRAMP is the first government program to help balance responsibility between government agencies and cloud providers.

For security, agencies must approach the cloud thoughtfully, with an unwavering commitment to evaluate threats, assess risks, and define security requirements in order to ensure risks are managed at acceptable levels. Accordingly, agencies must adapt and advance their information security programs and communicate the attendant requirements to their cloud providers so that cloud providers can demonstrate that appropriate security and other operational controls have been implemented.

The government also should require that providers from which it procures cloud computing services meet the government's operational requirements for security, privacy and reliability. As threats continue to evolve, it remains critically important that cloud providers demonstrate secure development practices and transparent response processes for their applications. More broadly, the government should, wherever practicable, ensure that the technologies it procures, acquires, and uses are built and maintained in accordance with industry best practices for secure development. It should also promote (with appropriate incentives) such practices for all application developers. Users — including government users — need to be sure not only that their "boxed" products are secure, but also that their software applications — including those rapidly developed for the cloud — are built and provided on the basis of sound fundamentals.

Despite best efforts to prevent and protect against threats, incidents will inevitably occur. Some of these incidents will require law enforcement investigations, which may be hindered by forensic and jurisdictional issues resulting from cloud architecture and characteristics. Cloud service providers face a number of challenges with respect to forensics. For example, the complexities of the technology and the distributed nature of the data can reduce both access to and the overall quality of forensics data, making audit and attribution of attacks more challenging. Users' data can be commingled on single pieces of hardware, in virtual machines, or distributed across multiple services in the cloud environment.

For investigations, government may not trust cloud providers to investigate an incident, but at the same time, the cloud provider may not be able to grant the government broad access to conduct an investigation into a multi-tenant environment since that might give the government access to confidential data it is not authorized to see. With respect to jurisdiction for law enforcement investigations, the location(s) of data, particularly when crossing national boundaries, may create significant challenges. These legal challenges can be managed, such as through use of geolocated private clouds, but probably cannot be fully resolved for all users in all cases. In some cases, new technologies, techniques, or standards for data forensics and data deletion may need to evolve for use in public, multi-tenant clouds.

In addition to these security requirements, government must identify appropriate controls to protect the vast amounts of sensitive personally identifiable information (PII) that it maintains and uses. Agreements with cloud providers are just one aspect of taking adequate precautions. A cloud provider can protect data as designated by the agency, but the agency itself must maintain policies and procedures for the identification and handling of data in-house, such as on employees' computers. In other words, privacy protections must be maintained seamlessly from the client to the cloud.

Protecting privacy also requires keeping pace with today's technological realities. Congress enacted the Electronic Communications Privacy Act (ECPA) — the primary federal statute regulating government access to subscriber information, stored communications, and real-time communications — almost 25 years ago, at a time when the vast majority of Americans had never heard of the Internet or e-mail. Electronic communications have evolved dramatically over the past 25 years and have become an essential mode of interaction for most Americans. But the law has not kept up with the changes in technology. When applied to the modern computing world, ECPA is complicated and unclear, and needs to be clarified and updated in order to properly account for consumers' reasonable privacy expectations. Microsoft supports the efforts to modernize ECPA that are being led by the

Digital Due Process Coalition, and we encourage the government and Congress likewise to take up responsible reform of ECPA.

As with security and privacy, reliability remains a concern of government. In geo-diverse cloud environments, redundancy can help limit situations where data becomes unavailable; yet at the same time, customers must address connectivity to and reliable performance of cloud services. As these services become more integrated into agency operations and mission critical functions, government officials must ensure that they can maintain connectivity to the cloud by having physically diverse communications paths and alternate methods for accessing data centers. In addition, agencies should consider their reliance on cloud services in their business continuity and disaster recovery planning, and establish the necessary SLAs with their cloud providers to ensure continuity of operations.

If requirements are properly defined, cloud computing could ease the compliance challenges facing government. Unfortunately, the federal enterprise struggles today to meet key compliance goals such as those required by the Federal Information Security Management Act (FISMA). With 23,859 government systems across 25 agencies, key compliance metrics continue to lag. For example, 46% of high impact systems and 45% of medium impact systems in the government have not been certified or accredited. That totals 11,548 uncertified systems. Furthermore, just more than half of all federal systems have had security controls tested or business continuity plans tested.[3] Cloud computing could help ensure government data and systems meet expectations for certification, controls testing, and continuity planning. The cloud also provides a platform by which government could reduce the number of duplicative systems — saving costs, ensuring consistent application of Federal security requirements, and improving services to citizens and compliance.

Shared Responsibilities

Protecting the public good in the cloud requires Congress, the Executive Branch, and industry to work together. Our collaborative efforts should focus on promoting transparency around cloud computing providers' security, privacy, and reliability practices and, in turn, helping to ensure that users can make informed choices. Together, government and cloud providers should also address access and consent in privacy practices, including by requiring notice of privacy policies to cloud computing customers and by promoting the harmonization of global data privacy and data retention laws. Finally, we should collaborate to strengthen criminal penalties against hackers of cloud computing, and define penalties for criminal misuse of legitimate cloud services, to provide more effective deterrence and to enhance prosecutors' abilities to investigate and prosecute malicious actors who place cloud computing customers and the broader ecosystem at risk.

Microsoft is committed to securing the ecosystem and works with government through multiple public private partnerships; we also regularly work with our industry peers to address the most challenging issues facing users. Forums such as the Cloud Security Alliance (CSA) bring together subject matter experts to discuss key cloud risks and challenges and share best practices to resolve them. The CSA serves to create a cohesive set of recommendations and provide education around cloud security issues for cloud providers and consumers both domestically and internationally. Industry participation with organizations such as the National Institute of Standards and Technology (NIST) and the European Network and Information Security Agency (ENISA) helps to define and communicate the security, privacy, and reliability requirements among governments, other cloud users, and cloud providers. Government and industry must continue these international efforts to define and harmonize standards that enable innovation, create opportunity, and power the modern economy.

These actions will not solve fully the security, privacy, and reliability challenges of integrating cloud computing into the federal enterprise. However, by strengthening the security, privacy, and reliability practices in cloud computing services, and providing greater transparency to users, cloud providers and government will help build confidence in cloud computing services and, in turn, help cloud computing services to reach their potential.

TRUST AND IDENTITY IMPERATIVES

I have spoken about responsibility with respect to security, privacy, and reliability, but one particular issue is worthy of further note. Today, there are over 1.8 billion Internet users in the world, or more than 26% of the population.[4] Internet users continue to grow at over 19% year over year,[5] yet the mechanisms to provide identity, authentication, and attribution in cyberspace do not yet meet the needs of citizens, enterprises, or governments in traditional computing environments or for the cloud. The lack of trust online stems in part from our inability to manage online identities effectively. The cloud only amplifies the need for more robust identity management to help solve some of the fundamental security and privacy problems inherent in current Internet systems. As people move more and more of their data to the cloud, and share resources across cloud platforms, their credentials are the key to accessing that data. Every day, Microsoft authenticates more than one billion Windows Live ID authentications and processes two to four billion Exchange Hosted Services e-mails. Cloud providers will need to develop technologies that allow us to better manage identities both within their own systems and in settings where identities must be federated across separate networks.

Cyber attacks are facilitated by the anonymity and lack of traceability of the Internet; malicious actors in cyberspace must be convinced that either the cost of their actions is not worth the return on investment or that there is a real chance of attribution and punishment. Mandating robust authentication for some Internet uses — such as accessing critical infrastructures — while ensuring anonymity at other times (e.g., when citizens want to access public information) can help strike the right balance between security and privacy. Modern identity systems increasingly permit users to provide elements of their identity without having to provide more information than is required for a given transaction. Additionally, in appropriate cases, hardware, software and data should be authenticated as well. For example, if someone wants to visit a website with content that is inappropriate for children, that person should be able to present reliable proof of age without having to reveal his or her entire identity. Granular attributes of identity that can be proven or asserted are called "identity claims."

While the industry and academia are advancing many technological capabilities for strong and robust identity and identity claims, a supporting ecosystem is also required. We must have mechanisms (and associated policies) for the issuance of digital credentials that provide stronger verification and are based upon in-person proofing. We must have interoperable identity systems so those who provide robust credentials and those who wish to consume them can do so easily, thus enabling better trust decisions. The need for i nteroperability also demands standards and formats for managing and exchanging identity information.

The draft*National Strategy for Trusted Identities in Cyberspace*,[6] recently released by the White House, represents significant progress to help improve the ability to identify and authenticate the organizations, individuals, and underlying infrastructure involved in an online transaction. Government and industry must continue to work together on this initiative, as well as on advancing standards and formats on both a national as well as a global basis to enable a robust identity ecosystem.

Conclusion

Integrating cloud services into the federal enterprise fundamentally advances government in the Information Age. The characteristics of the cloud can enable a new agility and responsiveness in government to meet the needs of its citizens, but only if government and cloud providers work together in this transformation to embrace the new responsibilities of the cloud.

As part of this transformation, agencies' business models will change and they will transfer responsibilities for security, privacy, and reliability, in varying degrees, to cloud providers. Evaluating and apportioning the risks resulting from this transfer depends largely upon the type of cloud computing service model(s) selected. The adoption of cloud computing in the government is not about the success or failure of any one agency, but about the federal enterprise transitioning functions in a thoughtful and healthy way. The success of this transition depends on two factors: (1) the ability to adapt and advance information security programs and to communicate requirements to agencies' cloud providers; and (2) the ability of cloud providers to meet customers' requirements with sufficient transparency to ensure that requirements for security, privacy, and reliability are met appropriately.

Government is not alone in the adoption and integration of cloud services. Enterprises of all sizes and consumers are dramatically increasing their dependence upon cloud services. As such, it is incumbent upon the government to work with industry to address our shared responsibilities. Addressing these new fundamentals will foster innovative uses of the cloud, cultivate confidence, and advance information technologies for the new economy. The alignment and understanding of responsibility in the cloud requires greater transparency from both cloud providers and cloud customers (including enterprises and governments). The more precise and transparent we are, the greater the trust we will build, and the greater opportunity we create.

End Notes

[1] For more information about Microsoft's commitment to privacy, see the Microsoft Trustworthy Computing Privacy page at www.microsoft.com/privacy.

[2] Microsoft's online Information Security Program has been independently certified by British Standards Institute (BSI) Management Systems America as being compliant with ISO/IEC 27001:2005.

[3] *See* OMB's Fiscal Year 2009 Report to Congress on the Implementation of the Federal Information Security Management Act of 2002, *available online at* http://www.whitehouse.gov/omb/ assets

[4] http://www.internetworldstats.com/stats.htm

[5] http://www.internetworldstats.com/pr/edi038.htm

[6] http://www.dhs.gov/xlibrary/assets

In: Cloud Computing and Government: Background, Benefits...   ISBN: 978-1-61761-784-3
Editor: George I. Nikolov   © 2011 Nova Science Publishers, Inc.

Chapter 10

TESTIMONY OF DANIEL F. BURTON, JR., SENIOR VICE PRESIDENT, GLOBAL PUBLIC POLICY, SALESFORCE.COM, BEFORE THE HOUSE COMMITTEE ON OVERSIGHT AND GOVERNMENT REFORM, HEARING ON "CLOUD COMPUTING: BENEFITS AND RISKS OF MOVING FEDERAL IT INTO THE CLOUD"

Chairman Towns and Chairwoman Watson, Ranking Member Issa and Ranking Member Bilbray, Members of the Committee, thank you for holding this hearing on cloud computing and for inviting me to share my views with you. Cloud computing is a revolutionary and disruptive new technology that is having a profound impact on how we use, manage and build computing applications. As the Senior Vice President for Global Public Policy at Salesforce.com, I am deeply involved in government discussions about cloud computing, and I applaud the efforts of this Committee and the Administration to enable federal agencies to take advantage it.

ABOUT SALESFORCE.COM

Salesforce.com is a leading enterprise cloud computing company that provides cloud solutions to organizations of all sizes in all industries globally. Our main service offerings are applications that allow organizations to input, store, process, and access data to manage their sales and customer services. In addition, we provide a platform (Force.com) that enables customers and developers to build and sell new cloud applications, as well as a collaboration tool (Chatter).

Salesforce.com delivers its services over the Internet through commercially available Web connections and browser software. Instead of building and maintaining costly IT infrastructure, our customers simply log on to the Salesforce.com Website and access their cloud services using a unique username and password. Over 77,000 organizations globally, including governments and businesses in highly regulated industries like financial services, healthcare, insurance and communications trust Salesforce.com with their data. Our U.S. federal government customers include the Bureau of Census, the Department of Army, the Department of Energy, the Department of Health and Human Services, the Department of Homeland Security, the Department of Navy, the Department of State, the Department of Transportation, the Environmental Protection Agency, the General Services Administration and NASA, among others.

In my remarks today, I will discuss the core characteristics of cloud computing. I will also address issues related to cost, data ownership, security and interoperability because I understand that they are of particular interest to the Committee. In doing so, I will make reference the Salesforce.com enterprise cloud computing model, not the consumer cloud computing model that companies like Amazon and eBay offer.

How Do You Know Cloud Computing WHEN YOU Seeit?

Descriptions of cloud computing are like the parable of the blind men and the elephant. Six blind men were asked to touch an elephant and describe it. One blindman grasped the elephant's trunk and announced that it resembled a giant snake; another felt the legs and said it was more like a tree; a third touched the tusksand insisted that it was similar to an enormous walrus; and so on. While each was correct in his own narrow description, each missed the larger picture.

This parable will sound familiar to anyone who has followed the discussion about cloud computing. Some focus on the fact that cloud computing involves third-party data centers and insist that because they hold their customer's data in remote data centers they are cloud computing providers; others emphasize the pay-as-you-go feature and conclude that because they charge their customers in increments over time they are cloud providers; others stress that it is accessed over IT networks and claim that because they provide applications over networks they are cloud providers.

While each of these descriptions is true as far as it goes, by themselves they do not constitute cloud computing. Nor are the companies that provide these discrete functions cloud computing providers any more than an elephant is a snake, a tree, or a walrus.

Cloud computing consists of a combination of these three features, plus something known as "multi-tenant" architecture.

- *Third-party data centers* – With cloud computing the actual computing takes place in a third-party data center, not on an individual's computer or within a company's own IT facilities. As a result, the user does not have to install or maintain a local copy of the software, invest in IT infrastructure, or maintain data centers.
- *Internet Access* – Users access cloud software over the public Internet with a browser. This means that they can retrieve their data and applications anywhere they have Internet access without dedicated networks or proprietary communication lines. It also means they can access information from multiple devices, like lap-top computers and smart-phones.

- *Pay-as-you-go* – Enterprise cloud customers do not purchase cloud applications, but subscribe to them, usually on a per-seat or a per-usage basis for a period of time.

MULTI-TENANCY

As important these three features are, unless they are combined with a multi-tenant architecture, they do not constitute true cloud computing

NIST alludes to the essential requirement of multi-tenancy in its definition of cloud computing, which reads as follows:

> *Cloud computing is a model for enabling convenient, on-demand network access to a shared pool of configurable computing resources (e.g., networks, servers, storage, applications, and services) that can be rapidly provisioned and released with minimal management effort or service provider interaction.*

The definitive reference to multi-tenancy comes when NIST defines resource pooling:

> *The provider's computing resources are pooled to serve multiple consumers* **using a multi-tenant model,** [emphasis added] *with different physical and virtual resources dynamically assigned and reassigned according to consumer demand.*

At the September 2009 Gov 2.0 Summit in Washington, DC Casey Coleman (CIO of GSA and Chair of the Federal Cloud Computing Executive Steering Committee) summed up the essential role of multi-tenancy when she stated that *"Cloud computing by its very nature is multi-tenant."*

A good analogy for multi-tenancy is the skyscraper. A skyscraper enables large numbers of different tenants to conduct their operations in the same building. The tenants do not have to lay the foundation, construct the building or maintain the underlying infrastructure. Instead, they simply lease office space and customize it to meet their needs, knowing that their business activities will be kept private from the other building occupants. The landlord is responsible for improvements to the building, and each time he upgrades the infrastructure all of the tenants benefit. If a tenant's needs change or if it becomes dissatisfied with the building services, he can terminate his lease and move.

Just like a skyscraper allows many different occupants to run their businesses discretely within a single building, a multi-tenant cloud computing platform allows many different users to run their computer applications discretely on the same computing platform. Because the users' data and applications are separated logically within the hardware and software, they can view only the data and cloud services that pertain to them. In this respect, multi-tenant cloud architecture is like online banking – it allows a number of consumers to use their individual accounts at the same time while keeping their banking information private through the logical (not physical) separation of data.

In order to appreciate the power of multi-tenant cloud computing, it is useful to compare it to traditional, single-tenant computing applications. Multi-tenant applications can satisfy the needs of numerous organizations with the hardware resources and staff needed to manage one large computing stack. By contrast, single-tenant applications require a dedicated set of resources for each organization. It is largely for this reason that the Application Service Provider (ASP) single-tenant computing model of the late 1990s failed. In the ASP model, the setup, maintenance and upgrades of computer applications were outsourced to a third-party service provider, just like they are with cloud computing. The difference was that the ASP had to maintain a separate infrastructure stack for each customer. As more and more customers were added, the sheer scale, cost and complexity of maintaining the aggregate computing infrastructure became unsustainable.

With multi-tenant cloud computing, the software applications are provided as a service to multiple customers on a single, large infrastructure stack. The configurations of each user are stored as metadata that describes the base functionality of their application and corresponds to their data and customizations. This metadata is then interpreted by the platform's runtime engine. In a robust multi-tenant, metadata cloud architecture there is a clear separation of the compiled runtime engine (kernel) and the application data. As a result, the kernel can be upgraded without disrupting customer's applications or data, thus allowing for continuous improvement in performance, reliability, security and scale. In short, multi-tenant computing yields massive cost, speed, scale and innovation advantages that single-tenant computing cannot match.

With its multi-tenant architecture, Salesforce.com is able to run approximately 230,000 applications for its more than 77,000 customers on just a few thousand servers. No other computing model delivers that kind of efficiency. A single-tenant computing model (sometimes referred to as a "private cloud") would require a minimum of 2 servers per application (one database server and one application server), plus additional servers for redundancy and disaster recovery. Consequently, a single-tenant computing model could require several hundred thousand servers to manage the computing needs of the customer base that Salesforce.com manages with just a few thousand servers.

The key advantages of the Salesforce.com multi-tenant enterprise cloud computing solutions include the following:

- *Secure, scalable and reliable delivery platform* – The delivery platform for our service has been designed to provide our customers with high levels of performance, reliability and security. We have built, and continue to invest in, a comprehensive security infrastructure, including firewalls, intrusion detection systems and encryption for transmissions over the Internet, which we monitor and test on a regular basis.
- *Rapid deployment* – Our service can be deployed rapidly since our customers do not have to spend time procuring, installing or maintaining the servers, storage, networking equipment, security products, or other infrastructure hardware and software necessary to ensure a scalable and reliable service.
- *Ease of integration* – Our platform is designed to enable IT professional to integrate our service with existing applications quickly and seamlessly. Our Force.com platform provides a set of application programming interfaces (APIs) that enable customers and independent developers both to integrate our service with existing third-party, customer and legacy applications, and to write their own application services that integrate with our service.

- *Rapid development of applications using the Force.com platform* – Our customers and third party developers can develop applications rapidly because of the ease of use and the benefits of a multi-tenant platform.
- *Lower total cost of ownership* – We enable customers to achieve significant upfront savings relative to their traditional enterprise software model. Customers benefit from the predictability of their future costs since they pay for the service on a per subscriber basis for the term of the subscription contract. All upgrades are included in our service, so customers are not burdened or disrupted by the periodic need to perform system upgrades. Because we implement all upgrades on our servers, new features and functionality automatically become part of our service on the release date and therefore benefit all of our customers immediately.
- *Increasing innovation* – By providing infrastructure and development environments on demand, we provide developers the opportunity to create new and innovative applications without having to invest in hardware and distribution. A developer with an idea for a new application can log onto our platform, develop, host and support their system on Force.com, and make the application accessible for a fee to our customers.
- *High level of user adoption* – We have designed our service to be intuitive and easy to use. Since our service contains many tools and features recognizable to users of popular websites such as those of Amazon, eBay and Google, it has a more familiar user interface than typical enterprise customer relationship management (CRM) applications. As a result, our users do not require substantial training on how to use and befit from our service.

For the U.S. government, these advantages translate into cost savings, flexibility, fast deployment and lower risk of project failure. Traditional government IT systems require significant up-front investments in hardware and software. Moreover, they can often take years to write, customize and install. As a result, they frequently fail to deliver the required functionality and are out-of-date by the time they are deployed, leading to newspaper articles about unsuccessful government IT projects with massive cost overruns. Because cloud computing eliminates large up-front capital investments, lets government agencies start with a few users to see if the application meets their requirements and enables them to scale rapidly if it does, there is much less chance of waste and failure.

Like any new technology, cloud computing raises several issues that must be addressed if it is to achieve its promise. Among these are cost, data ownership, vendor lock-in, security and interoperability. I will discuss each of these below. In doing so, I will refer to the experience of Salesforce.com as an enterprise cloud computing provider and our customer case studies.

COST

Because cloud computing services can be tailored to the specific needs of individual customers, it can be difficult to calculate precise cost comparisons between cloud solutions and traditional on-premise solutions. Nonetheless, most studies conclude that cloud computing offers substantial cost savings over on-premise computing. Moreover, there is broad consensus that cloud computing is far less risky than traditional on-premise computing – there are no massive up-front costs because users do not have to purchase software licenses or invest in expensive IT infrastructure. There is also general agreement that the on-going cost of cloud computing is much more predictable than traditional on-premise computing. Users of the cloud typically pay as they go, and pay only for what they use.

One of the best studies of the cost savings of cloud computing to the U.S. government is by Darrell West, *Saving Money Through Cloud Computing* (Brookings Institute, May 2010). This chapter concludes that there are significant cost savings associated with cloud computing.

> *Depending on the scope and timing of the migration, reliance on public versus private clouds, the need for privacy and security, the number of file servers before and after migration, the extent of labor savings, and file server storage utilization rates, savings generally average between 25 and 50 percent. Combined with cross-platform accessibility, scalability, and reliability, there is a strong argument for the federal government to place a greater emphasis on cloud solutions. Clouds bring convenience, efficiency, and connectability that are vital to government agencies.*

Because of these cost savings, Dr. West concludes that the amount of federal IT spending devoted to cloud computing will grow rapidly.

Salesforce.com case studies of government cloud implementations support these conclusions. For example, the U.S. State Department's Nonproliferation and Disarmament Fund (NDF) used Salesforce.com to create a cloud application to give program managers around the world ready access to up-to-date budget information. A 2009 Nucleus Research report estimated that the NDF cloud application cost one-quarter as much as it would have if it had been developed in-house. Furthermore, the report concluded that the return on investment was 216%, the payback time was 8 months, and the average annual benefit was $1,625,066.

NJ TRANSIT, which uses Salesforce.com to track and respond to service issues, offers a similar success story. Because of the communication and issue-tracking capabilities the cloud application enabled, NJ TRANSIT has been able to increase the number of inquiries it handles by 600% and reduce its response time by 35% without adding any additional staff.

These U.S. public sector examples are backed-up by case studies from the private sector and from other governments. For example, the Salesforce.com cloud-computing model saved Qualcomm an estimated $100,000 in hardware costs and allowed it to reduce support staff by 60%. Similarly, the Japan Post Network avoided $10 million hardware and software costs by deploying a Salesforce.com cloud solution and experienced a return in investment of 511% over three years. All of these case studies can be found on the Salesforce.com Website at www.salesforce.com.

DATA OWNERSHIP, COMPLIANCE AND VENDORLOCK-IN

As an enterprise cloud computing company, Salesforce.com manages massive amounts of information -- about 300 million transactions each business day. We use and process the information our customers enter into our system only as they instruct us to, or in order to fulfill our contractual and legal obligations. We claim no ownership rights to the information our customers submit to our cloud computing services. We disclose information submitted by our customers only if required to do so by law, and we provide affected customers prior notice of any such compelled disclosure to the extent permitted by law.

Salesforce.com also maintains strict confidentiality obligations and does not access customer data except under narrowly-defined circumstances. Like any organization that stores and processes data, we face a patchwork of U.S. state, federal, and international privacy requirements. Customer data may also be subject to these requirements.

Some critics have raised concerns that cloud computing will lead to vendor lock-in. It is unclear, however, that customers will be locked-into their cloud computing applications any more than they are to their traditional on-premise computing applications. At Salesforce.com, for example, if a customer decides that they no longer want to use our cloud services, we make their respective information available to them in a format that allows them to download it and take it elsewhere.

SECURITY

Security concerns are often cited as one of the main reasons to avoid cloud computing. Critics of cloud security emphasize that cloud computing is a new technology that lacks appropriate security standards and adequate controls. They also voice reservations about multi-tenant architecture and often point to private clouds as the best way to address the security issues associated with cloud computing. Others, however, believe that enterprise cloud computing is more secure than traditional client-server computing. They note that enterprise cloud computing allows for uniform high performance for all users, continuous improvements in the security of the underlying platform, features that can be tuned to match the sensitivity of the data being stored, a locked-down management network that is easier to secure than a distributed corporate network, and robust back-up systems.

In assessing the security of cloud computing platforms, it is important to look beyond generalizations to the specific security practices of individual cloud providers. Broad assertions about cloud security are like saying that trucks are safer than cars. Such a statement may appear to be true in the abstract, but it does not take into account the make, model and performance of the vehicles, where they will be driven, or who the driver is. Similarly, declarations like "private clouds are more secure than public clouds" are not very meaningful unless the security features of individual private and public cloud providers are carefully evaluated.

Salesforce.com views security as part of a trust equation that includes privacy, performance and reliability. Because trust also requires transparency, we have established a public trust site (https://trust.salesforce.com) that provides the Salesforce.com community with real-time information on system performance and security, including the following:

- Live and historical data on system performance
- Up-to-the minute information on planned maintenance
- Phishing, malicious software, and social engineering threats
- Best security practices for your organization

- Information on how we safeguard your data

The Salesforce.com security management system is based on an internationally accepted security framework that encompasses physical security, host security, logical network security, transmission level security, database security and operational security.

Salesforce.com is ISO27001 certified, SAS 70 Type II audited and SysTrust certified. We are a signatory to the US-EU Safe Harbor and have been certified by TRUSTe. We are also certified with the Japan Privacy Seal (JIPDEC).

Perhaps the best evidence of our security, however, is the fact that over 77,000 organizations around the world trust their information to the Salesforce.com enterprise cloud. Included among these customers are organizations that place a high premium on security, including financial services institutions, Fortune 500 companies, healthcare firms, technology companies, and governments.

We are encouraged by the actions the Obama Administration has taken to align the federal government security certifications with the cloud computing model and to streamline the security audit process. Programs such as FedRamp and Apps.gov are positive steps, and we look forward to working with federal agencies on these and other initiatives designed to facilitate the government's ability to use cloud computing.

INTEROPERABILITY

Interoperability is also frequently raised as an issue for anyone considering cloud computing. No matter how powerful an individual company's cloud services are, they will not be effective unless they interoperate with outside software programs. For this reason, interoperability is a core feature of the Salesforce.com enterprise cloud. Perhaps the best indication of the extent to which Salesforce.com interoperates with other software programs is the fact that over 50% of the transactions we process are handled through our application programming interface (API). In everyday terms, this means that about 150 million times each day our computers are talking with other computers outside our system – or "interoperating" – without the intervention of individuals.

Salesforce.com provides interoperability at several different levels. We offer application mash-ups with other software programs, such as Google and Hoovers; native enterprise resource planning (ERP) connectors with SAP and Oracle; and native desktop connectors with Lotus Notes and Microsoft Outlook. We maintain an integration partner ecosystem that includes companies like Deloitte, Accenture and Acumen, and offer developer toolkits for .Net and Java. In April 2010, we announced a partnership with VMWare that will allow the 6 million enterprise Java developers to write cloud computing applications on the Force.com platform in the Java programming language. Our cloud services also interoperate with other major cloud companies, like Google and Amazon, and can be used on desktop, laptop and notebook computers, as well as on mobile devices like the iPhone and the Blackberry.

In addition, Salesforce.com hosts AppExchange, which is like an iTunes for enterprise cloud software applications. AppExchange is an online directory that provides customers a way to browse, test-drive, share and install application developed on our Force.com platform. Partners and developers can offer their applications on the AppExchange directory. This directory gives our users a way to find and install applications to expand their use of the Force.com platform to areas that are complementary to or extend beyond customer relationship management solutions.

CONCLUSION

Cloud computing is a powerful technology that promises tremendous benefits for consumers, companies, non-profits, and governments. It has already been successfully implemented in organizations of all sizes around the world. According to Gartner, the cloud computing market was worth approximately $46 billion in 2009 and will increase to $150 billion by 2013. Gartner predicts that next year 25% of new software deployments will be based on software-as-a-service cloud computing applications. According to a recent Goldman Sachs technology software report, the shift toward cloud computing is "unstoppable." The remarkable growth of cloud computing is not limited to consumer and business applications. Numerous federal, provincial, and local governments in North America, Europe, and Asia have also implemented cloud computing solutions. Led by federal CIO VivekKundra, the U.S. federal government is emerging as a leader in public sector efforts to take advantage of cloud computing. I appreciate the Committee's interest in this issue and your efforts to advance the federal government's ability to take advantage of this important new technology.

In: Cloud Computing and Government: Background, Benefits... ISBN: 978-1-61761-784-3
Editor: George I. Nikolov © 2011 Nova Science Publishers, Inc.

Chapter 11

TESTIMONY OF MIKE BRADSHAW, DIRECTOR, GOOGLE FEDERAL, GOOGLE INC., BEFORE THE HOUSE COMMITTEE ON OVERSIGHT AND GOVERNMENT REFORM, HEARING ON "CLOUD COMPUTING: BENEFITS AND RISKS OF MOVING FEDERAL IT INTO THE CLOUD"

ChairmanTowns,ChairwomanWatson,Ranking Members Issa and Bilbray,and members of the Commitee.

Thank you for the opportunity to discuss with you the benefits of migrating more federal agencies to cloud computing. I lead the Google team that provides cloud computing services to the federal government.

Cloud computing is a relatively new term for some, but the cloud is being used today by significant numbers of consumers, businesses, and – increasingly – the public sector. In fact, more than two million businesses use our cloud service, Google Apps. In the cloud, everyday processes and information that are typically run and stored on local computers – email, documents, calendars – can be accessed securely anytime, anywhere, and with any device through an Internet connection. The cloud enables government agencies to replace in-house information technology – which is costly and complex to own, maintain, and secure – with externally provided computing power that offers better and secure performance at dramatically reduced costs.

Google's cloud service allows users to store data or run programs on our geographically distributed, well-secured data centers. Businesses increasingly are choosing to use Google's data centers the same way they now use their desktop computers or on-premise file servers, and in the process are saving money, becoming more efficient, and improving their security. For example, more than 50,000 companies, including 15 percent of the Fortune 500, rely on Google's cloud security service to filter billions of emails against malicious attacks.

In my testimony this morning I would like to make three basic points.

- First, government agencies are finding that the cloud can provide better information security than they have today. Agencies face significant challenges with lost or stolen laptops that contain sensitive data. The cloud enhances security by enabling data to be stored centrally with continuous and automated network analysis and protection. When vulnerabilities are detected they can be managed more rapidly and uniformly. Cloud security is able to respond to attacks more rapidly by reducing the time it takes to install patches on thousands of individual desktops or hundreds of uniquely configured on-premise servers.

- Second, the cloud offers cost savings, efficiency, improved collaboration, and scalability. By using multi-tenant cloud infrastructure, the costs of computing are spread out over many users instead of just the few users at a particular agency. Government data centers today are typically underutilized, which means they often waste money and energy.
- Finally, although the federal government is starting to adopt cloud computing, more could be done to broaden and accelerate the government's adoption of the cloud. Already, a path to cloud adoption exists, and federal government initiatives like Apps.gov and the Federal Risk and Authorization Management Pilot Program (FedRAMP) are making – or soon will make – progress towards accelerating cloud adoption. We support these efforts and thank the committee for the opportunity to explain the aspects of the government transition to cloud that are working as well as those that can be made even better.

We are excited about the cloud, and we are proud of our achievements in this space. But it is important to note that many companies are offering cloud services. Salesforce.com and Microsoft are just two of the many companies driving innovation and competition in cloud computing. Though most of my testimony will focus on Google products – which are the products I'm most familiar with – there are many cloud solutions out there. And, though we think we offer the best ones, we welcome and encourage the competition and innovation that we see every day in this space.

CLOUD COMPUTINGENHANCES SECURITY

One of the key benefits that cloud computing can provide to the federal government is improved security compared to the status quo model of desktop-centric and on-premise computing.

How we use banks is analogous to cloud computing. Under traditional computing models, we store our critical data on our computers either at home or at work. This is the equivalent of keeping cash under your mattress. Storing data with a cloud computing service provider is like keeping cash in a bank. These companies are security professionals and they typically provide much more consistent security than their customers can on their own.

In today's model of traditional desktop computing there is significant government data stored on portable devices like laptops and USB thumb drives, which can – and often do – get lost or stolen. There are dozens of examples of government computers having been lost or stolen. In 2007, a Transportation Security Administration external hard drive that contained the names, bank records, Social Security numbers, and payroll information of up to 100,000 TSA employees went missing. An Army National Guard laptop that contained the personal information of 131,000 soldiers reportedly was stolen in 2007. A Department of Veterans Affairs portable hard drive that contained sensitive VA-related information on approximately 535,000 individuals was also stolen in 2007. As these examples demonstrate, government agencies have struggled with security under the traditional desktop computing model.

A 2009 Government Accountability Office report on existing government security deficiencies confirmed that many of the data losses occurring at federal agencies over the past few years have been the result of physical thefts or improper safeguarding of systems, including laptops and other portable devices.

> *At least nine agencies also lacked effective controls to restrict physical access to information assets. We have previously reported that many of the data losses occurring at federal agencies over the past few years were a result of physical thefts or improper safeguarding of systems, including laptops and other portable devices.*
>
> *In addition, agencies did not always configure network devices and services to prevent unauthorized access and ensure system integrity, patch key servers and workstations in a timely manner, or segregate incompatible duties to different individuals or groups so that one individual does not control all aspects of a process or transaction. (GAO Report GAO-09-701T, at page 6).*

Cloud computing can protect against these security vulnerabilities. Moving data across portable devices becomes unnecessary, as cloud computing enables data to be accessed securely from anywhere with an Internet connection.

The most important component of feeling comfortable with one's data in the cloud is trusting a cloud services provider and the practices and policies they have in place. Most people probably do not realize that they have been doing this for years with web-based e-mail or common services like online banking. With Google products, users can set fine-grained access controls for documents, calendars, and other types of information commonly stored in the cloud.

Another important security benefit in the cloud is that agencies and other organizations can control security updates much more consistently and easily. Our research shows most organizations take between 25 and 60 days to deploy security patches, and some corporate chief information officers admit it can take up to six months. Google's cloud service allows everyone to get security updates as soon as they are available, not weeks or months later.

At Google data centers, data is stored on custom-built machines maintained by proprietary software that continually monitors systems. If a threat is found, the system can respond automatically. This structure provides scalability and helps make patching and upgrades more efficient. We can detect security threats across the web early and prepare appropriate defenses, sometimes even before antivirus companies know about them.

Security is at the core of Google's design and development process; it is built into the DNA of our products. Google is a company that came of age in the Internet era and consistently defends against and adjusts to Internet security threats. We use a combination of people, process, and technology to help secure our systems.

Google employs a dedicated, full-time security team with some of the world's foremost experts in information, application, and network security. The security team can collectively anticipate and fix security issues more quickly and effectively than most single companies or individuals. This team is responsible for maintaining the company's networks, developing security review processes, and building customized security infrastructure. It also has a key role in developing, documenting, and implementing Google's security policies and standards. Also, Google's security professionals are empowered by the design of our cloud – we are able to update all of our servers at once.

Google uses an access model designed to only grant as-needed access to customer data. Data centers themselves are equipped with security technologies like thermal imaging cameras, electronic card access systems, 24/7 guard coverage, video analytics, and access logs, among others. Data is obfuscated and split across numerous servers and data centers, making an attack much more difficult because no single user's data resides on a single disk or server.

The data in Google's cloud is stored in geographically distributed data centers. The data is replicated several times so that it will still be available if we are confronted with a power outage in one part of the country. If, for example, a hurricane or earthquake strikes one data center, the application keeps running in the other data centers, and the data stays safe. This has important implications for backup and disaster recovery from a continuity of government perspective. For example, the City of Los Angeles noted that for them, because of their location in an earthquake zone, Google Apps could provide more affordable and efficient backup and recovery solutions than they could otherwise have procured.

CostSavings, Efficiency, and OtherBenefits

Beyond enhanced security, the shift to cloud computing brings demonstrable benefits for saving the government money and increasing the efficiency and functionality of government services. In January 2009, Forrester Research, an independent technology research company, calculated that Google's cloud-based email service, Google Apps Gmail, costs businesses only $8.47 per user per month, versus $25.18 for traditional on-premise email. In case after case, real world examples show that cloud computing costs far less than the traditional desktop model.

For example, in 2009 the City of Orlando was facing aging infrastructure and budget cuts that led it to reconsider managing an in-house email system and running its own servers. In just two months, Orlando was able to switch its 3,000 employees over to a cloud computing service that cut the annual cost per employee from $133 to $50. Now, Orlando employees, from city planners to police officers, will use a web-based email system similar to Google's popular Gmail, but with more storage (25 Gigabytes) and more customized features.

Federal agencies also can reap these significant cost savings. Booz Allen Hamilton, a strategy and technology consulting firm, reported in October 2009 that federal agencies could save 85 percent of their yearly IT infrastructure budgets by moving operations to external cloud providers. In April of this year, the Brookings Institution found that government agencies that switched to some form of cloud computing saw up to 50 percent savings. To put that in context, the federal government is currently spending $76 billion per year on IT, with $20 billion of that devoted to hardware, software, and file servers. That's billions of dollars of taxpayer money.

Cost savings from switching to the cloud are especially relevant given the current under-utilization of government IT resources. The Office of Management and Budget emphasizes that while government data centers increased in number from 400 to 1,100 in a decade, server utilization at those data centers is on average a mere seven percent of full capacity. The cloud will be instrumental in reducing this kind of waste across the federal government's IT infrastructure.

In addition to being more cost efficient, the cloud is also more energy efficient. The City of Los Angeles, which contracted with Google to provide cloud-based email in October 2009, estimates that it will save $750,000 over the next five years simply from the reduction in energy costs.

For its part, the federal government, with over 1,200 of its own data centers, could significantly lower spending and energy consumption by moving some applications to the cloud. The Environmental Protection Agency estimated in 2007 that consolidated, energy-efficient servers and storage systems could cut electricity use by 55 percent. By 2011, the agency estimates that the cut in electricity use could save up to 74 billion kilowatt hours of electricity, $5.1 billion, and 47 million metric tons of carbon dioxide emissions.

Another way the federal government can help to reduce energy consumption is by promoting telework to reduce federal worker commute times and the energy consumed in that commute. As the series of snowstorms that blanketed the Washington, DC region this February showed, teleworking can prevent the government from shutting down completely in an emergency. Teleworking and the cloud can be important components of federal agencies' Continuity of Operations Plans. The cloud can allow teleworkers to easily and securely access their data and work from wherever they happen to be. During the February 2010 snowstorms, the Office of Personnel Management and GSA used cloud computing to share the load with other computer networks in order to keep OPM's Status Alert web site running.

The cloud also brings increased functionality. Federal employees can collaborate more easily and effectively because information and applications run in a shared, secure space online, making it easy for people to work together on documents. Two or more people can, for example, edit a web-based document together in real-time while they are hundreds or thousands of miles away from each other – rather than sending it back and forth as an attachment and going through the laborious process of incorporating edits on top of edits. Running applications online means that they can be accessed more easily and securely from any device – a netbook, a smartphone, or any desktop computer where a user happens to be located.

THE FEDERALGOVERNMENTRISKSFALLINGBEHIND THE PRIVATESECTOR

Today the private sector is using cloud computing to allow employees to access their information and run software applications from anywhere they might be, anytime they need it, from virtually any device that's connected to the Internet. With cloud, it is easier to communicate and work together on documents, calendars, and other collaborative projects. A 2010 report by Gartner, a leading IT research and advisory firm, confirms an acceleration of adoption of cloud computing with the scale of deployments growing. More than 3,000 businesses sign up for Google Apps every day. Businesses are able to save money by spending less on building and managing their own, often under-utilized, IT systems. The same benefits are available for the federal government, with the cost savings ultimately going to taxpayers.

Every day hundreds of millions of consumers use the cloud when they use email services like Microsoft's Hotmail, Yahoo! Mail, or Gmail, which are being run and stored on the Internet rather than locally on a specific computer. Similarly, consumers are using the cloud when they use online banking to look up bank records, balance check books, manage funds, or pay bills. A June 2010 Pew Research Center study projects that within ten years most Internet users will be doing the majority of their computing in the cloud instead of with software that runs and stores programs on a specific computer.

Businesses large and small are rapidly embracing cloud computing. Companies like Amazon.com, Salesforce.com, and Google are providing cloud platforms to allow business customers to improve efficiency and collaboration, lower operating costs, and secure data in ways that are simply not possible using the traditional, desktop-focused IT model.

Though the federal government is adopting at a slower rate compared to industry, we are beginning to see government cloud initiatives and pilot programs. The public sector is already adopting cloud at all levels of government to better serve citizens, reduce costs, lower energy consumption and make more effective use of taxpayer dollars overall. Federal entities currently using the cloud include the Department of Energy, Department of Defense, Department of the Interior, the National Aeronautics and Space Administration, the Social Security Administration, the Security and Exchange Commission, and the General Services Administration.

The DOE cloud computing migration is a good example of progress that is already being made. In 2009, DOE's Lawrence Berkeley National Labs (LBL) began exploring how to use cloud computing and LBL has already moved over 2,300 email accounts to Google Apps and will transition 5,000 accounts later this summer. This cloud deployment uses an identity management system to improve security. Also, the LBL cloud is empowering DOE scientific research teams to foster collaboration and community documentation through the use of Google Docs and other tools.

Simply put, cloud computing is already here and being used every day by individuals, business, and government. But we believe that the federal government could move more quickly, and by doing so it could reap benefits similar to those enjoyed by the private sector. The opportunity to switch to the cloud means that the approximately $80 billion per year market for federal government IT will see more innovation and competition – along with cost and energy savings, which are critical in today's environment.

CONCLUSION

We would like to thank Chairman Towns, Chairwoman Watson, Ranking Members Issa and Bilbray, and the members of the Committee for holding this hearing on the use of cloud computing by the federal government. The cloud can help agencies at all levels increase productivity, cut costs, keep pace with technology innovation, and improve security. We look forward to working with you and other government officials to continue to make cloud computing more efficient, cost-effective, and secure.

In: Cloud Computing and Government: Background, Benefits... ISBN: 978-1-61761-784-3
Editor: George I. Nikolov © 2011 Nova Science Publishers, Inc.

Chapter 12

WRITTEN TESTIMONY OF NICKLOUS COMBS, CHIEF TECHNOLOGY OFFICER, EMC FEDERAL, BEFORE THE HOUSE COMMITTEE ON OVERSIGHT AND GOVERNMENT REFORM, HEARING ON "CLOUD COMPUTING: BENEFITS AND RISKS OF MOVING FEDERAL IT INTO THE CLOUD"

Chairman Towns, Ranking Member Issa, Chairwoman Watson, Ranking Member Bilbray, and Members of the Committee, thank you for the opportunity to address the opportunities and risks associated with moving federal IT into the cloud.

My name is Nick Combs and I am the Chief Technology Officer for EMC Corporation's Federal Division. EMC is a global leader in cloud computing infrastructure and services. We enable the full realization of the inherent power of information by creating complete information environments that are reliable, efficient, and secure. With EMC, users and organizations can bring the power of information to life...information that illuminates what is possible and that moves the world forward. Prior to joining EMC, I served for more than 25 years in the Federal Government as a senior leader in the Army, Senior IT leader in the Defense Intelligence Agency and as an IT Director and CIO with the Director of National Intelligence. During my career in government and the IT industry, I personally experienced many of the IT the challenges facing federal agencies today, particularly as agencies transition to cloud services. In both the public and private sectors, I have worked with different types of cloud computing models, each of which had its own risk management, interoperability, and data portability requirements.

First, let me comment on the term "cloud computing" and its definition. Today, the term is one of the most common yet most misunderstood references to information technology and services. There are a number of definitions for cloud computing. For purposes of my testimony today, I will adopt the definition of The National Institute of Standards and Technology (NIST), which defines cloud computing as: "a model for enabling convenient, on-demand network access to a shared pool of configurable computing resources (e.g., networks, servers, storage, applications, and services) that can be rapidly provisioned and released with minimal management effort or service provider interaction."[1]

Given this understanding of cloud computing, I will address the various approaches to implementing the underlying infrastructure that facilitates cloud based solutions.

Confusion in the marketplace generally arises from discussion of different approaches to cloud deployment, that is to say discussions of Private, Community, Public, or Hybrid Clouds. Again, NIST has provided definitions of these delivery models that help provide more clarity

- **Private Cloud** is infrastructure deployed and operated exclusively for an organization or enterprise. It may be managed by the organization or by a third party, either on or off premise.
- **Community Cloud** is infrastructure shared by multiple organizations with similar missions, requirements, security concerns, etc. It also may be managed by the organizations or by a third party on or off premise.
- **Public cloud** is infrastructure made available to the general public. It is owned and operated by an organization selling cloud services.
- **Hybrid cloud** is infrastructure consisting of two or more clouds (private, community, or public) that remain unique entities but that are tied together by standardized or proprietary technology that enables data and application portability.[2]

The organizations represented at today's hearing collectively deploy all of these types of cloud computing models. EMC, for example, deploys solutions and services via private, community and public clouds. As an enterprise, EMC has used its solutions, as well as virtualization technology from VMware – the foundation of cloud infrastructure – as our IT organization leverages private clouds internally, reducing our IT costs and use of power resources. EMC has also been enabling customers to further their virtual datacenters and embrace cloud computing through the solutions and services it offers.

For example, through a public cloud, EMC's Mozy online backup and data recovery service provides peace of mind to over a million consumers and tens of thousands of individuals and businesses. EMC also teamed with Cisco and VMware to start the Virtual Computing Environment coalition, representing an unprecedented level of collaboration in development, services, and partner enablement that reduces risk in emerging cloud infrastructures in both the public and private sector. Just last month EMC announced the formation of a new Technical Advisory Board to shape the strategic vision of private clouds and beyond. This Board, comprised of recognized industry experts from business and academia, will focus on long-term technology strategy, industry trends, and advanced development opportunities and initiatives. Members were selected for their expertise and thought leadership in such key areas as server, networking, storage, virtualization, cloud computing, data structures, security, application middleware, and technical computing.

THE BENEFITS OF CLOUD COMPUTING

Cloud computing provides the characteristics that every IT organization needs by enabling IT infrastructures to be flexible, on-demand, efficient, and resilient. Organizations have been building IT systems the same way for the last 40 years and it is time for a change.

However, we can no longer afford to have these legacy and stove-piped, monolithic systems in which each requirement has its own IT system. Organizations have attempted to utilize Service Oriented Architectures (SOA) to bring these disparate IT systems together, but have struggled due to the lack of interoperability standards in designing IT systems. Cloud computing, based on open systems architectures and aligned to evolving cloud standards, can provide the foundation for future interoperable systems.

These new environments can dramatically reduce the largest costs associated with IT systems, particularly those related to operations and maintenance. According to the analyst firm IDC, more than 70 percent of organizations' IT budgets are dedicated to just keeping the lights on and only 30 percent of budgets are available to bring new capabilities to the organization. The Federal Government has spent billions of dollars for computers to create and process information, internal networks to move that information around, and hardware to store it. And don't forget about the application software for those internal processes and accounting. We are at a point where government agencies are spending a majority of IT budgets just to maintain our current systems and infrastructure. During my service in the federal government, I saw some government organizations with operating and management costs as high as 85 percent of their overall IT budget. Cloud Computing offers the means through which to address this imbalance.

Through the cloud, organizations can centrally manage their IT systems and provide uniform policy implementation. They will reduce their operating and management costs, thus freeing up resources to address other needs. For example, money previously devoted to simply maintaining the infrastructure could be used to increase the infrastructure's security posture. Cloud computing brings a level of automation to IT that dramatically reduces costs by sharing resources and frees up more resources to deliver the capabilities that organizations need.

FEDERAL STRATEGY FOR CLOUD COMPUTING

The transition to cloud computing will not occur overnight; rather it requires a journey to realize all the benefits the cloud has to offer. The federal government has many unique environments, but these organizations can benefit greatly from the successes that commercial organizations have already achieved through the adoption of cloud computing. The economies of scale, flexibility, and efficiencies of these cloud infrastructures will not only save us significant amounts of capital and maintenance costs, but enable us to apply and use information across our enterprises as never before.

One can only imagine all the ways in which information technology could be applied in the government if federal IT professionals were freed from the task of managing today's complicated and antiquated infrastructures. OMB Director Orszag made a similar point last month when he highlighted the fact that government organizations are unable to match the productivity and innovation of the private sector because of archaic and complicated computing infrastructure.[3] Cloud computing provides a mechanism to address this technology gap, allowing the federal government to unleash new innovations and improve productivity.

Many federal organizations have already begun to build a bridge to the cloud by adopting some form of virtualization. In fact, virtualization has become the foundation of the cloud and in my view, is the great enabler of cloud services across the various deployment models. Cloud computing is virtualization taken to its most logical extreme, creating the ultimate in flexibility and efficiency, and revolutionizing the way we compute, network, store, and manage information. Virtualization capabilities are also evolving outside the server realm. In fact, EMC recently announced breakthrough capabilities that enable virtual storage over distance. The industry's first distributed storage federation will provide unprecedented business agility by eliminating the current boundaries of physical storage. This is a key enabler to future cloud architectures.

CLOUD SECURITY AND RISK MANAGEMENT

Information security is by far the biggest concern of federal CIOs considering implementing cloud infrastructure and services. According to an April 2010 Lockheed Martin Cyber Security Alliance survey of U.S. federal government, defense, and intelligence agency decision makers, respondents were most concerned by data security, privacy and integrity in the cloud.[4] In addition, 46 percent of respondents to the Ponemon Institute's November 2009 "Cyber Security Mega Trends" survey of IT leaders in the U.S. federal government indicated that cloud computing increases security risk within their organization.[5] The biggest security concern noted by Ponemon survey respondents (30 percent) was the inability to protect sensitive or confidential information and the second most significant concern (20 percent) was to restrict or limit the use of computing resources or applications.

Admittedly, with cloud computing come sophisticated automation, provisioning and virtualization technologies that have significant security implications, so we must look at security in a whole new way. In March of 2010, RSA the Security Division of EMC, unveiled a shared vision with Intel Corporation and VMware for building a more secure and transparent infrastructure for business-critical cloud services. While perimeter and point security products will still be used by organizations, companies such as EMC and VMware are embedding controls and security management in the virtual layer, creating an environment in the virtual world that is far safer than what exists in the physical. Industry must continue to develop and deliver technology components that support centralized, consistent management of security across the technology stack. Security must be dynamic and intelligent. The static, reactive environment developed in the past simply will not work.

With virtualization and cloud computing, applications have become completely disassociated from the IT infrastructure on which they run. It provides the flexibility to have the same application run in the datacenter next door on one day, in a centralized datacenter hundreds of miles away the following day, and in a service provider datacenter another day. For that reason, security cannot solely rely on the controls of the IT infrastructure such as the network perimeter. Security must evolve to become much more centered on the users and on the information they are accessing. For that reason, emerging technology practices, such as adaptive authentication and data loss prevention, are both widely used in the commercial world. However, they are only beginning to be adopted in federal government organizations. Such practices must be more broadly deployed. This environment must be transparent to the enterprise and to the user. Security cannot be an after thought; it must be embedded in the fabric. It must be built into the products and infrastructure by the vendor community.

For a decade, fraudsters have been crafting malware to steal users' passwords and perform fraudulent actions on their online bank accounts. Cloud computing can increase the risk of exposing corporate assets to fraudsters and cybercriminals. The automaker's next design is worth more on the black market than online bank accounts. The same malware used to steal online banking password is also being used to steal corporate passwords. In the age of cloud computing, solely relying on passwords to protect access to cloud applications is not sufficient. Additional best practices like risk based authentication must be employed and we think that that approach will fit well within the Trusted Identity strategy that is currently being developed by the Obama Administration.

When implemented correctly, cloud environments can be much more secure than today's IT environments, which are often protected by inadequate perimeter security practices. The level of transparency cloud vendors provide is a critical aspect when choosing a cloud partner. While there is a lot of talk about Service Level Agreements (SLA) helping to satisfy federal government information security needs, this alone is inadequate. The federal government must take a trust-but-verify approach. Cloud vendors should be required to provide the tools and capabilities to allow customers visibility into their cloud environments to ensure compliance with those SLAs. SLAs should be clearly defined and monitored by government customers to ensure maximum service value is received for budget dollars spent. For instance, SLAs in areas of performance, availability, backup and recovery, archive, continuance of operation, and disaster recovery must be clearly stated, measured, and monitored by the government agencies. Additionally government risk and compliance capabilities need to be deployed and dash boards provided to the customer to ensure that our information is protected and our policies are being followed.

Security must be risk-based and driven by flexible policy that is aligned to the business or mission need. The need for a common framework to ensure that security policies are consistently applied across the infrastructure is critical to the success. That is one of the principle reasons that EMC supports updating the Federal Information Security and Management Act or FISMA, important legislation that will update the law to enable more operational risk management, which is essential in both today's environment and the evolving cloud computing infrastructure.

Technologies and effective best practices exist today to deliver private cloud environments inside federal organizations to gain dramatic improvements in IT efficiency, while also providing the security required to protect sensitive information within the government enterprise. Multi-tenant federated clouds can be deployed where similar security requirements exist. However, placing information on a public cloud today should be limited to public facing information only and then only if the providers can provide the level of auditing and protection procedures needed to deal with breaches of sensitive information.

CONCLUSION

I again thank the Committee for allowing EMC and I to contribute to this very important effort. IT is on the verge of dramatic change; cloud computing has the potential to have the most significant impact on IT since the development of the microprocessor. We have to remain focused to ensure we get it right. This will be a journey and we will realize benefits at many points along the way and it will provide organizations with much greater flexibility to meet the demanding needs of our federal government. Admittedly, security is a top concern, but the technology and best practices exist to address that risk. A critical part of the solution lies in engineering security into the cloud, not bolting it on as an afterthought. Ultimately, cloud computing offers great potential for federal information technology, and federal departments and agencies should be encouraged to embrace that potential.

End Notes

[1]: "The NIST Definition of Cloud Computing" by Peter Mell and Tim Grance, Version 15, 10/7/2009.
[2] "The NIST Definition of Cloud Computing" by Peter Mell and Tim Grance, Version 15, 10/7/2009.
[3] Remarks by Peter Orszag, Center for American Progress, June 8, 2010, Washington, DC.
[4] "Awareness, Trust and Security to Shape Cloud Adoption," a survey commissioned by the Lockheed Martin Cyber Security Alliance and conducted by Market Connnections, Inc., April 2010
[5] "Cyber Security Mega Trends: Study of IT leaders in the U.S. federal government", Independently conducted by Ponemon Institute LLC; Publication Date: November 18, 2009.

In: Cloud Computing and Government: Background, Benefits... ISBN: 978-1-61761-784-3
Editor: George I. Nikolov © 2011 Nova Science Publishers, Inc.

Chapter 13

WRITTEN TESTIMONY OF GREGORY R. GANGER, PROFESSOR OF ELECTRICAL & COMPUTER ENGINEERING AND COMPUTER SCIENCE, CARNEGIE MELLON UNIVERSITY, BEFORE THE HOUSE COMMITTEE ON OVERSIGHT AND GOVERNMENT REFORM, HEARING ON "CLOUD COMPUTING: BENEFITS AND RISKS OF MOVING FEDERAL IT INTO THE CLOUD"

I thank you for the opportunity to testify about the benefits and risks of using cloud computing for federal IT functions.

About me: My name is Gregory (Greg) R. Ganger. I am a Professor of Electrical & Computer Engineering and Computer Science at Carnegie Mellon University (CMU). For the last ten years, I have also served as Director of CMU's Parallel Data Lab (PDL). The PDL is a world-renowned research center focused on storage and large-scale infrastructures, such as cloud computing and more traditional data centers, regularly working with and annually supported by most of the major developers of technology in these areas. Current industry sponsors include Google, Microsoft, Yahoo!, VMware, HP, IBM, Intel, Oracle, Facebook, APC (of Schneider Electric), EMC, Hitachi, LSI, NEC, NetApp, Seagate, and Symantec.

I have been conducting research on large-scale computing and storage infrastructures (e.g., cloud computing) and their operation/administration for over a decade. Among the cloud computing projects I lead are CMU's Data Center Observatory (DCO) and the CMU portion of OpenCirrus. The DCO was conceived as a consolidated data center and private cloud for research computing/storage needs, but heavily instrumented and forward-looking to enable research into efficiency, and it is being realized with active collaboration from several of the PDL sponsor companies. OpenCirrus (https://opencirrus.org/) is an open cloud computing testbed currently consisting of ten sites worldwide, each of which provides public cloud computing resources via open interfaces and open source software.

Testimony roadmap: I have been asked to testify about the use of cloud computing for federal IT needs, including potential benefits, risks, challenges, and consequences. My written testimony is organized as follows. First, I provide a brief review of cloud computing generally, highlighting a few forms that it can take, including the highly relevant concept of a so-called "private" (or "internal") cloud. Second, I discuss the large potential benefits of using cloud computing for federal IT functions, which are similar (in many cases) to those for large corporate organizations. I highlight the benefits first because, while I suspect that most questions will focus on the risks and challenges, overall thinking about the concept of using cloud computing resources for federal IT functions should not lose sight of the large potential benefits of this young, maturing technology. Third, I discuss various risks, challenges, and consequences. Some of these (e.g., resistance to change) will require continuing education and strong guidance, possibly including explicit incentives. Some of these (e.g., lock-in and management complexity) will require patient and incremental approach to moving federal IT into the cloud, as advancement in both technology creation and standards bodies address unresolved issues. A few (e.g., security) may require certain IT functions to never migrate fully to a public cloud. None, however, preclude rapid partial migration of federal IT function into the cloud and expanded migration over time.

It is important to keep in mind, while considering pros and cons of moving federal IT into clouds, that it is far from an all-or-nothing decision. For some federal IT functions, it will be the right choice, and for others it may not be. The choice need not be the same for all IT functions, and movement can happen independently for each, allowing incremental movements that each yield benefits.

A. CLOUD COMPUTING BASICS

Very broadly, "cloud computing" involves using someone else's computers (and possibly software setups), shared with yet other groups, for some task instead of using your own. There are many technical issues involved, which have delayed the realization of this long-sought notion of computing services as utilities, but the basic concept of outsourcing work is natural in today's service-based economy.

The "cloud" aspect refers to the fact that the computers used are on the network, somewhere, but that the cloud computing customer need not be aware of where they are or details of how the outsourced work is completed – it is referred to as "in the cloud", because large networks (e.g., the Internet) are often illustrated as clouds in technical diagrams.

The term "cloud computing" has been applied to a broad class of IT outsourcing activities, leading to broad definitions. For example, NIST's definition[1] is more technical than my very brief description above, but it closes with "and is composed of five essential characteristics, three delivery models, and four deployment models." Just the cross-product of the three delivery and four deployment models yields twelve configurations that fit the definition. I will not detail the full breadth here, but I will highlight a couple configuration options in an attempt to help clarify cloud computing and important issues involved.

Raw resources vs. software services: The delivery model axis relates to the form of computing service purchased from a cloud computing provider. One option, called

"Infrastructure as a Service (IaaS)" by NIST, is to rent raw computing resources, such as computer time or storage capacity. Which programs a customer runs in their rented computer time,[2] or what data is stored in rented storage capacity, is entirely up to the customer (who must, therefore, configure and maintain the programs themselves). Setting aside technical details, the IaaS concept should be familiar to anyone who has rented a car, exercised in a fitness center, or stayed at a hotel. The other two options, called "Software as a Service (SaaS)" and "Platform as a Service (PaaS)" by NIST, provide complete applications (e.g., email) and/or building blocks (e.g., database systems) for use by customers (and perhaps provided by customers to third parties). Setting aside technical details, these concepts are akin to outsourcing of food services, patent litigation services, or accounting services.

Public cloud vs. private cloud: The deployment model axis focuses on who shares the cloud. One option, termed a "public cloud" by NIST, is made available to the general public by a provider selling cloud computing services. This is the option usually in mind when people first think about cloud computing, since it matches the general accessibility of the Internet. But, it is not the only option. Another option, termed a "private cloud" by NIST, is operated solely by one organization and shared by its various sub-parts. For particularly large organizations, such as the federal government or a large Internet service company (e.g., Google or Microsoft), many of the benefits of cloud computing can be realized with a private cloud model – for such organizations, the economies of scale and aggregation are sufficiently present without sharing externally, because of their many sizable sub-organizations.[3] Of course, an organization can use more than one cloud, including of different types, and can also used both cloud and non-cloud (i.e., their own) computer resources.

B. POTENTIALBENEFITS OF MOVINGFEDERAL IT FUNCTIONSINTO THE CLOUD

Cloud computing has the potential to provide large efficiency improvements for federal IT functions. As with outsourcing in non-IT domains, such as rental cars and food services, the efficiency arises from having multiple customers (organizations) share the provider's offering instead of each providing for itself. Efficiency improvements come from multiple fundamental sources, including: (1) increased utilization of resources, since sharing allows the portions unused by one customer to be sold to (used by) another, while each customer pays for just what they use; (2) economies of scale, since operational costs usually do not scale down linearly with resource size – for example, one cannot use a part of a car, and cooking for two takes nearly as long as cooking for five; (3) increased specialization, since experts working for the provider can focus on the one offering rather than being "jacks of all trades"; (4) low entry cost (in terms of time, effort, and dollars) for new customers, since the resource is already set up by the provider and ready for use. These benefits can all be present for cloud computing, with large potential reductions in IT costs (both capital and personnel), energy demands (due to the need for fewer total computers), and time to establish new IT functions.

Although concision precludes full analysis here, two examples can help illustrate potential infrastructure efficiency benefits of even just one or two of these sources:

- Although an imperfect example, because of artifacts of CMU's smaller size and relative resource-poorness, our experiences making a case for using cloud computing for research computing at CMU provide some insight. In surveying the separate infrastructures used by research groups on campus, we found average utilizations around 25% -- that is, ¾ of the work potential of the computers went unused, over time, even in a University research environment that struggles to find funds to purchase equipment.[4] A private IaaS cloud computing approach with 75% utilization would reduce the number of servers needed by 66% or allow three times the work to be completed during heavily active times, which has induced us to aggressively pursue deployment of such a private cloud at CMU. Such numbers are normal, even laudable for the traditional "every group for themselves" approach, not a sign of misbehavior. Indeed, a GSA presentation[5] indicated "Average Server Utilization" values of 7-15%, offering even more room for improvement.
- HP's recent data center consolidation effort provides a second example. In 2006, HP identified their "many separate data centers" deployment (85 data centers across 29 countries) as a significant source of inefficiency. They noted plans to consolidate into six large data centers, estimating $1B/year savings in IT expenses and significant energy savings as a result.[6] Recently, HP's CIO Randy Mott shared some outcomes of this successful consolidation effort, including 60% reduction in overall data center costs.[7] Despite ever-growing demands for computing, HP reduced their number of server computers by 40%, which would combine with their improved cooling approaches to yield significant energy savings.

The savings in these examples do not even account for the much improved IT staff efficiency (#3 above) or the faster pace of deployed IT improvements (a consequence of #3). With consolidated infrastructures, IT staff specializing in particular aspects can focus on those aspects – because of the large scale, such specialization does not lead to excessively sized IT staffs. Since the particular aspects (e.g., network management or storage management) are handled by the provider, none of the customers need to employ staff focused on those aspects – one set of staff handles them for all, eliminating redundancy across customers and allowing customer IT staff's to focus on the customer's missions instead. Also, because specialized staff have fewer aspects to manage, they can focus more attention on improving their specific aspects, leading to more rapid adoption of new technologies and best practices from which all customers immediately benefit.

In addition to significantly increasing efficiency across a set of current customer IT functions, cloud computing can greatly improve the situation for new IT functions (#4 above). Traditionally, a lengthy start-up process is often involved with establishing a new IT function, including procuring new computers (and sometimes building machine room space to power and cool them), installing and configuring the computers, and only then finally starting to set up the IT function in question. With cloud computing, one can rent pre-setup computer resources as soon as one has budget to do so, leading to much quicker progress on new directions. Moreover, one does not have the danger of incorrectly guessing how many computers are needed (which can lead to waste or delays), since the cloud provider allows rapid incremental scale-up (charging only for what is used) as long as the customer is willing to pay for what they use. Among other things, therefore, cloud computing could significantly accelerate deployment of e-government applications.

Overall, the potential benefits from cloud computing are huge, both for global efficiency (total equipment and energy used) and for each customer (dollars and mission focus).

C. RISKS, CHALLENGES, AND CONSEQUENCES

Cloud computing is very different from the traditional approach of each organization (e.g., agency) creating and maintaining their own computing resources, from top to bottom. Naturally, there are many challenges to be faced in making the significant transition to outsourcing aspects to external providers, particularly given the relative youth and rapid evolution of cloud computing. Of course, there are security concerns when an external provider is made part of an agency function. There are also "lock-in" concerns caused by lack of standardization and (in some cases) the difficulty of moving large data sets. Another significant source of challenges is the massive IT culture change inherent in a transition to cloud computing, which will require overcoming resistance to change and retooling IT staff skill sets.

Security concerns: Security is an issue for all networked computer activities. It is natural to imagine that security might be weakened by involving an external provider, particularly when confidential data are involved. But, it is not necessarily the case in all, or even most, circumstances. As in the real world, computer security is about risk management, not absolutes – most of us feel relatively secure in our homes, for example, despite glass windows on the ground floor.

Having federal agencies maintaining infrastructure does not guarantee their security, both because humans are imperfect and because no perfect computer security technologies exist. Public cloud providers are capable of employing the same best practices and technology as government agencies and potentially upgrading more rapidly to new advances (because of #3 above). The question is whether or not they can be trusted to do so. To establish that trust, there will need to be certification of the degree of trust that can be placed in a given provider, using established (e.g., FISMA) and perhaps new mechanisms – standardized approaches to doing this is an area of necessary, and ongoing, effort in technology working groups. Movement of IT functions to providers must be limited to those pairings with acceptable risk. Certain functions, and certain data, will perhaps never be appropriate for public clouds – highly classified intelligence activities, for example. But, for many federal computing activities, security needs are likely to be consistent with those of corporate customers of public clouds.

It is worth noting that private clouds, maintained by the government, can be used for IT functions that may require security efforts beyond those that public cloud providers are willing to employ (e.g., because they go beyond what corporate customers require).

Lock-in concerns: Currently, cloud computing offerings are diverse – one can choose among several to which to migrate a function, and then go thru the effort to migrate, but often there is no easy way to switch from one provider to another. Today, such a switch can involve time-consuming extraction of one's data, reprogramming of one's application to fit the new provider's interfaces, and uploading of one's data to the new provider. Each step can be onerous.

One big part of the problem is standardization or, rather, lack thereof. Although various working groups are now focused on standardization, it is still early in the process.

Indeed, cloud computing is sufficiently new that there is some danger in standardizing so quickly, with such a short window of experience from which to draw. Nonetheless, standardization is an important part of promoting compatibility and competition among cloud computing providers.

A technical issue, for IT functions that involve very large data sets, is the time required to upload or download the data. For example, at commonly available wide-area networking (WAN) rates, transferring multi-terabyte datasets to or form a public cloud could require multiple weeks, which would make the concept of migrating a high hurdle. This is a challenge that federal customers share with corporate customers, and technical solutions will undoubtedly be developed.

Resistance to change: Some of the trickier challenges faced when efficiency-seeking leaders push their IT staff to move some functions to a cloud are non-technical, relating to human nature. Some (not all!) IT staff resist changes to currently working practices that they control and understand. I suspect that, where it exists, this resistance will be stronger in consistently-funded government IT settings, where business-style pressures and incentives (e.g., bonuses) for innovative steps leading to tangible savings are not present. Simply demanding an IT change rarely yields desired outcomes, as unhappy IT staff can become inefficient in a variety of ways. A mixture of push (e.g., requests and insistent education) and pull (e.g., incentives) may be needed to effect rapid and positive adoption.

Perhaps the most common form for such resistance to take is aggressive arguing against the change in question, on technical grounds and by overstating the effort required to enact the change. The awkward aspects of such arguments are usually twofold: the IT staff raising them generally know more than anyone else in the organization about the technical issues in question, and the arguments raised generally are at least partially correct. A mixture of education (for the IT staff and their managers) and a technical mindshare (for both to utilize) may be needed to separate the legitimate concerns from those based primarily on a desire to avoid change.

The technical mindshare should also provide for sharing of effort on issues like certification/accreditation (e.g., for security issues discussed above), verifying continued good practices, negotiating Terms of Service (ToS), and procurement (e.g., multiple bids obtained and okayed periodically). Forcing every agency to independently deal with such issues truly could become a significant barrier, but a shared clearinghouse is a natural way to eliminate redundant effort for common needs. Note that none of my discussion is meant to imply that actions, including those that I mention, are not already being pursued in the context of the Federal Cloud Computing Initiative; indeed, some are (e.g., see apps.gov).

IT culture changes: A consequence of moving to cloud computing is major change for IT staff. Note that even full transition to cloud computing would not mean elimination of all IT staff – not by a long shot. Expert IT personnel will be needed to assist with planning, to provision, and to manage IT functions outsourced to the cloud. But, the expertise that they will need is going to be different. Rather than expertise in managing the aspects now outsourced (e.g., physical computers, networks, and building-block applications), for example, IT staff and managers will need new expertise in working with cloud-based activities, projecting usage costs rather than capital costs, and there may be reduced separation between application engineers and IT staff. Continued education for IT personnel, and perhaps a new breed of staff, will be an important part of such transition.

Not only will new IT expertise be needed to manage functions outsourced to the cloud, but a hybrid IT model is most likely for quite some time − some functions will be moved to one or more clouds, while others remain "in house". Thus, the IT staff will need to manage a set of functions spread across multiple environments, using new integrated management tools. Creation of such tools can be expected, as particular cloud interfaces become very popular and/or standardized.

D. Concluding Remarks

Cloud computing is an exciting realization of a long-sought concept: computing as a utility. Pursuing judicious use for federal IT functions is important, given the large potential benefits. Patience, perseverance, incremental adoption, and continued investment in research, education, and standardization related to cloud computing will be needed in realizing that potential. Some specific recommendations for consideration that follow from my observations include:

- First, cloud computing is a big change, and realizing its large potential will require significant formal technical and change management training for IT staff and managers. This need may warrant expansion or adaptation of programs like "scholarship for service" as well as targeted executive education initiatives.
- Second, standardization is important to address lock-in concerns, but continued experimentation (including research, testbeds, and case studies) and innovation are also crucial given the relative youth of cloud computing and the presence of unresolved technical questions (e.g., in security, data transfer, and management). The natural tension between these two needs may warrant focused programs for each in order to avoid lack of progress on either.
- Third, information and effort sharing across federal agencies considering cloud computing will be an important aspect of overcoming resistance to change. Explicit support should exist for shared technical mindshare, provider tracking/clearing, and case study reporting.

It is my hope that my testimony has helped to clarify some of the major technical matters and logistics associated with the idea of using cloud computing for federal IT. For non-technical practitioners, I recognize that digesting the concepts and evaluating the merits of cloud computing is no easy feat. Yet, I understand how important it is for members of the Committee to have trust and confidence in the IT directions taken by federal agencies, given the expense and mission importance of IT. As leaders in the realm of technology and innovation, please know that we at Carnegie Mellon University stand ready to assist you in dealing with technical questions as they relate to your efforts to craft sound public policy and oversee federal IT activities. We applaud your diligence in reviewing this specific matter.

Again, thank you for the opportunity to testify. I will be happy to answer any questions the Committee might have.

End Notes

[1] The full NIST definition is two pages long, but the primary paragraph states "Cloud computing is a model for enabling convenient, on-demand network access to a shared pool of configurable computing resources (e.g., networks, servers, storage, applications, and services) that can be rapidly provisioned and released with minimal management effort or service provider interaction. This cloud model promotes availability and is composed of five essential **characteristics,** three **service models**, and four **deployment models**." Most of the remainder details the five, three, and four. The latest version (v15) can be found at http://csrc.nist.gov/groups/SNS/cloud-computing/cloud-def-v15.doc .

[2] Rented raw computer time in most cloud offerings is used to execute software encapsulated in a so-called "virtual machine", which appears to the customer as a physical machine. Indeed, all cloud resources are "virtualized" in the sense that details of how they are provided are hidden from customers and may not match the appearance given to the customer – such virtualization enables improved efficiency and is fine for customers, so long as the behavior promised to the customer is realized.

[3] As one example, the National Business Center (NBC) of the Department of the Interior now provides some private cloud capabilities (http://cloud.nbc.gov/).

[4] But, during active times, they tend to be overburdened.

[5] "GSA Presentation on the Federal Cloud Computing Initiative" by Michael Goodrich (Project Manager, FedRAMP and Apps.gov, General Services Administration) on Software & Information Industry Association panel. See slide 22. Available at http://www.siia.net/blog/index.php/2010/06/gsa-presentation-on-the-federal-cloud-computing-initiative/

[6] http://news.cnet.com/HP-plans-data-center-consolidation

[7] http://www. Enter prisenetworkingplanet. com/news/article.php/3878966

In: Cloud Computing and Government: Background, Benefits...   ISBN: 978-1-61761-784-3
Editor: George I. Nikolov   © 2011 Nova Science Publishers, Inc.

Chapter 14

CLOUD COMPUTING: OVERVIEW OF INFORMATION ASSURANCE CONCERNS AND OPPORTUNITIES

National Security Agency

CLOUD TECHNOLOGY INTRODUCTION

Cloud computing is an emerging trend which has progressed to the point of serious adoption in both public and private sector organizations, yet it remains a relatively immature paradigm, one which dictates a revision to the traditional characterization of risk in information technology environments. As a means of an introduction to those changes, this paper offers an overview of the information assurance aspects of cloud computing with a focus on potential security advantages and pitfalls. While many of the security concerns associated with cloud computing are shared with traditional computing models, this paper will focus on those issues unique to cloud computing or that are exacerbated by it. The intended audience is anyone who is considering the adoption of cloud computing and who needs to understand the security risks and potential opportunities cloud computing provides as part of a risk management process.

Cloud computing is an evolving concept and various definitions have been offered, some with widely varying scope. However, boiled down to the basic concepts and simply stated, cloud computing can be described as a style of computing in which dynamically scalable and often virtualized resources are provided as a service over the network.[1] Examples of cloud computing delivery models vary from *infrastructure as a service* (IaaS) where one can lease capabilities such as storage or computing resources (e.g., Amazon Simple Storage Service and Elastic Compute Cloud), *platform as a service* (PaaS) where one can lease an application development environment (e.g., The Microsoft Azure Services Platform) and *software as a service* (SaaS)which offers network basedapplications (e.g., Facebook, Google docs). The figure at the right illustrates how these various classes of cloud computing offerings build upon one another and offers additional examples from the commercial space.

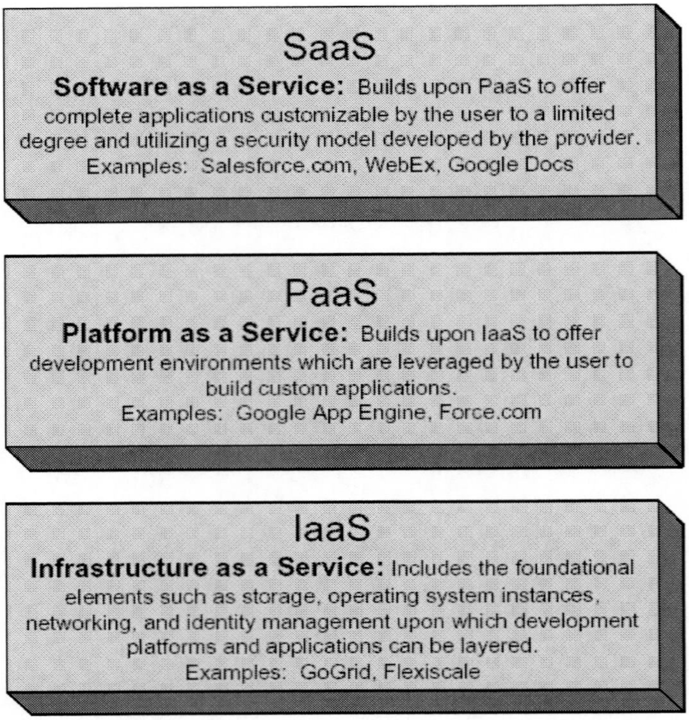

Figure 1. Cloud Service Delivery Models

IA CONCERNS

When considering the risk associated with cloud computing, the most fundamental element that must be considered is how the cloud environment affects the trust boundary. In thinking about this question, first consider a traditional computing model, one where applications reside on client machines or somewhere else on the infrastructure owned and controlled by the enterprise. In this environment it is possible to levy a host of countermeasures to mitigate the security risks that exist in the information technology world. Those countermeasures can include firewalls, data encryption, antivirus solutions, tight access permissions, separation of networks either virtually or physically, and more. Coupled with those technical countermeasures are the use of trusted administrators, trusted application developers, and internal processes which should reflect the value of the network and the data which resides on it. Now consider what happens when the application is moved to a cloud infrastructure provided by an outside provider, one whose business model is typically driven by the provision of a common service to a wide variety of customers. At this point the security of that data is largely a function of the skill, willingness, diligence, and fiscal ability of the provider to protect the data and provide reliable service.

The trust boundary will vary depending on the type of cloud service in question as shown in Figure 2, a presentation adopted from one offered by the Cloud Security Alliance [13]. This illustrates the software development process and notes that for traditional applications which are developed and deployed in-house, the architecture and design, development, testing, and deployment can be accomplished with trusted individuals using tools and processes integral to the enterprise. Certainly risks remain, even outside of the application development process, but the high degree of control and ownership allows a layering of process and technical countermeasures. At the other end of the spectrum, SaaS allows the user very limited control over the application, with customizations typically limited to a narrow set.

Due to this issue of the movement of the trust boundary, public clouds (whereby cloud resources are dynamically provisioned over the Internet) represent the greatest challenge from a security perspective. While the specific concerns will vary somewhat depending upon the type of cloud service (IaaS, PaaS, or SaaS) there are some general issues incumbent in all three:

- *Trust Boundary:* Just how far does the trust boundary extend? This can be a lot further than is immediately obvious - for example, a separate provider might be utilized for aspects of the service, as is the case with Facebook applications which can utilize Amazon Web Services [4, 7] for storage and other services. This notion of utilizing layers of providers is one that has many tentacles, each of which can ensnare a user in ways that are perhaps not immediately obvious. For example, how do the laws in those countries where the data is ultimately stored affect the security of data in the cloud?Do competitors or other adversaries now have easier access to that data by virtue of the country used for physical storage?
- *Access Control*: How is access control within the cloud environment maintained and how are users' various cloud environments isolated from each other? What provision is made for remote administration? At the cloud provider's site, how is administrative access to the infrastructure policed? If the provider is acquired by another company or engages in an alliance that would change the dynamic of this access, would customers be notified and be allowed time to react, perhaps by switching providers?
- *Incident handling:* What are the provider's responsibilities when an intrusion, suspected intrusion, or security vulnerability is noted? How does the move to a cloud infrastructure impact any forensic procedures associated with incident recovery? As an example of the latter, in the event an employee is suspected of violating a company policy or law, or in response to a suspect intrusion, it may be standard practice to immediately create an image of the user's client machine. If that platform exists in the cloud, will that option still be available?
- *The "ilities":* Can the cloud provider offer adequate reliability, availability, and quality of service? The cloud can complicate questions such as availability in ways perhaps wholly unexpected by those accustomed to traditional computing paradigms. Take the case of the FBI's execution of a warrant against a data center, targeting individuals suspected of fraud and confiscating computers related to the suspects, but also housing the digital presence of a dozen other businesses, at least one of which was unable to execute their business [16].

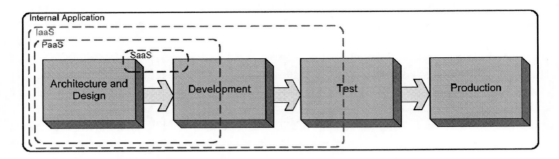

Figure 2. Public Cloud Trust Boundaries

- *Data backup:* Are backups of data and other perishables such as source code and configuration files the responsibility of the provider or the consumer? If the responsibility of the provider, how quickly can one expect data to be recovered? Can the entire image be restored as well as individual files?
- *Data purging:* Do you need a means of ensuring that deleted data is truly deleted and does not remain in an archive? For example, in a cloud application, is there an ability to truly delete an account or is it simply deactivated [6]?
- *Security Management:* Who is responsible for security management issues such as auditing and patch management? This is particularly topical when dealing with situations where security management may be a shared responsibility such as in the case of PaaS where the final installation may be a blend of network elements, operating systems, and tools offered by the cloud provider with a smattering of customer applications riding on top.
- *Provider's Pedigree:* What is the history of the provider with regards to security, incidence response, and availability? While past performance is no guarantee of future behavior, it can be an indicator. Also consider the security related certifications obtained by the provider - while the value of such certifications can be debated, if their limits are understood they can offer value.
- *Data Rights:* What rights are relinquished to data stored in the cloud? Some user access agreements have given the cloud provider unlimited rights, in perpetuity [14].
- *Accreditation:* What impact does using the cloud have upon the user's ability to obtain necessary accreditations or certifications for their applications? One simple example is storage - in some environments there may be a requirement that certain data types cannot be transmitted or stored overseas.
- *Business Continuity:* What happens if the cloud provider goes out of business or simply decides to exit the business? Will users be given an opportunity to migrate applications and retrieve data before the provider's site goes down? Are users now locked into proprietary formats that hinder that movement to another provider? Do users own any domain names that are used to access data or applications?

Rest assured this is more than a case of paranoia. As more and more data moves to the cloud, the attackers are following, with high profile attacks against several cloud computing sites already in the proverbial history books of the web. References to several real-world examples have been provided at the end of this document [5, 8, 15, 17]. Other proverbial "war stories" include lost photographs when a vendor exited the on-line image storage business, the organization who thought "it was *their* responsibility to do backups", and a site where access control mechanisms have been thwarted repeatedly. In fact, nearly all - if not all - of the issues identified above have real-world examples associated with them.

Unfortunately, in the predator-prey relationship that so aptly characterizes security, the story of the attacker's reaction to cloud computing doesn't end with attacks against the cloud services, but extends to using those services as launching pads for compromising client computers. Their techniques include enticing users to download malicious code, posting links to malicious web sites that have the capability of achieving drive-by downloading attacks, cross-site scripting, and more.

COUNTERMEASURES

So, how does one counter the uncertainty and risk of using public cloud resources? There are a range of options:

- *Limit Use:* Don't use the public cloud for sensitive data. For example, one might limit the data placed on a social networking site to data that one truly intends to be publicly available and not rely on any privacy or data confidentiality features the provider might offer. User training is a key element here.
- *Encryption:* Encrypt data before uploading it to the cloud. This could be a good solution for folks who are looking at the cloud as a means of data storage.
- *Characterize the Vendor:* Attempt to gain confidence in the provider and obtain answers to the security concerns posed by this document and others that may be unique to a situation. The question of enforcement of the expectations one obtains through such insight is paramount and, while service level agreements and contract mechanisms can play a role, such legal distinctions are well beyond the scope of this document. Note there may be a practical limit to the insight and control one can gain through such means when dealing with providers who are in the business of providing a common service to the masses.
- *Utilize Safe Web Surfing Practices*: Since that attacker's motivation is not focused solely on compromising cloud services, but using those services as a platform for compromising client computers, following safe web surfing practices is paramount. NSA's *Mitigation Monday #2, Defense against Drive-By Downloads* [11] describes technical steps that can be taken to reduce such risks, and US-CERT offers guidelines which also extend into the behavioral aspects of safe web surfing [3].
- *Use Private Clouds:* Avoid, or limit, dependence on public cloud services by utilizing a private cloud. While in a public cloud, the service is open to possible exploitation by the internet community at large, moving to a private cloud has the effect of limiting the threat exposure by restricting access to a much greater degree through layers of protection mechanisms such as firewalls and routing restrictions. Practically speaking, for many organizations a mix of public and private clouds will prove optimal. In essence, organizations might use their risk management and return

on investment analysis to choose the most cost effective architecture that meets their security needs.

IA OPPORTUNITIES

To security practitioners, this notion of using private clouds - cloud services implemented behind the firewall on the enterprise's networks - eliminate the most perplexing security issues of cloud computing by avoiding the extension of the security boundary that is at the heart of public cloud security issues. Hybrids, which include characteristics of both public and private clouds exist as well, but will not be explored here.

Private clouds are catching on. Security concerns are part of the reason they are chosen over public clouds, but cost is also a consideration as some organizations have concluded the fiscal benefits of using a public cloud disappear in the context of a long term, large scale project - they conclude it's cheaper to roll their own private cloud [2].

From a security perspective, what potential benefits can cloud computing provide, specifically in the context of a private cloud? If it's done right, there are several:

- Manageability may be improved by the consolidation incumbent in moving disparate applications to an enterprise cloud. Some organizations have realized significant simplification of their application space by consolidating their business apps into a much smaller number of cloud assets [2]. Others talk about how they have used the cloud to simplify the application of patches - clone the environment, patch, test, and deploy.
  One of the most fundamental steps one needs to take toward securing a network is making certain it is manageable - understanding what is on your network and being able to perform security management. Consolidation and simplification aid manageability and are nice security enablers.
- Auditing and security monitoring may be simplified in this more consolidated environment.
- Scalability, and therefore availability, may be improved. Some of the key tool providers in the cloud computing space advertise a capability to easily add storage and processing capability to the pool of resources available to cloud applications.
- Some aspects of data protection can be simplified. It may be easier to protect data at rest if it exists in a limited number of locations vice being spread out across the enterprise on an untold number of desktop or laptop hard drives.
- It is possible to leverage particular aspects of cloud services to provide some unique security benefit. For example, the DISA RACE cloud infrastructure offers the ability to obtain an operating system image pre-configured to recommended security guidelines [12]. Utilizing such an image can assist developers in ensuring that applications are compatible with securely configured platforms and can help establish that systems used operationally begin in a sound configuration. One can also consider provisioning such images with the proper security tools as appropriate to the intended usage of the platform - that could include everything from code scanning tools for developers to antivirus solutions.

IN CLOSING

Thoughts on the information assurance impact of cloud computing are continuing to evolve as this technological model matures. The Cloud Security Alliance's *Security Guidelines for Critical Areas of Focus in Cloud Computing* [13] delves much more deeply into many of the issues raised here, representing the census thoughts of many experts in the cloud computing and information assurance arenas. It is highly recommended reading.

REFERENCES

Amazon Web Services: Overview of Security Processes. http://s3.amazonaws.com/aws_blog/ AWS_Security_Whitepaper_2008_09.pdf

Capturing the Private Cloud. A description of the fiscal motivations driving some to choose private clouds over public. http://gcn.com/Articles/2009/07/13/Private-cloud-computing-for-government.aspx

Cyber Security Tips. A variety of technical and behavioral guidelines for safe usage of the Internet. http://www.us-cert.gov/cas/tips/

Facebook and AWS. A description of how developers can use Amazon Web Services to build Facebook applications. http://aws.amazon.com/solutions/featured-partners/facebook/

Facebook Hit by Five Security Problems in One Week. http://www.pcworld.com/article/ 160545/facebook_hit_by_five_security_problems_in_on e_week.html

Facebook Needs To Improve Privacy Practices, Investigation Finds. A look at Facebook security as compared to Canadian privacy laws. http://www.priv.gc.ca/media/nrc/ 2009/nr-c_090716_e.cfm

Hosting Facebook Applications on Amazon EC2. A tutorial describing how to host a Facebook application utilizing cloud services from Amazon. http://developer.am azonwebservices.com/connect/entry.jspa?entryID=1044

Imageshack Hacked By Anti-Full Disclosure Movement. Describes an attack whereby users where redirected to a single image explaining why the site was hacked. http://blogs.zdnet.com/security/?p=3725

Lawyers Shine Light On Real Cloud Concerns. A summary of legal issues surrounding the use of cloud computing. http://news.cnet.com/8301-19413_3-10286028-240.html?part= rss&subj=news&tag=2547-1_3-0-20

Microsoft's Azure Cloud Platform: A Guide For The Perplexed. A terse overview of Azure. http://blogs.zdnet.com/microsoft/?p=1671

Mitigation Monday #2, Defense against Drive-By Downloads. A set of guidelines for safer web surfing. http://www.nsa.gov/ia/guidancesecurity_configuration_ guides/ fact_sheets.shtml

Rapid Access Computing Environment. DISA's portal for access to a DoD platform as a service cloud. http://www.disa.mil/race

Security Guidelines for Critical Areas of Focus in Cloud Computing. Cloud Security Alliance. Offers detailed discussions of the security considerations associated with Cloud Computing. http://www.cloudsecurityalliance.org/guidance

The Good, Bad, and the Ugly of SaaS Terms of Service, Licenses, and Contracts. Includes specific excerpts from user agreements dealing with the rights users of software as a service platforms retrain - or forfeit - as a condition of using the site. http://peterlaird.blogspot.com/2008/06/good-bad-and-ugly-of-saas-terms-of.html

The Twitterhack Is Cloud Computing's Wake-Up Call: Time for Security That Works. Describes an attack the cloud that resulted in the compromise of sensitive files belonging to Twitter employees. http://mediamemo.allthingsd.com/20090715/the-twitterhack-is-cloud-computings-wakeup-call-time-for-security-that-works/

When the FBI Raids a Data Center: A Rare Danger. A story of how the FBI's execution of a warrant had serious consequence for 3rd parties in a data center. http://www.itworld.com/legal/67004/when-fbi-raids-data-center-rare-danger *17. Why Cloud Computing Needs Security.* Describes the challenges that consolidated cloud computing sites pose for security. http://gigaom.com/2008/06/10/the-amazon-outage-fortresses-in-the-clouds/

End Notes

[1]Derived from http://en.wikipedia.org/wiki/Cloud_computing.

In: Cloud Computing and Government: Background, Benefits...   ISBN: 978-1-61761-784-3
Editor: George I. Nikolov   © 2011 Nova Science Publishers, Inc.

Chapter 15

CLOUD COMPUTING AND CYBER DEFENSE

Bob Gourley

Advancing technology has the potential of dramatically changing the security posture of the federal enterprise and, if engineered correctly, the entire IT fabric of the globe. Potential security enhancements in the communications infrastructure, the software codebase, and cloud computing all hold great potential for dramatic positive change. This paper provides an overview of the cloud computing components relevant to security and proposes items for both awareness and action by the Federal IT team.

What is cloud computing? The term is used two different ways in the IT community. To most users, cloud computing is any capability delivered over the network. If it is not local computing it is from the cloud. To these users, almost all enterprise IT is cloud computing. Technologists and enterprise architects use the term in a different way. To them, cloud computing implies new ways of providing capability on demand by use of virtualized resources. It involves pools of storage, network, processing and other computational resources that can be efficiently allocated on demand. It also implies far more agility in support of operational missions. Technologists view cloud computing as a means to most efficiently deliver computer power via an application program interface (API).

What follows is a snapshot of the current glideslope of technology in this area, an update on relevant activities in the private sector which can further federal enablement of cloud computing security, and a new look at key principles for federal implementation of cloud computing.

Industry Visions: Major IT powerhouses, including Microsoft, Sun Microsystems, IBM, Google, and Oracle are all addressing the major shift to Cloud Computing in slightly different ways, but all capture the essence similarly. All pay great attention to industry thought leaders like Tim O'Reilly, CEO of O'Reilly Media, and writer Nicholas Carr.

- **Tim O'Reilly**'s position as a leader of technology publishing and as facilitator of Silicon Valley's greatest technology expositions informs his continuing assessments on the state of computing. He considers Cloud Computing as the foundation for the next generation of computing, which he has been calling Web2.0. Cloud computing has long been a vision industry was building towards, with a network of networks seen as the platform for all significant computing (in 1982 Sun Microsystems established its company with the vision that "The Network Is The Computer"). O'Reilly articulates the ideal goal of cloud computing being that every device we think of as a computer today is really just a device that connects into the grid of connected computers to deliver required services. To O'Reilly, cloud computing is about increasing functionality using the power of the entire grid and all the people it connects to.

- **Nicholas Carr** is one of the most popular and most controversial writers on IT today. His books and articles have forced strategic discussions for years by examining concepts like the true strategic value of IT to an organization. In 2003 he penned a Harvard Business Review article "IT Doesn't Matter" in which he argued that the strategic importance of IT has diminished in inverse proportion to the use of IT, since it is now so commonplace. In 2004 he published another controversial piece on "The End of Corporate Computing" in the MIT Sloan Management Review where he argued that increasingly companies will purchase IT as a utility service from outside suppliers. Carr is now documenting the move to Cloud Computing is a book titled "The Big Switch" where he draws parallels to the shift to the use of electricity as a utility. A hundred years ago, companies stopped generating their own power and plugged into the newly built electric grid. The cheap power provided by utilities didn't just change how businesses operate. It set off a chain reaction of economic and social transformations that brought the modern world into existence. Carr writes that today a similar revolution is under way. Hooked up to the Internet's global computing grid, information-processing plants have begun pumping data and software into our homes and businesses. So now computing is turning into a utility.[1]

Commercially available cloud services: Every company that provides IT hardware, software or services now contributes to cloud computing. We can measure the state of Cloud Computing by a survey of capabilities available right now from Google, Amazon, Microsoft, Salesforce.com and VMware.

- **Google:** The core of Google's business is all in Cloud Computing. Services delivered over network connections include search, e-mail, online mapping, office productivity (including documents, spreadsheets, presentations, databases), collaboration, social networking and voice, video, data services. Users can subscribe to these services for free or pay for increased levels of service and support. As an example of the types of cloud services provided, this paper is being written in the Google cloud. As it was written it was securely saved and backed up in a way that only the author could access, then when the draft was near complete it was shared with a small number of reviewers. When it was finalized the paper was stored as a PDF file for distribution. All this was done in a cloud with better security and privacy features than home PCs. Privacy and security on Google cloud services have many weaknesses, including the fact that data on Google's servers is not protected with strong encryption. However, the dramatic improvement over security of content when left on PC hard drives is a very positive trend and as Google continues to enhance security of its cloud services protection will only increase.

- **Amazon:** As the world's largest online retailer, the core of Amazon's business is ecommerce. While ecommerce itself can be considered Cloud Computing, Amazon has also been providing capabilities which give IT departments direct access to Amazon compute power. Key examples include S3 and EC2. S3 stands for Simple Storage Services. Any internet user can access storage in S3 and access stored objects from anywhere on the Internet. EC2 is the Elastic Compute Cloud, a virtual computing infrastructure able to run diverse applications ranging from web hosts to simulations or anywhere in between. This is all available for a very low cost per user. Amazon invests highly in security, however, current criticisms of its cloud approach including issues with availability (outages of even a moment can be costly for cloud services consumers). Another key concern is the ability of malicous attackers to leverage Amazon and the power of their processors in ways that Amazon can not detect or monitor. For example, attackers who might want to leverage the power of a super computer to crack encryption keys could lease large numbers of servers from Amazon and cut down the processing time required for brut-force attacks, and Amazon might only know that processors are being used.

- **Microsoft:** Traditionally Microsoft's core business has been in device operating systems and device office automation software. However, Microsoft has also always been in the server business and is in almost every data center today. Since the early days of the Internet Microsoft has also provided web hosting, online e-mail and many other cloud services. Microsoft now also provides office automation capabilities via a cloud ("Office Live") in an approach referred to as "Software Plus Services" vice "Software as a Service" to allow synchronous/asyncrhonous integration of online Cloud documents with their traditional offline desktop-resident versions. The next evolution of Microsoft's offerings are built on a foundation they call "Azure" but this foundation is still in a development release and is not a reliable offering yet. A criticism of Microsoft's approach has been that weaknesses in their desktop products and operating systems might be replicated into their cloud environment, however, the strength of cloud computing security models will eventually mitigate these weaknesses.

- **Salesforce.com:** The core mission of Salesforce.com has been in delivery of capabilities centered around customer relationship management. However, in pursuit of this core Salesforce.com has established themselves as thought leaders in the area of Software as a Service and is delivering an extensive suite of capabilities via the Internet. A key capability provided is the site Force.com, which enables external developers to create add-on applications that integrate into the main Salesforce.com application and are hosted on Salesforce.com's infrastructure. Salesforce.com is critical to track since they are functionality leaders in the delivery of cloud computing power.

- **VMware:** Provides several technologies of critical importance to enabling cloud computing, and has also started offering its own cloud computing on demand capability called vCloud. This type of capability allows enterprises to leverage virtualized clouds inside their own IT infrastructure or hosted with external service providers.

- **Cisco:** Has long provided the switch fabric of the Internet and the interconnect inside datacenters and is now offering enhanced collaborative tools and unified computing capabilities that bring the foundation of cloud computing to any datacenter.
- **Sun Microsystems:** With almost 100% of Sun's R&D budget being focused on data center enhancements the company has positioned itself to be the primary provider of large scale compute power and it forms the foundational elements of most cloud offerings today. Sun enables secure access to clouds via identity management approaches and also offers delivery of cloud compute power via thin clients.

There are many other companies contributing to cloud capabilities, but the survey above captures the direction of the industry. All major players are onboard and clear mega trends have emerged.

Industry Trends Relevant to the Federal Approach: Industry cloud computing designs provide reliable services delivered through data centers that make extensive use of virtualization to deliver services. These services are available anywhere in the world, with connection to a network giving access to compute power as if it were local. Commercial offerings are increasingly based on quality of service agreements which spell out expected levels of performance and availability. Open source software and open standards are foundations for most cloud computing today (even Microsoft has announced its own increased commitment to open standards and full publication of standards and interfaces in support of its cloud computing).

Consumers of cloud computing capabilities are not budgeting or paying for infrastructure, they pay for capability, frequently on a subscription basis. Utilization of computing resources is optimized though capabilities like virutalization, since virtualization allows for hardware to be used more than it is when left idle. Consumers do not have to engineer for peak load, the IT providers must engineer for that.

Industry experience with cloud computing has resulted in extensive documentation on key characteristics that users should expect from cloud computing. Key characteristics include[2]:

- Customer **capital expenditure** is minimized which lowers barriers to entry, as infrastructure is owned by the provider and does not need to be purchased for one-time or infrequent intensive computing tasks.
- **Device and location independence** enables users to access systems regardless of their location or what device they are using, e.g., PC, mobile.
- **Multi-tenancy** enables sharing of resources, and costs, among a large pool of users, allowing for:
  - **Centralization** of infrastructure in areas with lower costs, e.g., real estate, electricity, etc.
  - **Peak-load capacity** increases (users need not engineer for highest possible load levels)
  - **Utilization and efficiency** improvements for systems that are often only 10-20% utilised.
- **On-demand allocation** and de-allocation of CPU, storage and network bandwidth

- **Performance** is monitored and consistent
- **Reliability** is enhanced by way of multiple redundant sites, which makes it suitable for business continuity and disaster recovery
- **Scalability** meets changing user demands quickly without users having to engineer for peak loads. Massive scalability and large user bases are common, but not an absolute requirement.
- **Sustainability** is achieved through improved resource utilisation, more efficient systems, and carbon neutrality. Nonetheless, computers and associated infrastructure are major consumers of energy.
- **Security** typically improves due to centralization of data, increased security-focused resources, increased ability to patch and upgrade, increased ability to monitor, increased ability to encrypt and many other reasons. However, there are concerns about loss of control over certain sensitive data. When designed in at the beginning, security of cloud architectures is significantly higher than non-cloud approaches. Enterprises requiring significantly enhanced security should consider private clouds, where the data center is controlled by the enterprise vice outsourced.

Industry experiences in cloud computing are underscoring that all these characteristics are achievable and can be optimized by well engineered, central planning activities that focus on organizational mission.

A new look at key principles for Federal implementation of cloud computing: The security of the federal enterprise, as well as its functionality, can be significantly enhanced by smartly implementing cloud computing. The following are some key principles that can facilitate this:

- The importance of mission-focused engineering. Private clouds inside the federal enterprise can enhance mission support, but mission-focused engineering should be a first step in this pursuit.
- The continual need for security, including data confidentiality, integrity and availability. All federal computing approaches must be engineered to be in total consonance with IA guidelines to assure federal information, information systems and information infrastructure. Cloud Computing, when engineered right, makes dramatic, positive changes to the mission assurance posture of the federal enterprise. Cloud computing enables stronger end point security and better data protection. It also enables the use of thin clients and the many security benefits they provide. Identity management and encryption remain of critical importance.
- The need for always instantaneously available backup of data in the cloud. Ensured availability under all circumstances is a key benefit of smart cloud computing approaches.
- The continual need for open source and open standards. Most cloud infrastructure today is based on open source (Linux, Solaris, MySQL, Glassfish, Hadoop) and this positive trend will help in net centric approaches. According to the IDC Group, open source software (OSS) is "the most significant, all-encompassing and long-term trend that the software industry has seen since the early 1980's" Gartner projects that by

2012, 90 percent of the world's companies will be using open source software. This all indicates open source and open standards should be a key principle for federal cloud computing and other net centric approaches.

- The continual need to evaluate both low barrier to entry and low barrier to exit. As approaches to cloud computing are evaluated, too frequently the cost of exiting an approach is not considered, resulting in lock-in into a capability that may soon be inefficient. Cloud computing capabilities should be adopted that do not result in lock-in.

- The need for open standards. Cloud computing contributions to enhanced functionality for the federal workforce and increase intereoperability as the code, API's and interfaces for cloud computing are secure but are widely published for all participants to interface with. Federal involvement in open source and open standards communities should continue and be accelerated, since increasingly cloud computing open standards are being discussed and designed by open standards bodies like W3C, OASIS, IETF and the Liberty Alliance. Document and other formats used by federal cloud computing activities will be open and available for all authorized users on all devices.

- The need to understand the cost of "private clouds". For at least the near term, the federal government will remain a provider of "private cloud" capabilities where security dictates ownership levels of control over compute power. This fact means the federal enterprise must continually engineer for change and technology insertion, which underscores the need for low barriers to exist in design criteria.

Regarding security, cloud computing holds the potential to dramatically change the continuous loosing game of continual workstation patching and IT device remediation by reducing the amount of applications on desktops and changing the nature of the desktop device from fat client to thin client. Devices can now have their entire memory and operating system flashed out to the device from private clouds and can have the power of the cloud presented to users as if the user is on an old fashioned desktop. This can be done in a way that never requires IT departments to visit the workstation to patch and configure it. And since all data is stored on private clouds it can be encrypted and access only provided to authorized users. No data can ever be lost when laptops are stolen and no data can ever be lost when desktops are attacked by unauthorized users. Security by well engineered use or cloud computing and thin clients or cloud computing and smart fat clients is dramatically enhanced.

This all leads to a key conclusion for the federal enterprise: as we move forward in cloud computing for support to the mission, the federal enterprise should continue to strengthen formal processes to ensure that lessons learned from both industry and the governments's own successful cloud computing initiatives are continually examined and broadly adopted across the enterprise.

Bob Gourley is the former CTO of the Defense Intelligence Agency and is a recipient of Infoworld's Top 25 CTO award for 2007. He won AFCEAs award for meritorious service to the intelligence community in 2008 and is now the lead writer at http://ctovision.com and is the CTO of Crucial Point LLC, an IT consultancy. Contact Bob at bob@bobgourley.com

End Notes

[1]See http://www.youtube.com/watch?v=6PNuQHUiV3Q for a video of Cloud Computing context featuring interviews with luminaries like Tim O'Reilly.

[2] See http://en.wikipedia.org/wiki/Cloud_computing for more info.

In: Cloud Computing and Government: Background, Benefits...   ISBN: 978-1-61761-784-3
Editor: George I. Nikolov   © 2011 Nova Science Publishers, Inc.

Chapter 16

THE NIST DEFINITION OF CLOUD COMPUTING

Peter Mell and Tim Grance

Note 1: Cloud computing is still an evolving paradigm. Its definitions, use cases, underlying technologies, issues, risks, and benefits will be refined in a spirited debate by the public and private sectors. These definitions, attributes, and characteristics will evolve and change over time.

Note 2: The cloud computing industry represents a large ecosystem of many models, vendors, and market niches. This definition attempts to encompass all of the various cloud approaches.

DEFINITION OF CLOUD COMPUTING

Cloud computing is a model for enabling convenient, on-demand network access to a shared pool of configurable computing resources (e.g., networks, servers, storage, applications, and services) that can be rapidly provisioned and released with minimal management effort or service provider interaction. This cloud model promotes availability and is composed of five essential characteristics, three service models, and four deployment models.

Essential Characteristics

On-demand self-service. A consumer can unilaterally provision computing capabilities, such as server time and network storage, as needed automatically without requiring human interaction with each service's provider.

Broad network access. Capabilities are available over the network and accessed through standard mechanisms that promote use by heterogeneous thin or thick client platforms (e.g., mobile phones, laptops, and PDAs).

Resource pooling. The provider's computing resources are pooled to serve multiple consumers using a multi-tenant model, with different physical and virtual resources dynamically assigned and reassigned according to consumer demand. There is a sense of location independence in that the customer generally has no control or knowledge over the exact location of the provided resources but may be able to specify location at a higher level of abstraction (e.g., country, state, or datacenter). Examples of resources include storage, processing, memory, network bandwidth, and virtual machines.

Rapid elasticity. Capabilities can be rapidly and elastically provisioned, in some cases automatically, to quickly scale out and rapidly released to quickly scale in. To the consumer, the capabilities available for provisioning often appear to be unlimited and can be purchased in any quantity at any time.

Measured Service. Cloud systems automatically control and optimize resource use by leveraging a metering capability at some level of abstraction appropriate to the type of service (e.g., storage, processing, bandwidth, and active user accounts). Resource usage can be monitored, controlled, and reported providing transparency for both the provider and consumer of the utilized service.

Service Models

Cloud Software as a Service (SaaS). The capability provided to the consumer is to use the provider's applications running on a cloud infrastructure. The applications are accessible from various client devices through a thin client interface such as a web browser (e.g., web-based email). The consumer does not manage or control the underlying cloud infrastructure including network, servers, operating systems, storage, or even individual application capabilities, with the possible exception of limited user-specific application configuration settings.

Cloud Platform as a Service (PaaS). The capability provided to the consumer is to deploy onto the cloud infrastructure consumer-created or acquired applications created using programming languages and tools supported by the provider. The consumer does not manage or control the underlying cloud infrastructure including network, servers, operating systems, or storage, but has control over the deployed applications and possibly application hosting environment configurations.

Cloud Infrastructure as a Service (IaaS). The capability provided to the consumer is to provision processing, storage, networks, and other fundamental computing resources where the consumer is able to deploy and run arbitrary software, which can include operating systems and applications. The consumer does not manage or control the underlying cloud infrastructure but has control over operating systems, storage, deployed applications, and possibly limited control of select networking components (e.g., host firewalls).

Deployment Models

Private cloud. The cloud infrastructure is operated solely for an organization. It may be managed by the organization or a third party and may exist on premise or off premise.

Community cloud. The cloud infrastructure is shared by several organizations and supports a specific community that has shared concerns (e.g., mission, security requirements, policy, and compliance considerations). It may be managed by the organizations or a third party and may exist on premise or off premise.

Public cloud. The cloud infrastructure is made available to the general public or a large industry group and is owned by an organization selling cloud services.

Hybrid cloud. The cloud infrastructure is a composition of two or more clouds (private, community, or public) that remain unique entities but are bound together by standardized or proprietary technology that enables data and application portability (e.g., cloud bursting for load-balancing between clouds).

Note: Cloud software takes full advantage of the cloud paradigm by being service oriented with a focus on statelessness, low coupling, modularity, and semantic inter-operability.

CHAPTER SOURCES

The following chapters have been previously published:

Chapter 1 – This is an edited, excerpted and augmented edition of a United StatesGovernment Accountability Office publication, Report Order Code GAO-10-513, dated May 2010.

Chapter 2 – This is an edited, excerpted and augmented edition of a United StatesCIO Council publication, dated May 20, 2010.

Chapter 3 – These remarks were delivered as Statement/Testimonyof Chairman Adolphus Towns, given before the House Committee on Oversight and Government Reform dated July 1, 2010.

Chapter 4 –These remarks were delivered as Statement/Testimonyof Chairwoman Diane E. Watson, given before the House Committee on Oversight and Government Reform dated July 1, 2010.

Chapter 5 – These remarks were delivered as Statement/Testimonyof VivekKundra, given before the House Committee on Oversight and Government Reform dated July 1, 2010.

Chapter 6 – These remarks were delivered as Statement/Testimonyof Dr. David McClure, given before the House Committee on Oversight and Government Reform dated July 1, 2010.

Chapter 7 – These remarks were delivered as Statement/Testimonyof Cita M. Furlani, given before the House Committee on Oversight and Government Reform dated July 1, 2010.

Chapter 8 – This is an edited, excerpted and augmented edition of a United States Government Accountability Office publication, Report Order Code GAO-10-855-T, dated July 1, 2010.

Chapter 9 – These remarks were delivered as Statement/Testimonyof Scott Charney, given before the House Committee on Oversight and Government Reform dated July 1, 2010.

Chapter 10 – These remarks were delivered as Statement/Testimonyof David F. Burton, Jr., given before the House Committee on Oversight and Government Reform dated July 1, 2010.

Chapter 11 - These remarks were delivered as Statement/Testimonyof Mike Bradshaw,given before the House Committee on Oversight and Government Reform dated July 1, 2010.

Chapter 12 - These remarks were delivered as Statement/Testimonyof Nicklous Combs,given before the House Committee on Oversight and Government Reform dated July 1, 2010.

Chapter 13 - These remarks were delivered as Statement/Testimonyof Gregory R. Ganger, given before the House Committee on Oversight and Government Reform dated July 1, 2010.

Chapter 14 - This is an edited, excerpted and augmented edition of a United StatesNational Security Agency publication, dated December 18, 2009.

Chapter 15 - This is an edited, excerpted and augmented edition of a Crucial Point LLC publication, written by Bob Gourley, Chief Technology Officer.

Chapter 16 - This is an edited, excerpted and augmented edition of a National Institute of Standards and Technology publication, dated October 7, 2009.

INDEX

D

E

logistics, 155

M

machinery, viii, 77
majority, 79, 122, 142, 145
malware, 147
management, viii, ix, 5, 7, 8, 9, 13, 14, 15, 18, 19,
28, 36, 40, 52, 53, 58, 59, 60, 62, 81, 82, 83, 84,
85, 93, 94, 99, 100, 109, 117, 118, 124, 129, 133,
134, 142, 143, 145, 146, 150, 152, 155, 156, 160,
162, 168, 169, 173
mapping, 68, 166
Marine Corps, 52
marketing, 50
marketplace, 92, 93, 95, 144
media, 3, 4, 12, 13, 19, 57, 92, 109, 110, 163
memory, 40, 57, 87, 101, 105, 170, 174
messages, 57, 70
metaphor, viii, 79
methodology, 4
Mexico, 61, 62, 73, 74
Miami, 61, 67, 68, 72, 73, 75
Microsoft, vi, ix, 9, 57, 64, 66, 68, 69, 70, 74, 115,
116, 117, 119, 120, 122, 123, 124, 125, 126, 134,
138, 142, 149, 151, 157, 163, 165, 166, 167, 168
migration, 63, 64, 66, 69, 70, 71, 132, 142, 150
military, 51
missions, x, 43, 52, 56, 57, 119, 144, 152, 165
mobile device, 66, 67, 68, 134
mobile phone, 11, 40, 87, 100, 173
modernization, 82, 91
MPI, 57
multimedia, 83

N

National Aeronautics and Space Administration, 3,
12, 24, 35, 36, 50, 55, 72, 73, 74, 114, 142
National Science Foundation, 35, 36, 114
national security, 6, 39, 80, 82, 84, 104, 105
natural disasters, 55, 67
negotiating, 154
network elements, 160
networking, 43, 88, 95, 100, 101, 130, 144, 154, 174
next generation, 166
nodes, 57, 106
North America, 135

O

Obama Administration, vii, 39, 86, 134, 147
obstacles, 91, 92, 93
Office of Management and Budget, v, 1, 2, 5, 24, 29,
74, 81, 96, 107, 108, 111, 140

online information, 58
operating system, 9, 36, 42, 43, 88, 101, 114, 117,
160, 162, 167, 170, 174
opportunities, x, 4, 48, 54, 109, 116, 117, 143, 144,
157
outreach, 56, 57, 105
outsourcing, 118, 150, 151, 153
oversight, 16, 60, 91, 94, 111
ownership, 59, 67, 85, 95, 128, 131, 133, 159, 170

P

paradigm, x, xi, 102, 157, 173, 175
password, 127, 147
performance, vii, ix, 4, 13, 24, 36, 39, 43, 57, 69, 82,
84, 89, 91, 100, 110, 121, 123, 130, 133, 137,
147, 160, 168
perseverance, 155
personnel costs, 55
photographs, 161
plants, 166
platform, 9, 13, 16, 25, 51, 52, 56, 57, 58, 59, 63, 65,
68, 70, 71, 95, 96, 109, 111, 115, 117, 118, 123,
127, 129, 130, 131, 132, 133, 134, 157, 159, 161,
162, 163, 166
portability, x, 8, 14, 20, 21, 22, 39, 42, 43, 44, 45,
78, 79, 84, 87, 102, 103, 105, 113, 143, 144, 175
predictability, 131
prevention, 146
procurement, 1, 2, 19, 22, 41, 51, 55, 63, 82, 85, 86,
91, 107, 108, 112, 113, 154
programming, 42, 57, 88, 101, 130, 134, 174
programming languages, 42, 88, 101, 174
project, vii, 19, 39, 45, 52, 53, 54, 59, 82, 95, 103,
106, 131, 162
public policy, 155
public schools, 69, 70
public sector, ix, 39, 40, 48, 65, 132, 135, 137, 142
punishment, 124

Q

quality control, 85
quality of life, 99
quality of service, 159, 168
quality standards, 103

R

real estate, 90, 168
real time, 50, 90
reality, 50, 119
real-time basis, 83
recommendations, iv, 1, 6, 7, 20, 44, 82, 102, 107,
123, 155